HOW TO WRITE FAST

HOW TO
WRITE
FAST
(While Writing Well)

....

DAVID FRYXELL

Writer's
Digest
Books

CINCINNATI, OHIO

For my parents,
who taught me to love words.

96 95 94 93 92   5 4 3 2 1

Library of Congress Cataloging in Publication Data

Fryxell, David A.
  How to write fast (while writing well) / David Fryxell.
    p.   cm.
  Includes index.
  ISBN 0-89879-514-1
  1. Authorship.   I. Title
PN151.F79   1992
808'.02—dc20   92-15077
                                        CIP

Edited by Catherine Brohaugh
Designed by Sandy Conopeotis

The following page constitutes an extension of this copyright page.

ABOUT THE AUTHOR

• • •

David A. Fryxell is the author of nearly 1,000 magazine and newspaper articles — including work for *Playboy, Travel & Leisure* and *Reader's Digest* — and a book of midwestern humor, *Double-Parked on Main Street.* He's been an editor of *TWA Ambassador, Horizon, Pitt,* and *Milwaukee* magazines and is currently features editor of the *Saint Paul Pioneer-Press* newspaper. His writing and editing have earned him more than eighty national and regional awards. While writing this book, he changed jobs, bought and sold houses, moved, nursed his wife through a broken leg — and still turned in the manuscript early.

TABLE OF CONTENTS

• • •

WHY WRITE FASTER (AND BETTER)?

• • •

MAKING IT LOOK EASY

I have a confession to make. Remember the kid in school who regularly turned his homework in early, the troublemaker who always had the fifty-page report for Mrs. Griswold done the week *before* it was due? That was me. You know the co-worker who gets his fiscal-year plan written seemingly mere hours after the boss requests it, who knocks out proposals without breaking a sweat, who even—for gosh sakes—*finishes* his expense reports *before* anybody else has unpacked? That's me, too. Or, since this is a book about *writing*, have you ever noticed the writer who never misses a deadline, who never has to burn the midnight oil, who never stares at the blank page in an agony of writer's block? You guessed it: It's yours truly.

I bring this all up not to make you feel bitter and resentful all over again (I *saw* those looks when Mrs. Griswold said, "Now, why can't everyone be like David here?"), or even to gloat. No, I'm confessing to being a deadline-beater, to being someone who "makes it look easy," because I'm convinced that I can make you the same kind of writer. You, too, can make writing look easy—because it doesn't have to be hard. You, too, can learn how to write fast.

I bring this up partly out of self-justification. Writing fast has never been particularly admired—except by those (teachers, editors, publishers) who actually need the writing done. In fact, rapid writers have always been looked down on in arty circles. If you write quickly, without spilling blood, sweat and tears on the manuscript page, the results can't possibly be any good—or so the thinking goes. Quality of writing ought to rise in direct proportion to the time invested in creation. A novel "knocked out" in six months can't possibly compare to a work agonized over, written and rewritten, for the better part of a writer's career. Can it?

The folks in these arty circles have a word for fast writers: *hack*. I maintain that a better term for a writer who works efficiently and who consistently meets deadlines is *professional*.

The benefits of learning to write faster and more efficiently ought to be obvious to anyone who's ever written for a living (or as a dedicated pastime). While much has been said and written about how to write *better*, the hard reality for most working writers is that it is at least as important to strive to write *faster*: to slice the time between the thrill of getting an assignment and the joy of dropping a completed manuscript into the mailbox, and counting the days until the check arrives. For many writers, writing faster is simply a matter of survival. Writing faster can mean the difference between making a go of a challenging career as an author and going back to your old job as an accountant, or asking "Smoking or nonsmoking?" down at Bill's Big Boy.

For the writer in a one-person wordsmith's shop, productivity is every bit as important as it is for a huge factory churning out widgets instead of words. And it can be just as challenging: Between you and each finished manuscript lies an obstacle course of psychological traps, phone calls from hectoring editors, interruptions from spouses and children, and—worst of all—your own swamp of notes and files, threatening to overwhelm the basement nook or kitchen corner you laughingly call your office.

This book is your step-by-step guide through that obstacle course. From generating workable ideas to maximizing your research results, from efficient interviewing to organizing your notes, from lead to revision, you *can* learn how to write fast.

You can also learn how to write better, and this book will teach you that, too. For writing faster and writing better are not, as those snooty arty types mentioned above would have you believe, inimical. Quite the opposite: The same techniques that will make you a faster writer also will make you a better writer. That's because the secret of speeding up your writing is learning what makes good writing—and doing it right the first time.

The late *New Yorker* reporter A.J. Liebling used to boast, "I can write better than anybody who's faster, and faster than anybody who's better." Once I heard that line, I immediately adopted it as my personal credo. It's the ultimate goal of every kid who's ever turned in his homework early, of every bright-eyed employee who's beaten the rest of the staff to the punch, of every writer who knows the satisfaction of turning in superior work before the deadline instead of under the gun and the editor's ire.

Writing faster. Writing better. That's my definition of becoming a *professional* writer.

DEVELOPING (UGH) DISCIPLINE

I'm talking about myself in this chapter not only to make a point about the virtues of writing faster, but to give you some idea of who this guy is who's purporting to show you how to revolutionize your writing habits. Other than having been an obnoxious kid and teacher's pet, where do I get off telling you how to write faster and better?

Obviously, I wasn't born writing fast. I didn't reach for the typewriter along with my pacifier. And, despite my annoying propensity for finishing school assignments early (which you are by now thoroughly sick of reading about, and which I promise not to mention again for 75,000 words), I don't think I took any sort of systematic approach to my writing until after college. Out in what guidance counselors euphemistically refer to as "the world of work," I learned by doing—in what another cliché would call "the school of hard knocks."

I got my first hard knocks as a fledgling assistant editor on a pair of in-flight magazines. Editing other people's work, I soon discovered, was as hard as writing my own and twice as frustrating. When writers couldn't meet their deadlines (*my* deadlines!) or when they turned in a mess instead of a manuscript, their problems suddenly became *my* problems. I still remember my shock at dealing with the highly respected financial columnist of a leading Manhattan magazine, who was freelancing a column for our in-flight publication. To my horror and amazement, this renowned writer couldn't seem to put one paragraph after another, or to deliver any assortment of paragraphs even remotely on time. I wound up getting the last several pages out of him over the phone, one paragraph at a time: I would figure out what material needed to come next, call him, and he'd comply (more or less). It was like building a story the way Dr. Frankenstein built bodies.

Editors, I learned, have to look at writing analytically. In figuring out after the fact how stories *ought* to be assembled, I got better at putting my own stories together right the first time. Paradoxically, I found that understanding this sense of a story's structure was ultimately liberating. By writing more efficiently, I could be free to write more creatively. I began to see that, yes, it is possible to write faster *and* better.

After three years helping to put magazines in airline seats, I spent thirteen months applying what I'd learned to the now-defunct *Horizon* magazine, an arts monthly that was busily defuncting even when I was there. From *Horizon* I escaped to a writer's dream job: newspaper columnist.

But that job could have been a nightmare instead of a dream-come-true, and not because it was in the unlikely Eden of Dubuque, Iowa. The job description was simple: write three feature columns, each about twenty inches long, every week. That meant three columns a week, fifty-two weeks a year—156 deadlines to make, 156 bullets to dodge each year, more than 3,000 inches of copy annually. Anybody who couldn't write fast would be eaten alive by such a "dream job."

By the time I left Dubuque, I was writing *four* columns a week. I had learned, if I hadn't already known, how to write fast. But I also did some of the best writing of my life. Under deadline pressure, under the constant demand to meet my weekly quota, I was forced to develop the discipline that makes a superior writer. "Discipline" is not a word you hear bandied about much in writing circles—it's neither as fashionable nor as easy as talking about your "muse" or "inspiration." But, as Archibald MacLeish once noted, "all art begins and ends with discipline . . . any art is first and foremost a craft.

"We have gone far enough," MacLeish continued, "in the road to self-indulgence now to know that. The man who announces to the world that he is going to 'do his thing' is like the amateur on the high-diving platform who flings himself into the void shouting at the judges that he is going to do whatever comes naturally. He will land on his ass. Naturally."

In the pages that follow, I hope to show you how *not* to land on your ass. Naturally.

SPEEDY LITERATURE 101

When it comes to discipline—and sheer swiftness of writing—nobody, according to the *Guinness Book of World Records*, tops Charles Harold St. John Hamilton (1876-1961). *Guinness* calls Hamilton the most prolific author in history. Hamilton, an Englishman, wrote the adventures of "Billy Bunter" under the pseudonym Frank Richards. At his prime, from 1915-26, he often knocked out 80,000 words a week—about the length of this book—for a trio of boys' adventure magazines. Over his lifetime, Hamilton produced about 75 million words.

The fastest female writer was a South African woman, Kathleen Lindsay. During her lifetime (1903-73), Lindsay somehow penned 904 novels under three married names and eight pen names. Please note, she died just before the advent of the modern word processor. Librarians can only shudder at the thought of what she might have produced if fully armed with modern technology.

Neither Hamilton nor Lindsay nor any of their army of pseud-onyms may ring a bell with today's readers, and it's true that their prodigious output is unlikely to find a spot (heck, it'd have to be a darn big spot) in the annals of great literature. But swiftness of writing isn't strictly the province of what some might call "hacks." Yes, many great authors have been painfully slow at their art, creating only a handful of laboriously crafted works in their careers. Many other fa-mous writers throughout history, however, give the lie to the preju-dice that good writing, like fine wine, can only be produced slowly.

Often the greats of the literary past were driven to rapid productiv-ity by the same forces that may inspire you: the need to pay bills, to simply make a living. Samuel Johnson (1709-84), for example, wrote his "philosophical romance," *Rasselas* in a week to pay his mother's debts and the costs of her funeral. Honoré de Balzac (1799-1850), one of the most prolific authors of his day and a master of the novel, literally wrote his way out of the garret. Even when he had achieved some literary success, Balzac continued to labor sixteen hours a day, starting at midnight after a few hours sleep and continuing into the next afternoon. Fueled by countless cups of black coffee, he created the masterpiece of *La Comédie Humaine* — a tapestry of some 2,000 characters in nearly a hundred novels written over twenty years. Lit-erature is lucky that Balzac was a terrible investor, losing his shirt time after time in get-rich-quick scams and forced back to his writing desk to keep ahead of the bill collectors.

Not only the debt-ridden in literature's pantheon knew how to write fast. Even many of the elite created at an impressive pace, blessed with a muse that worked overtime, perhaps, or simply a solid share of discipline. The Spanish playwright Lope de Vega (1562-1635) wrote several of his plays overnight, and penned more than a hundred of them in no more than a day a piece. Though "only" about 500 of de Vega's works survive, he's believed to have written more than 2,000 — an output that caused an envious Miguel de Cervantes to dub de Vega "a monster of nature." (Even way back then nobody liked the kid who turned in his homework early.) Sir Walter Scott (1771-1832), it's said, dictated his novels so rapidly that his secretaries could barely keep pace; he wrote two of the novels in his Waverly series in just three weeks. And Alexandre Dumas (1802-70) once won a wager, the story goes, by writing the entire first volume of his *Le Chevalier de Maison-Rouge* in only seventy-two hours.

More recent writers have kept up the pace. In fact, some have called Perry Mason creator Erle Stanley Gardner (1889-1970) "the world's fastest writer." Gardner once worked on seven novels simultaneously; at 140 books, though, he falls a few million words short of the "most prolific" title. (Maybe he took a lot of vacations.) Fellow mystery writer John Creasey (1908-73) could probably have given Gardner a run for his money, speedwise: Creasey once cranked out two novels in a single week. It's worth noting that Creasey collected what's likely a world record 743 rejection slips before publishing the first of his 564 books—and went on to write more than 40 million words in about forty years. Georges Simenon (1903-89), the French mystery writer and creator of Inspector Maigret, also topped 500 books. Before settling down to work, Simenon would have a complete medical exam—it slows one down to keel over the typewriter, n'est-ce pas?—and then lock himself in a room to write. Precisely six days later, he would emerge with a completed novel. (And on the seventh day, one presumes, he rested.)

Like mystery writers, science fiction authors have a tradition of doing their best work in almost no time at all. Lester del Rey, a great editor as well as an accomplished writer, could knock out a 6,000-word story for the pulp magazines of his day in only two hours. Del Rey once rolled a sheet of paper into the typewriter after breakfast, wrote all day, and dropped a 20,000-word novelette into the mailbox that night.

The speed record for science fiction writers, though, is surely held by Isaac Asimov, who, until his death, was steadily working his way onto the most prolific list as well. In the first decades of his career, Asimov wrote ten hours a day; he managed five books in 1957 alone. By 1979, when he celebrated his 200th book with the publication of *Opus 200*, he had written 15 million words. That total includes Asimov's much-praised nonfiction books, most of which he said he wrote in less than three days apiece.

Many humor writers also seem able to be funny at a frantic pace. This, too, takes discipline, though that sounds contradictory to the whimsical world of humor. P.G. Wodehouse (1881-1975), the creator of Jeeves and Bertie Wooster, planned his frothy entertainments with almost military precision, relying on many pages of notes to make sure his jokes fired at the right time and place. Once a novel was strategized, Wodehouse would start work at 7:30 A.M., seven days a week, and write 2,000 words a day. This regimen allowed him to produce a finished book in three months.

Today, most of our funniest writers—Dave Barry, Calvin Trillin and

Russell Baker, to name only a few—work in newspapers and magazines, where no sooner is today's or this week's chuckle put to bed than the demand arises again: Make somebody laugh *tomorrow* or *next week*. Somehow, column after column, these writers manage to turn out not only some of the funniest writing in America, but some of the best. Inspired by their incessant deadlines, with no time to agonize and overanalyze ("Is this really funny or does it just seem funny because I wrote it?"), they find humor all around them.

But today's genre writers don't have a monopoly on speed. Probably the best-known prodigy of production among contemporary literary novelists is Joyce Carol Oates, who wrote thirty-three books and three plays by age forty. Critics often chide Oates for producing *too much*, on the dubious supposition that her work would be better if there were less of it. Oates is not, in fact, a model of authorial efficiency, despite her output: She rises at dawn and works until mid-afternoon before having breakfast (so much for "the most important meal of the day"), writing in longhand. She rewrites some pages more than a dozen times and has even revised some stories *after* publication, before they are gathered into a collection. Imagine what Oates could do if she learned to type those first drafts and learned to leave well enough alone after the second revision—and imagine how the critics would harp then!

Not to pick on a remarkable writer, but Oates is a good example of the folly of slavish imitation of successful authors' writing habits. You, too, could start writing right through breakfast time, abandon your computer for a pen and pad, and rework your words until you can barely read your own scribblings. But it would not make you Joyce Carol Oates, and it certainly would not boost your productivity to match hers. Some writers are able to turn out a great deal of work *despite* their writing habits.

CHANGE YOUR INK? BUY A BATHROBE? GET A SYSTEM!

Wouldn't it be lovely, though, if we could just imitate the habits of a writer and get the same results? This temptation is what Francine du Plessix Gray once called "the wisdom of the keyhole": If only you knew how such-and-such a successful writer worked, and copied his or her tools and techniques, surely you could write like that, too. George M. Cohan used to rent an entire Pullman car and travel until he finished whatever he was working on, hammering out 140 pages a night to the rhythm of the rails. Ah, if only the great days of rail travel were still with us, you could rent a Pullman car, start writing and arrive as a Yankee Doodle Dandy! Right?

The technique, the "secret," doesn't have to be so elaborate or stylish to tempt emulation. Rudyard Kipling could write only with pitch-black ink—mere blue-black, he said, was "an abomination" to his "demon." Maybe that's it! Maybe you're using the wrong color ink! Balzac wore a favorite dressing gown as a sort of authoring good-luck charm; perhaps a trip down to Kmart for a new bathrobe would cure your writer's block. Joan Didion has to sleep in the same room as her manuscript-in-progress. Move the office into the bedroom! Gore Vidal, plain-spoken as ever, has said that he cannot summon his muse without coffee and then a bowel movement. Crank up the Mr. Coffee and. . . .

Well, you get the idea. It's only natural to hunger for some magic trick, some easy alternative to discipline and hard, steady work, that will energize your writing. And of course that may be why you picked up this book in the first place: "Here's some simple stuff I can do to speed up and improve my writing. Maybe he'll tell me to use pitch-black ink instead of that abominable blue-black. . . ."

Sorry. Writing doesn't work with a magic wand. But before you toss this book back on the shelf in favor of *How to Cure Writer's Block With One Trip to Kmart*, let me be quick to tell you what you *can* learn from the masters, and even from me: a fundamental approach to organizing and accelerating your writing. A way of thinking more clearly about the writer's task. A method of arranging both the physical resources of your writing—your notes, reference books and interview materials—and the dynamics of your story, from start to finish and all the twists and turns in between—a system.

Yes, no less than the widget works across town, you need a system to manage your work as a writer. Think about it: What does a writer (like me) really mean when he says, "Writing comes easily to me"? It's not some hardwiring in his brain that sets him apart from those who echo fellow writer Gene Fowler in saying, "Writing is easy. All you have to do is stare at a blank sheet of paper until drops of blood form on your forehead." No, it's a way of working, a combination of experience and insight that tells him what he needs to get the job done and how, in turn, to put those ingredients together.

Some of it *can* be picked up from reading interviews with writers and forewords to books, that "wisdom of the keyhole." For my own career, reading the introduction to *The John McPhee Reader* gave me a framework for organizing and thinking about my writing, a framework that I have since adapted to my own needs and thought processes. Learning how McPhee, the gifted *New Yorker* reporter, approached his work helped crystallize my own thinking about the process of writing. But it wasn't the arrangement of his office or the color of paper he used that I borrowed from McPhee; it was his sense of a system.

I know, a system sounds inimical to the mysterious art of writing — much less magical than finding the right color of ink, renting a Pullman car, or drinking coffee until either your muse or nature calls. *Did Flaubert have a system?* you ask. *Balzac had a bathrobe, but did he have a system?* The point of developing a systematic approach to your writing, however, isn't to turn you into a keypunching version of those assembly-line robots you see in automobile plants: *Insert Verb A into Sentence B, then punctuate.* Just the opposite: By getting organized — by wresting order out of the chaos of your writing process — you will be freed (to borrow a phrase) to be all that you can be as an author. Once you have a system that lets you find and plan where a story is going and how you'll get there, it's a lot easier to pay attention to the scenery en route.

In other words, with a system instead of a wishful-thinking magic wand, you'll be able to write not only faster, but *better*.

"I can write better than anybody who's faster, and faster than anybody who's better," boasted Liebling. I don't know if Liebling was a model of planning and well-thought-out execution — in fact, I rather suspect not — but then not all of us have his gifts. So what we would-be Lieblings need is an organizational approach to the work of writing that clears up the creative confusion and enables us to focus on the task at hand. We need a way to uncover the structure that's inherent in every story. We need a guiding light for our research and interviewing. We need, in short, a system.

And the system begins, as you might expect, at the beginning.

GETTING ORGANIZED: YOUR KEY TO WRITING FASTER

• • •

THE "D" WORD AND THE "O" WORD

It was Aristotle who observed that the most characteristically human activity is planning one's life. He may have been right, but it's also all too characteristic of most of us that we tend to put off such planning — preferring, say, the characteristic activities of a sloth. Even when we do finally get busy, too many of us approach life without a plan. We plunge forward in a frenzy of activity — like a bouncy puppy unleashed in a roomful of doggie toys, to continue the animal metaphor — and then, when we're exhausted, look with dismay at the mess all around us, and wonder why nothing got accomplished.

You're going to get tired of hearing me use the word "discipline," but here I go again: The secret to planning your writing life, and successfully executing that plan, is discipline. I could be upstairs right now, watching an NFL playoff game, but my "game plan" for writing this book called for me to write at a certain pace. To keep up that pace, I have to write so-many-thousand words today, playoffs or no playoffs. It took discipline to make that plan, and it takes discipline to follow through on it. (Though, if you'll excuse me just one second, there was just a roar from the crowd on the TV upstairs, and I'm going to run up and see who scored. I'll be right back. Honest.)

"Discipline," says screenwriter and time-management and creativity consultant Kenneth Atchity, using that "D-word" again, "is the key . . . the bedrock of productive writing. Talent is not a rare commodity. Discipline is."

Forget about the muse, he might have added. Good writing, not to mention rapid writing, results from following your own inner master, not from waiting for the muse. If you wait for the muse to strike, you'll get a lot of dishes washed and watch a lot more NFL playoff games, but you won't get much writing done. If you write only when the muse deigns to visit, the writing—what there is of it—isn't yours at all; it belongs to the muse. Rather, you must become your own muse. You must nurture an inner inspiration you can summon for half an hour before you catch the morning bus, for a spurt of writing during your lunch hour, or even when you'd really rather be watching the Big Game.

Being a writer—as another screenwriter, Lawrence Kasdan, once noted—is like having homework for the rest of your life. If you ask my mom what I was like as a kid, she's been known to mention that she never had to bug me to do my homework. Somehow I developed, early on, an internal taskmaster that made me get my homework done; today, that taskmaster still nags me to finish the "homework" of being a writer.

But mastering your writing life is not simply a matter of sitting down and working. Success as a writer also includes learning to gauge how long a given project will take you—so you know when you must start your "homework"—and how to organize each task for completion in the least possible time.

The "O-word"—organization—is the other face of the coin of discipline. Like discipline, it affects every aspect of a successful writer's work: How you organize your time. How you organize your workspace and your notes. How you organize your work itself, both in the simple sense of putting point B after point A, and in the deeper sense of the thematic structure of your work.

Because organization, in all its aspects, is so crucial to learning to write fast, before we take a step-by-step look at the secrets of writing faster we're going to examine how those steps get laid out in the first place. You can't begin to write faster and better until you get organized. And once you get organized, you'll be amazed at how such dilemmas as writer's block and deadline terror suddenly seem more chimerical than critical. For an organized writer meets his deadlines even as he is wresting meaning out of the chaos of everyday life. A successful writer, an organized writer, always turns in his homework on time—and always merits an "A."

KNOCKING OUT A NOVEL BEFORE DINNER

Let's start with organizing your time, since many writers never get over this basic hurdle. How many people believe they could be great writers, if only they could find the time? How many working writers spend their entire careers under the gun, unable to do their best work because they have one eye on the clock? (And how many, unable to master their own time, fool themselves into thinking they "work best under pressure"? In fact, that's the only time they work at all!)

If your problem is finding time to write, it means you are losing time: The pieces of your life that could be spent writing are being lost instead to watching television, sleeping late and sitting around thinking about being a writer. Yes, modern life is hectic, but that's all the more reason to take control of your time and stop losing it to minutiae. As Proust observed (and, admittedly, this was before the invention of televised sports), "The time which we have at our disposal every day is elastic; the passions that we feel expand it, those that we inspire contract it; and habit fills up what remains."

Even tiny chunks of time, reclaimed, can add up to the hours necessary to write. The French chancellor D'Aguesseau, it's said, once noticed that his wife was habitually ten minutes late coming down to dinner. He decided to make use of those ten minutes (3,650 minutes a year, or more than sixty hours). While he waited for dinner, D'Aguesseau wrote a three-volume book, which became a best-seller when it was published in 1668. Anthony Trollope spent most of his life working as a postal clerk, but he would get up at five o'clock each morning and write 3,000 words in the three hours before beginning with the mail. If Trollope finished penning a novel before it was time to go to work — and he finished nearly fifty books this way — he'd simply begin another. More recently, the British crime novelist Michael Gilbert managed to craft twenty-three books during his daily fifty-minute commute to his "real job" as a solicitor.

For you, finding the time to write may mean staying up an hour later each night, closeting yourself with the typewriter one night a week, or tapping on a laptop computer on airplane rides. Even just an hour a day can add up to a solid first draft of a novel in a little over three months. (If that pace — say, 750 words — sounds like more than you can possibly manage in an hour, well, you haven't read the rest of this book yet.) At four books a year, you'd match Anthony Trollope's output in not much more than a decade.

This mundane mathematics is exactly how the greats of literature have found the time to create their masterworks. Irving Wallace, early in his career, used to keep detailed records of his output — to spur himself to greater productivity if he started lagging behind his self-assigned quotas. Even when the words won't come, it's important to keep to your schedule: "Force yourself to sit four hours at the table,"

James Jones advised. "Sometimes you get nothing. But the self-discipline is good for you. Somewhere inside, you'll be working."

Of course, like anything else, finding the time to write becomes easier once it becomes a habit. If you can make yourself jog or spend time on the Nautilus machine every night, you can make yourself write. The former will make you live longer; the latter will give you a reason to live.

LEARNING TO LIVE WITH DEADLINES

Ah, but what about deadlines? Surely, deadlines will be the, er, death of most people who take up the challenge of calling themselves writers. And yet many writers feel they work best (or solely!) under the pressure of what Kenneth Atchity calls "end time." William Saroyan, for example, wrote his classic *The Human Comedy* in only a few days — because he had a deadline to meet. Why are deadlines so difficult to meet, and why do so many writers need one to fire up their creative juices?

First of all, contrary to what you might think, chronic deadline-missers are seldom simply lazy. The writers I've had working for me who suffered the most trouble meeting deadlines were often the hardest workers on my staff. They'd spend long hours at the library, conduct in-depth interviews and laboriously transcribe them, and write all weekend. Yet somehow their stories never arrived at my desk on time. By contrast, I would start on a story at the same time, edit other stories and do a ton of administrative work in addition to my writing assignment, and go home promptly at five. To an outside observer, *I* was the lazy one — but my stories were always finished a couple of days early, giving me plenty of time to listen to my staff writers moan and make excuses.

The point of relating this isn't to pat myself on the back. The point is that I organized my time; the other writers didn't. They finished their stories in a deadline-fueled adrenaline frenzy; I rarely missed my bus home.

It's easy to be glib about "organizing your time." Throughout this book, however, I will be giving you specific techniques you can use to better organize your writing time — as well as a whole philosophy that will link organizing your time to the way you organize your work as a writer. For now, I just want to concentrate on organizing your time as it relates to meeting those dreaded deadlines.

In working with writers as an editor, I've found that the most common trait among deadline-abusers is that they really have no idea how long any given writing assignment will take them to complete. Oh, they *think* they do: "Sure, I can get that to you in three weeks." But the gap between self-expectation and reality is almost total. I've had writers, typically with a story already late, blithely assure me, "It just needs one more good afternoon of work." A week later, I'll pop my head in to check on the story, which is still missing in action: "Oh, it just needs one more good afternoon of work," the writer will insist again. "You'll have it by tomorrow at the latest."

These writers are not lying, to me or to themselves. They are utterly sincere. They are also utterly in the dark about the road their work must take and the speed they can travel. They lack an inner measuring stick by which to gauge the complexity of a subject, how much research it entails, and how long a story will take at the keyboard. They begin an assignment the way Columbus set sail for the Indies: without a map and with no concept of the journey's duration, only a firm faith that they'll get there somehow. Is it any wonder that so often they wind up late, and at the wrong destination? (Columbus's discovery of the Americas may have been a boon to history, but it was not, after all, his assignment. Editors who want spice from the Indies will lose patience if you keep sending them surprises from the Americas.)

You must have a map. To return to my writer who thinks his story needs only one more afternoon of work: If he had an outline of his story, with his notes carefully tagged to each portion of the plan, he would know darn well how much ground he had yet to cover. (Writers who miss deadlines also, ironically, are always turning in copy that's too long. Both the lateness and the wordiness are merely symptoms of the same problem: If you're writing a 4,500-word story and you don't know where it's going, no alarms go off in your head when you hit 3,500 words and the story's not yet half done. You *don't know* it's not yet half done. For all you know, you could be steaming toward the conclusion.)

With a "map"—not only for the actual writing, but for all the steps that come before—you can plan your work routine from day one till the deadline. With a "map" and a little experience, you'll know when you must wrap up your research and start writing. You will learn to work under the pressure of many small intermediate deadlines, instead of in the panic of "end time." And if your challenge is "finding time," you will see how the bits and pieces of time you find for writing can add up, for each one represents a clearly defined step along the road to completion. Like D'Aguesseau, who wrote while waiting for his wife to come down to dinner, you'll get there, one bite at a time.

ORGANIZING OSCAR MADISON

Before we turn to the grand issues of organizing your themes and ideas — creating your "maps" — I want to say a few words about the mundane issues of organizing your desk and your files. Again, in my experience, writers who miss deadlines and exceed the assigned length are almost inevitably, well, slobs. Dare to peek in their offices when they are in the throes of creation, and you'll run to call 9-1-1: Surely some catastrophe has taken place here! Files and photocopies lie about the floor like the aftermath of an avalanche. Books (half of them overdue from the library) rise in Babel-like towers. Yellow sticky notes cluster ten deep on the desk, like bees who've chanced upon a particularly rich vein of clover.

Remember Oscar Madison, the sloppy half of Neil Simon's *Odd Couple*? He was a writer, of course. Typecasting.

But I don't mean to sound like Felix Unger, the fussy neatnik coupled with Oscar Madison. You don't have to be prissy to get organized as a writer. You don't even have to have a clean desk.

In an article I did once about the links between the look of executives' desks and their efficiency, the experts I consulted concluded that the optimum approach was Aristotle's Golden Mean. Too much chaos wastes time; an excess of neatness is counterproductive. These experts advocated instead what one called "organized piles." Most of the truly efficient people I know practice this technique, whatever they call it: To a visitor, the desk might appear slightly messy, with small piles of work here and there. But to its occupant, the desk has a place for everything, and everything is in its place. Those piles of papers are meaningful, not random, and any item on the desk can be retrieved in a flash.

Your whole writing life should be organized in much the same way. Your office doesn't have to look clean enough for your mother-in-law to come visit; it just has to be functional. Yes, you need a filing system, but the important thing is how quickly you can lay your hands on material you need — not how neatly the labels on the folders are calligraphied. You need a folder for each writing assignment, labeled specifically and clearly enough so you'll recognize it a few years from now, and a couple of folders for ideas and clippings for future stories. (A filing system is also important for recycling your own ideas, once written, which is the fastest way to generate "new" stories. How can you write a full-length piece on that psychologist you featured in a sidebar if you can't find your notes from the first story? I keep all my notebooks and all my old story files, on the "you never know" theory, and it's amazing how often that one tidbit I need for a new article turns out to be in my notes for a long-ago assignment.) For most projects—an article assignment, for example—one catchall folder is probably enough. For big chores—a book or a series—it makes sense to subdivide your files into multiple folders.

When I started this book, for example, I ran out and bought several packs of large, ruled index cards, two dozen manila folders, and a plastic file box to keep it all in. I labeled each folder with the name of a chapter (plus a few for "Misc.") and taped the description of the chapter, from my book proposal, on the front. As I took notes and thought of things I wanted to say in the book, I scribbled them down on index cards. Whenever I got a small handful of finished cards, I'd file them by chapter. When I was ready to start writing, I picked up the folder for chapter one and sorted the cards into a logical sequence. And bit by bit the book materialized.

This notion of getting your materials organized goes hand-in-hand with organizing your time. The project takes shape one piece at a time, index card (or whatever) by index card. So, too, your time is organized, taking one step at a time, one folder at a time, one writing session at a time. Ultimately, the organization of your writing itself follows the same pattern: sentences into paragraphs, paragraphs into scenes, scenes into a completed work. Paradoxically, it is this painstaking, methodical approach that allows you to write faster.

The obvious metaphor is building a wall. You don't build a wall forty bricks at a time. One by one the bricks are mortared into place; when you're done, the whole is greater than the sum of the parts, stronger than the pile of bricks and mortar with which you began. The more carefully and skillfully each individual brick is laid, the finer the finished wall will be. Nothing is gained by rushing ahead and building the top before the lower sections are complete.

At the same time, however, nobody builds a wall without a plan. How high will it be? Where will it join the rest of the house? The individual bricks, laid one by one, can't make these decisions for themselves.

ARCHITECTONICS: THE HARDEST PART OF BEING A WRITER

It was Aristotle, again, who said that the work of a writer should have structure the same way the work of a bricklayer or a potter or a carpenter has an underlying structure. A number of modern writers have borrowed the term "architectonics" to describe this deep, fundamental structure so necessary to their work—the ultimate sense of "getting organized" as a writer. The architectonics of a piece of writing, said Norman Sims in his book *The Literary Journalists*, is "the structural design that gives order, balance and unity to a work, the element of form that relates the parts to each other and to the whole." In the simplest sense, it is the scheme that links and orders your index cards or scribbled notes. In the broadest sense, it is the map behind the map—the meta-map, if you'll pardon a dip into jargon—that guides your writing.

In any sense, it is perhaps the most difficult part of being a writer. "The kind of architectonic structures that you have to build," says Pulitzer Prize winner Richard Rhodes (*The Making of the Atomic Bomb, Farm*), "that nobody ever teaches or talks about, are crucial to writing and have little to do with verbal abilities. They have to do with pattern ability and administrative abilities—generalship, if you will. Writers don't talk about it much, unfortunately." Fellow journalist Joe McGinnis's (*The Selling of the President, Fatal Vision*) agrees: He says that the decision-making process before he ever begins to write, deciding about "the unity of the book," is the hardest part of every project.

To understand architectonics, you have to take apart a piece of writing and see its structure. Sometimes the structure is so intricately woven into the fabric of a work that it's lost; even the writer can't find all the subtle patterns once he's finished, and indeed the work has developed unanticipated patterns and synergies of its own. But other writers make their structure more plain. "Formula," you might say with a smug sneer in your voice. "They're writing according to a formula." Ah, but when the formula works, it's a thing of beauty.

Consider the front-page features of the *Wall Street Journal*, masterly examples of a straightforward but versatile structure—a formula, if you must. If the *Journal* has a story on some mega-dollar trend in the shoe industry—the revival of "Beatle boots," perhaps—it rarely relies on the old five-Ws-and-H-lead: "Shoe-industry experts say Beatle boots are making a comeback, with sales up . . ." and so on. No, the *Journal* is more likely to start with a scene in a shoe store, and with a personality to catch reader interest:

> Joe Blow remembers Beatle boots. He remembers wearing them as a teenager, much to the dismay of his less-than-hip parents. Blow, now an account executive with Schmoe, Doe & Smith Advertising in Manhattan, bought Beatle boots again the other day, for the first time in twenty-five years.

Blow is part of a growing nationwide revival of interest in the boots. . . .

Which story are you more likely to read?

Notice that the prototypic *Journal* story gets to the point—what I like to call the "hook"—pretty quickly after introducing Joe and his buying habits. While you can entice readers with anecdote, you also must give them a larger reason to read on (namely: this is a national trend, not just one crazy guy who can't get out of the sixties). So you go from the particular to the general, and you make the leap before readers give up and flip to the mutual fund listings.

It's a pretty basic example of "architectonics," but it works. To really see how a *Journal* story is organized, and how that structure helps not only hold the reader but provide a framework for the information that must be imparted, we need to dissect a real *Wall Street Journal* story.

From Aristotle to Maggots

Imagine you've been given the assignment of writing a front-page feature about (ugh) maggot farming. Yes, maggot farming. That was the unpleasant task given *Journal* reporter Barry Newman a few years ago. The result—2,000 words about, yes, (ugh) maggot farming—is a classic example of *Wall Street Journal* style that was subsequently anthologized in *The Literary Journalists*.

Newman opens his story with an unusual scene, laced with details, found a mile outside the old mill town of Leigh, England: Kevin Ashurst's cinder-block-shed maggot farm, set incongruously in a field of pink wildflowers. The contrast of maggots with pretty pink wildflowers presages the contrasts to come, where the lowly life of maggot farming is linked with the higher glories of, of all things, sports.

Newman spends three more paragraphs, packed with intriguing particulars, before he hits us with his "hook." The lead takes us right into the by-now-obvious question: Why on earth would anyone raise maggots? The answer, of course, is bait.

And here the article pivots, switching from Kevin Ashurst's maggot farm to three paragraphs on what maggots are bait *for*: so-called "coarse fish," which are great sport in England. With more specific details, Newman makes clear why this is a big deal—four million people fish for coarse fish, fishing matches are shown on British TV—and thus why, beyond a grotesque interest in maggots, you should keep reading.

In paragraph nine, these two strands of the narrative that pivot on the "hook" paragraph—maggot farming and coarse fishing for sport—come together as neatly as the warp and woof of a weaving. Last year's champion coarse fisherman, we learn, was none other than Kevin Ashurst, our old friend the maggot farmer from Leigh.

The details and elaboration fit naturally into the structure from here down to the finish. Next we're back at Ashurst's maggot farm (with everything put into context), listening to Ashurst and watching him (ugh) work. Newman plays skillfully on the irony of a maggot farmer as national champion, an irony he's prepared us for by the very two-part structure of the opening. He makes the irony manifest in the closing sentences, in which his protagonist is seen sprinkling chicken heads into a box of dead fish. Ashurst waxes philosophically about the appeal of success, what keeps him in this (ugh) business. It's not the money, he concludes; it's "prestige."

Newman's story unfolds with the grace and precision of a ballet, or of a mathematical proof. You could chart it: M (for maggot farm) + P (for prestige, the national stature of championship fishing) + M/P (the two come together in the character of Ashurst) = D (details about Ashurst, maggot farming and coarse fishing) + I (the ironic juxtaposition of maggot farming with prestige).

Now, I don't know how Barry Newman works. Maybe he's so enormously gifted, or experienced, as a reporter and a writer that such structures come to him automatically. But I suspect that his work is in fact quite carefully planned, that the architectonics are laid down before the writing ever begins.

That's why you need to get organized. Speeding up your writing becomes merely a bonus, a side effect of knowing where your story is going and how you'll get there. So let's look at two different ways in which you can approach the architectonics of your own stories. . . .

FINDING STRUCTURE — OR CREATING IT

Organic Structure: Built-In Answers

The structure of your story may be inherent in the subject—what Coleridge called the "organic" principle of organization—or imposed by you upon the subject matter ("mechanic," in Coleridge's distinction). Newman's story about the maggot farmer is a straightforward example of organic architectonics: Presented with the twin, seemingly disparate themes of maggot farming and championship sport, he introduced first one and then the other, then brought them together and left us with a powerful ironic effect. We might follow much the same course with our mythical story about the great Beatle boot revival. Here, the twin themes are the old (the sixties, represented by

Joe Blow as a teenager) and the new (the boom in Beatle boots, epitomized by adman Blow—an executive in an archetypally with-it pro-
fession). They are brought together, symbolically, by the moment in
the shoe store where Joe buys his first pair of Beatle boots in a quarter-century. This dichotomy could continue throughout the story,
playing off an "everything old is new again" refrain. The ending might
then recombine the elements with a fresh twist—maybe Joe's mom
still doesn't approve of his choice in footwear, or perhaps now she
likes his boots.

Other organic organization schemes are suggested not by the dramatic tensions of the story but by the subject itself. Our story on Beatle
boots, for example, could resemble the shape of a boot: a long, straight
stretch of narration that turns (at the "heel," to continue this farcical
example) and then continues in a perpendicular course, with a curve
upwards again at the "toe." A story of a horse race could easily end
at the same scene where it started, suggesting the oval course of the
race. I once wrote a story on the chess champion Walter Browne that
alternated in scenes between proof of his prodigious ability at games
and the darker side of his career (he labored in the shadow of chess
master Bobby Fischer, and besides it's hard to make a living that way).
The bright and dark episodes suggested the alternating, white and
black progression of a chess game.

John McPhee is a master of the organic form. His book *Oranges*,
for example, simply parallels the life cycle of the fruit he's writing
about; of course, there's nothing simple about the way in which
McPhee weaves a world of information about the citrus industry into
this organic organizational scheme. In *The Search for Marvin Gardens*,
McPhee uses a Monopoly board—originally patterned after Atlantic
City, New Jersey—to structure his story about the real-life, run-down
Atlantic City of today. The contrast between the cardboard, mega-
bucks game and the down-in-the-dumps reality is driven home
through an imaginary Monopoly game that's played throughout the
story. At the dramatic center of another McPhee book, *The Pine Barrens*, about the wilds of New Jersey, stands a chapter on the town of
Chatsworth—"The Capital of the Pines," which sits virtually at the
geographic center of the Pine Barrens, just as the chapter forms the
center of *The Pine Barrens*.

Look for your organizing principles within your subject itself to
build the architectonics of your story. Think about the shapes and
structures inherent in your idea. Doodle on a notepad: What form
does your story suggest? Some stories are naturally linear, with a clear
progression from beginning to end, and when you have such a story

you should grab onto that linear structure for all it's worth. Other tales are more circular, tending back to where they began. Many represent intertwinings of disparate forces or characters, and that intertwining should suggest your story's shape. A few stories — McPhee's Atlantic City/Monopoly article, my black-and-white chess profile — have a structure at the heart of their subject, which you should embrace as long as you're careful not to let it become a gimmick.

"The piece of writing has a structure inside it," McPhee has observed. "It begins, goes along somewhere, and ends in a manner that is thought out beforehand. I always know the last line of a story before I've written the first one. Going through all that creates the form and shape of the thing. It also relieves the writer, once you know the structure, to concentrate each day on one thing. You know right where it fits."

We'll return to that important latter point in the pages to come, as we look at how knowing where you're going banishes writer's block and speeds up your work. But first I want to look at stories that *don't* organize themselves, where some organic principle doesn't spring up out of the material — at what Coleridge called "mechanic" structures.

Mechanic Structure: The Do-It-Yourself Approach

It should come as no surprise by now that I think McPhee is a virtuoso of the mechanic approach as well. Consider his book *Encounters with the Archdruid,* a lengthy profile of Sierra Club president (and "archdruid" environmentalist) David Brower. The mechanical form of the book is exposed in the drawing on the cover: three triangles in a row above a line, below which stands a lone, centered triangle that seems to act as a fulcrum. The three upper triangles represent the three antagonists that McPhee set out to pit Brower (the fulcrum triangle) against. He brought Brower together with, in turn, a mining advocate, a resort-development booster, and a proponent of a dam project, each at the site of their environmental conflict. These three "encounters" form the organizational plan of the book.

McPhee works the same mechanical magic with chronology in several books, most notably in *Travels in Georgia.* Handling chronology, whether in nonfiction or fiction, is one of the toughest tasks a writer faces. The ancient Greeks came up with the notion of *in medias res* (in the middle of things), a scheme on which McPhee does a skillful riff in *Travels in Georgia.* It's the story of, among other things, a woman who dines on the critters she finds squashed in the road. Yes, she eats road kill. (Ugh! Shades of the maggot farm story! I guess you need a strong stomach to be a great writer.) McPhee could have begun by describing an unappetizing scene of the woman devouring road-killed weasel and muskrat, which in fact was the actual chronological start of his travels with her. But while that would certainly have been a grabber, it might have been a little strong for a lead scene, turning off as many readers as it intrigued. It also uses up one of the most powerful scenes in McPhee's tale right at the start: Where could the story possibly go from there, to top that? So instead he begins *in medias res*, with a more acceptable yet still striking anecdote of the woman eating a snapping turtle (better than a *weasel*). Then he goes on to visit, with his protagonist, the stream-channelization project that brought him to Georgia and this story in the first place. (In a sense, here's the "hook" of the article.) Only then does he take us to the actual opening scene of weasel-eating. Skipping past the snapping turtle and the channelization project, the story then proceeds in chronological order. Its mechanical structure, imposed by McPhee for dramatic and reader-interest reasons, could be charted as: B-C-A-D-E-F. . . .

When should you opt for a mechanical rather than organic structure for your own stories? Certainly, if no organic structure suggests itself, it will fall to you to impose some organizing principle on your story. But the mechanical approach needn't be viewed only as a last resort. You should also impose a structure, rather than relying on something inherent in the material, if the result is a more dramatic, gripping way of telling your story. You're a writer, after all, not a camera: Your nonfiction ought to be *more* interesting than unedited real life, and your fiction must be larger and more compelling than the material from which it springs.

The choice may also depend on how your story originates. If you observe something and then deem it worthy of writing about, an organic approach may suggest itself. But if instead you set out to find or create a story—as McPhee did in pitting his environmentalist against three antagonists—you may wind up building a dramatic framework into which you pour the details of your story. Either approach can work; the key is to have a structure once you sit down to write.

Metaphors as Maps

McPhee's *Travels in Georgia* is also a good example of another organizational device you may find useful: the use of language itself as a structural link. McPhee repeats the term "D.O.R." ("Dead On the Road") throughout the road-kill anecdotes, so that later it packs an ironic kick when he describes himself stuck in traffic at the Newark airport: "*Homo sapiens*, D.O.R." You could think of this as symbolism, but it also works in an architectonic sense.

I used this kind of device to connect and animate a story on the symphony conductor in Dubuque. The local symphony boosters had suggested a story on the conductor, since he was celebrating his twenty-fifth anniversary in town. I'd already learned that when you're doing four columns a week, you don't look a gift story idea in the mouth. So I set up an interview with the maestro, a temperamental Iranian immigrant, expecting to do a nice little puff piece on his quarter-century holding the baton. Instead I got a diatribe about what a mistake he'd made coming to Dubuque, how awful his experience there had been, and how his career had been cut short.

But what really stuck in my mind was the image of his first rehearsal with the symphony upon arriving in Dubuque, held in the cafeteria of a local college. So here's how I started:

> Parviz Mahmoud first raised his baton to conduct the Dubuque Symphony Orchestra, twenty-five years ago, atop a rickety stage of roped-together cafeteria tables. At night, when his makeshift orchestra could rehearse in the University of Dubuque's cafeteria, the maestro and the music had to compete with the chop-chop-chop of a butcher cutting meat for the next day's meals.

Then I seized on that image, and made the dramatic "*Chop!*" the organizing motif of the story. This recurring motif worked both to move the story along and as a fundamental metaphor for the maestro's unhappiness with how his career had turned out: "Parviz Mahmoud wonders if he shouldn't have heeded the slap of the butcher's cleaver as an omen, hopped off that wobbly stage and never looked back. *Chop!*"

After a summary of Mahmoud's early career, I brought him to Dubuque and quoted his unhappiness at being stuck there: "Where else do you go from the University of Dubuque? Linwood Cemetery." Almost as punctuation, I repeated: "*Chop!*"

And so on through the story. At last, I ended with one more full-circle reference to the discordant sounds of his first rehearsal:

> He thinks sometimes about how the symphony will replace him. How will they again entice someone to take up the baton here? A Parviz Mahmoud magically made twenty-five years younger would not come, or at least would not stay.
>
> He would hear the chop-chop-chop for what it is—a career

cut short—and flee to where the pastures are greener, the music sweeter.

The point here is that once I hit upon the "chopping" motif, the rest of the story fell together. It was as natural and simple to write as the telling of a familiar anecdote, its parts rolling across my word processor and its narrative bound together by my organizational scheme. As the motif sped my writing, it also lent it power—as demonstrated by the firestorm of controversy that swept the town and especially the symphony after the story appeared. The Dubuque Symphony, incidentally, soon went in search of a new maestro. *Chop!*

A happier example of a simple metaphorical organizational trick is a story I wrote on Captain Grace Murray Hopper, the feisty Navy computer scientist who coined the term "bug" for a computer glitch. I'd read before the interview that the clock in Hopper's Navy office runs counterclockwise. Hopper's explanation: "That's so nobody in the office can say, 'We've always done it that way.' " I seized on that for my lead—as epitomizing Hopper's attitude toward life—and continued playing off the "clock" notion throughout the article. The metaphor, or mix of metaphors, kept the story ticking right along.

"Unlike the backwards clock in her office, the computer revolution Hopper helped wind up has been racing forwards . . ." I wrote, as a transition from her early career to her current comments on computers. The latter included her dramatization of a nanosecond (a billionth of a second), another clock concept woven into the story: "She held up a sheaf of copper wires, each 11.8 inches long: Her nanoseconds, which she distributes at every lecture. 'This is the maximum length electricity can travel in a billionth of a second.' "

Finally, I brought Hopper's career up to her retirement (later rescinded by a special act of Congress): "The saddest day in Grace Hopper's life came soon after her sixtieth birthday, when the clock ran out on her career. . . ."

These examples, abstracted out of context, may seem mechanical or artificial, but in fact they rang true to their respective stories. Thus they worked not only mechanically but organically; like fence posts, they held up the story at crucial points and let it flow along forward.

WHERE ARE THOSE FENCE POSTS, ANYWAY?

How can you find your own "fence posts"? It's mostly a matter of keeping your eyes and ears open for them, of being alive to the possibilities. Is there an image that keeps recurring as you research (or imagine) the story? Does one picture or phrase seem to sum up what you're saying, giving you that *frisson* of "Yes, that's it!"? Is there some place or some thing at the center of your story, the physical or metaphorical locus of your theme?

Don't panic if you can't seem to recognize these possibilities at first glance. Often they won't occur to you until you sit down to mull over your material, to shape what you've gathered into a story. Remember that notion of building a fence: You can't build a fence without first figuring out where it will go. And fence posts don't find themselves — you have to organize your material in such a way that the strongest, tallest points stick out before you ever start to write. Then the story will seem to build itself, stringing out ahead of you. Write fast? You'll have to, just to keep up.

PLANNING FOR SPONTANEITY

Whether you're writing a book, a newspaper article, or anything in between, the same basic principles apply. You need to organize your time, both in terms of finding the time and planning your work to meet a deadline. You need to organize your tools, from your desk to your files, from your notes to your research materials. And you need to organize your story, in the simplest sense of what comes after what and in the deeper architectonics of what it all means.

Once you get organized, you'll find — almost magically — that your writing is better. The time, the tools, and the themes will work *with* you instead of against you. Instead of worrying about meeting deadlines, finding notes among the clutter, and figuring out where your story goes next, you'll be able to concentrate on the pure act of writing. You will achieve what psychologists who study work and creativity call *flow*: that almost effortless, out of time and place, unity of yourself and your work.

And you will write faster. You will write faster because you'll write with confidence. You'll have a "map" of where you're going. You'll be organized in your efforts to get there. No detours. No false starts.

That's the goal. Now let's take it step by step, starting with that old familiar question writers always get asked: Where do you get your ideas?

It's a natural question, but not the most important for the would-be speedy writer. The *real* challenge, as we'll see in the next chapter, is this: Where do you get *fast* ideas?

CHAPTER THREE

FINDING FAST STORIES

• • •

IDEAS ARE EVERYWHERE

When I was writing my newspaper column, knocking out three or four stories a week, people would ask me, "Where do you get your ideas?" They would see this stream of stories, week after week, and wonder what the headwaters could possibly be like. Who has so many ideas, anyway?

It was hard to explain to people not in the writing or reporting business, but the fact was, *getting* the ideas was never the problem. Ideas are everywhere. My first day on the job, I started a manila file folder labeled "Ideas." The pace of my column-writing never caught up with the stuffing and replenishing of my ideas file. When I left for greener pastures, in fact, I bequeathed to my successor not one but two bulging folders full of ideas for columns.

No, getting the ideas wasn't the challenge. The tough part was getting ideas that I could execute within the time constraints of a thrice-weekly feature column. Translating a glimmer of an idea into a do-able column meant figuring out what preliminary research I needed to do and whom to interview, setting up the interview(s), and, usually, driving a hundred miles or so out to East Pigsty, Iowa, and back. Some ideas, often ones that seemed like a good idea when I scribbled them down or tore a nugget of inspiration out of some weekly newspaper, never could survive that leap from idea into action. I'd come to them in my file, think about how hard they would be to execute, shake my head, and flip past to something more realistic for my deadlines. I'll admit: Many of the ideas I bequeathed to my successor fell into this category, and she probably passed them along in turn to whoever followed her on the column.

I don't mean to say I was lazy, or to suggest that laziness is the proper approach when evaluating ideas. Rather, I want to advise against biting off more than you can chew under the circumstances. The circumstances might be your current job or writing schedule, or they might include the limits of your knowledge and abilities. If I'd been a staff writer for a major magazine at the time, for example, with only one story to do that month (or every few months, even), many of the ideas I passed over again and again as unworkable might suddenly have made good stories for me. If I had known more about certain fields—agribusiness, for example—I might have tackled some more substantive ideas in those fields, or tackled the same ideas in a different way.

Write only the stories you can write sounds like a truism, like a statement so obvious and self-evident it hardly bears saying. But accepting this premise and making it a part of your approach to your work is actually a crucial step along the path to writing faster. If you try to write stories that, for one reason or another, you really can't write— whether because you don't have the luxury of time at the present or because the subject is too big for you—you'll do more than slow yourself down and waste time. Ultimately, you will injure your self-esteem as a writer. You will damage the confidence so vital to successful, speedy writing. Yes, you should always stretch as a creative person. But don't try to climb Mount Everest before you can handle the hill in your own backyard. Robert Burns may have been right in principle when he said, "A man's reach should exceed his grasp, else what's a heaven for?"—but that won't impress editors when you can't deliver on an assignment. ("Gee, I only took that assignment on superconductors to grow as a writer. Can I get the manuscript to you in heaven?")

Writing only the stories you can write means you must be a lot choosier when you go looking for ideas. Since ideas seldom come ready-made with you in mind ("Inside this issue of the *New York Times*: Three story ideas just right for Jane Wordsmith"), however, you'll need to learn to see ideas in different ways, to turn them around and adapt them to what you can write.

MAKING IDEAS DO-ABLE

Narrow the Focus

One way to take an idea from the "intriguing but impossible" pile and turn it into something you can write is to narrow the focus. At the time I was in Iowa, for example, farm debt was a big problem. Farmers were going under right and left, and there were serious questions about the long-term survival of the family farm. So, naturally, I thought about doing a big story on farmers and debt—the ultimate "Will the family farm survive?" story. Interview a few dozen farmers, government experts, economists and bankers. Chart the course of farm debt over the past century. Talk to some more experts to see how farm debt relates to the national economy. Visit several family farms as well as large, corporate-owned farms. Go to farm implement dealers and small-town businesses, to see how the sagging agricultural economy had affected their sales. . . . Before I knew it, I had a story that would take months to accomplish—a story that, frankly, was probably beyond my ability to intelligently research and that went deeper than my own interest in the subject.

I could have just tossed my couple of newspaper clippings on farm debt into the "intriguing but impossible" section of my file, and moved on. Instead, however, I thought about how I could narrow the focus of this idea. How could I make it a story that I could write? (Just as important, how could I make it a story that I would *want* to write?) Often, narrowing the focus is as simple as moving from the general to the particular, from the sweeping to the specific. Instead of writing the ultimate round-up story on farm debt, I would write about one farm family in our area. I would bring this big, complex subject home to newspaper readers by showing how it affects some folks pretty much like them. Then, to put my specific farm family into the broader picture, I would include some basic statistics on the scope of the problem, quote a few experts, and compare the family's situation to the national average.

That was a story I could write. Incidentally, it was also a much better and more interesting story than my first take on the idea. It was human; it was real; it was about faces instead of abstractions. I think readers learned more about the crisis confronting the family farm from my little story than from any big story that I, at least, could have written. I wrote the story I could write and did my very best with it, instead of attempting something that was bound to fail and trying to sell my editor and my readers on the results.

Similarly, at the city magazine I edited, we'd been kicking around ideas for a story on the troubled inner city. It was a story potentially as big and complex as the problem. It would not, however, be a story entirely new to our readers, since, of course, the local newspapers have reported extensively on urban and racial problems. My staff writers kicked around ideas for a blockbuster: the definitive take on the gap between Milwaukee's rich and poor, black and white. But I argued that that's a story too mammoth to do right even as a major magazine feature—and that even if we could somehow get our arms around the topic, few readers would slog through such a long and difficult read on a story they might feel they know all too well. Narrow the focus, I advised. Write the story you can write—and that the readers will read. So instead we focused on one inner-city neighborhood, no more than a couple of blocks, and wrote quite specifically about the residents both good (the lawyer sticking it out in her old neighborhood, the high school graduate going on to college) and bad (the gangs, the drunks). We actually showed readers something up close that they hadn't seen before in sweeping, generic stories about urban blight. Instead of trying to eat the whole pie, we made the most out of a single slice.

The same principle applies to fiction. Maybe you aren't really up to writing the ultimate World War II novel—and besides, Herman Wouk has beaten you to it. Instead of spending a decade or two trying to outdo *The Winds of War* and *War and Remembrance*, maybe you should write a novel inspired by your mom's experiences living near a camp for German POWs. Or perhaps you visited, on vacation, a small French town that would be a perfect setting for a romantic story of the Resistance. You don't have to include every shot fired from Pearl Harbor to Hitler's bunker, particularly not if this is your first novel.

With every idea that you attempt, narrow it until you know you can do it right. Test every project against the rule: *Write only the stories you can write.* If it doesn't fit, narrow the focus until it does.

Similarly, fit the idea to the task, instead of expanding the assignment to try to encompass some grand idea. Don't try to make a magazine feature out of a ten-inch newspaper story, or a book out of a magazine feature assignment. Don't try to make a novel out of a short story. Don't play Cecil B. DeMille with a one-act, two-character play. Find the story you can write, and concentrate on writing it right.

The Ignorance Angle

A second way to transform an unworkable idea into a story you can write is to turn your ignorance to your advantage. If the first technique is a question of focus, this is a matter of *angle* or *viewpoint*. I've done a number of stories on businesses or industrial operations—from inside a cheese factory to how Rolls-Royce automobiles are made. For me to try to learn everything there was to know about the chemistry of cheesemaking or the fine points of internal-combustion engines was clearly impossible. (And it would have been a waste of time, since few readers would sit still for a lecture on cheese chemistry or engine design.) Instead, I tackled the stories as simply a skilled observer: Hey, folks, here's what cheesemaking looks, sounds, and smells like. Here's what you would see if you got a guided tour of the Rolls-Royce automobile plant, as I did. Few readers have ever been in a cheese factory, and fewer still have ever gone to England and watched Rolls-Royce cars being made. But everyone's eaten cheese and everyone knows the cachet of Rolls-Royce — so I could take for granted a certain modest level of reader interest in my "inside story." Then I approached these stories from the same viewpoint as most readers: a basic curiosity about where familiar things — cheese, famous cars — come from, about what makes them the way they are.

No, you won't learn how to make cheese or how to build a car from reading my stories. But you'll learn what I did (at least the most interesting parts), see what I saw, and come away knowing something more about the world. I wrote these stories simply by keeping my eyes open, asking questions, and trying to keep in mind what the average reader would want to know.

The ultimate example of this ignorance-is-bliss approach, for me, was my first visit to a dairy farm. I grew up in South Dakota, so people always assume that I know my way around a barnyard. But in fact I was a city kid, the offspring of college professors, not farmers. I grew up thinking that milk came from the grocery store, and the hardest work I associated with milk was struggling to open a carton without ripping the spout. Cows were something to sing about (ee-yi-ee-yi-o).

So one day, as a newspaper writer in Iowa, I got the idea to write about dairy farming. Now, it would have been as ludicrous for me to write an in-depth report on the dairy business as for me to explain general relativity. (Indeed, relativity might have been an easier assignment; at least I'd studied physics in school.) That was not a story I could write — not and meet any of my other deadlines for a few months. The story I could write, instead, was the story of a city kid getting his hands (and, er, shoes) dirty on a dairy farm for the first time. By *using* my ignorance — my honest amazement, in fact — about the hard work that puts milk on my table, I could bring the world of dairy farming alive. Readers who, like me, had little experience with dairy farms could see something new through my eyes; readers who knew dairy farming could enjoy a greenhorn's discovery of something familiar to them.

I don't mean to suggest that all idea problems can be solved by playing George Plimpton. But Plimpton's amateur's-eye-view (in *Paper Lion* and other books) does point up the power of having a fresh angle, of picking a viewpoint appropriate not only for the story but for the writer. Experts often know *too much* about a subject to communicate it effectively (or interestingly!) to a lay audience. Open eyes and an open mind can be potent tools for a writer looking for the fastest and best way to turn an idea into a story.

Much the same principle can be applied to ideas for fiction. Suppose you want to write a spy novel, inspired by the literate espionage sagas of John le Carre. But of course le Carre writes from the inside looking out, based on his firsthand experience of the shadowy world of British intelligence. For you to learn enough to write credibly from that viewpoint would be impossible (particularly with this secret subject!). So perhaps your protagonist ought to be an ordinary citizen — like you — who unwittingly falls into the world of espionage, as in Alfred Hitchcock's *North by Northwest*. You could probably learn enough about the spy game to keep one step ahead of your hero, and your readers. Part of the story then becomes the unfolding of this secret world, paralleling the discoveries you make in your research.

Any time you consider a complex subject, think about whether it's worth your while to become an expert before writing about it. Maybe you can write an even better, more engaging story just by learning more than your readers know. Try on a new viewpoint and see how your story looks now. Remember: It's the angle from which you approach an idea that makes for a story you can write, and write fast.

The Hierarchy of Audiences

A third technique for turning ideas into fast stories — assuming you're a freelancer and not a staff writer — is changing the intended audience. (Obviously, staff writers are stuck with their publication's given audience.) This is a variation on the shifts in focus and viewpoint: You change the story that you have to write by changing who you're writing for.

For example, suppose that you have an idea to write about nuclear power. As always, the next step is to find the story that you can write about this idea. You might have found that there's a terrific market for an up-to-date textbook on nuclear power, but — unless you have a degree in nuclear physics or engineering — that's probably not something you can write. It's certainly not something you can write fast. So you could aim instead for a general audience, attempting a popular-science book on nuclear power or possibly a major magazine piece. But again, unless you have some background in this field — say, you've covered it before — that would be a daunting undertaking.

Take the idea one step further in the hierarchy of audiences: How about a children's book on nuclear power? Or a visit to a nuclear power plant for a juvenile science magazine? Those ideas might be do-able given your current knowledge of the subject and some quick research. Best of all, actually doing such a story could give you the additional expertise necessary to then pitch the idea for a general adult audience.

The same kind of hierarchy applies to local, regional and national stories. Suppose you have an idea on quilting — say you've noticed that several younger women you know have taken up quilting. The first and fastest story you might write could be a trend article for your local newspaper, based on the people you already know plus a visit to local stores that sell quilting supplies. Then you might try to broaden the story for a regional audience: Take what you already know and do some research in neighboring cities, then pitch the story to a state or regional "shelter book" (*Sunset* or *Midwest Living*, for example). Ultimately, you might even be able to write and sell a national story ("Quilting Boom Sweeps U.S." or "Quilting: It's Not Just for Grandma Anymore").

The important thing is to try walking before you sign up for the Boston Marathon. Write the fastest version of the idea first, then look for ways to write it for a different audience. Each subsequent treatment of the original idea will be faster to write because you've already done at least some of the homework.

Look at every idea with your mental writer's time clock in mind: How can you translate this idea into something you can write quickly? Narrow the focus, change the viewpoint, and alter the intended audience. Every idea has a hundred, a thousand permutations. In each idea, there is a story that you are uniquely suited to write, the story only you can write fast.

HOW THE IDEAS GET YOU

But hold on a minute. Haven't we put the cart before the proverbial horse here? We've been talking about how to evaluate ideas, how to turn them on their heads and twist them inside out to create fast stories. What about *finding* the ideas? You've got an empty head and a bunch of empty file folders; the heck with evaluating ideas — how do you get them in the first place?

You've forgotten that finding ideas is the easy part. Without any framework of what to do with them — with what makes a fast story — you could wade out into the ocean of ideas and come back with a net so full you'd spend all your time sorting through your catch. Before you go fishing for ideas you can write fast, it's best to know something about what your prey looks like, its habits, and where it hides.

You're still skeptical. OK, let's take the life-style section of a major metropolitan Sunday newspaper — the "Tempo" section of the *Chicago*

Tribune, since that's what happens to be lying on the floor by my coffee table — and find some ideas. Please note that these aren't necessarily fast story ideas, or even ideas that you or I could reasonably write without lots and lots of research. These are just raw, unfiltered ideas found in eight pages of newspaper, including ads:

- An item on how much CBS-TV will have to cut from the movie *Sea of Love* to make it suitable for broadcast: How about a story on TV censors, the men and women who wield the scissors and determine how much we do and don't see?

- Skitch Henderson turns seventy-three: How about a reminiscence of great band leaders?

- A letter to Dear Abby praises a national nonprofit adoption program for handicapped children: Is there a chapter in your town? Why not profile some parents who've taken on this challenge?

- Another letter to Abby complains about a bad experience with baby-sitters: What about a guide to finding a good sitter? Or a story for teens, telling them how to get started as baby-sitters? Or an economics story, on whether jobs at fast-food franchises and shopping malls have lured teens away from baby-sitting, causing a shortage?

- A front-page story talks about how much harder winter was to get through a hundred years ago in Chicago: What was winter like a century ago in your town? Or is there an anniversary of a historically bad blizzard, hot summer, flood, or cold wave coming up?

- An ad from the University of Chicago Hospitals talks about the progress that's been made in the war against cancer: What's your nearest university medical center or research hospital doing about cancer?

- Another ad promotes tutoring centers for kids who have trouble in school: Do such places really work? What's available in your area?

- A TV note mentions that a cable channel is showing a James Bond film festival. How about a whimsical piece on how 007 would be different today, in the era of glasnost and real high-tech gadgetry?

And so on. That's something like fourteen ideas, or better than one per page. And I was just getting warmed up. With a little practice, you too can find more story ideas than you know what to do with.

So the point is to know in advance what to do with the ideas you find, whether to pursue them or ignore them. Otherwise, you'll waste a lot of time and energy clipping and considering ideas you can't realistically write. *Gee, wouldn't it be great to write a profile of Tom Cruise?* you might think, and then start making a file on this big-time movie star. But unless you have some reasonable expectation of being able to interview Cruise, you'd be wasting your time. Ideas are cheap; your time isn't. Part of learning to write fast is learning to concentrate your efforts on the art of the possible.

That attitude affects, in turn, your whole process of searching for stories. First, once your inner "radar" gets tuned to fast stories vs. unlikely ideas, you'll be a smarter idea scanner. You will start to see an immediate "fit" between your knowledge and skills and any would-be story that floats across your horizon. As author Robert Payne put it, "The ideas get you."

Second, concentrating on the art of the possible affects where you start your search for ideas. Some sources are simply more ripe for workable ideas than others. To use an extreme example, your daily newspaper is probably a more fruitful and efficient place to seek stories than the *Bulletin of Atomic Scientists* — unless you're an atomic scientist who can translate items therein for a lay audience. (Conversely, a national newspaper such as the *New York Times* or *Wall Street Journal* is another good source for national ideas that, in turn, can be localized or regionalized for your market — better, say, than more parochial out-of-town papers or magazines.)

HOME IS WHERE THE FAST IDEAS ARE

As Dorothy learned in *The Wizard of Oz*, there's no place like home — and that's true in the idea chase as well. Start with what you know, what's close to home. (No, I didn't know anything about dairy farming, to pick up on an earlier example, but it was certainly close to home. The ignorance-is-bliss approach to an idea doesn't make much sense if you can't get ready access to the subject. Sure, you'd like to take a fresh approach to Tom Cruise, but will he let you?) Not only does the adage "write what you know" speed up your writing; it also adds to the authenticity of the finished product. In the case of fiction, your make-believe will be more believable if you're not making it *all* up. Consider giving your protagonist the same job that you, a friend or a relative actually hold. Think of the success suspense novelist Dick Francis, a former jockey, has had writing books set in the racing world. Or Elizabeth Peters — an archaeologist in real life — and her series of archaeology-based thrillers. And don't set your whole story in a land or time period that's utterly foreign to you. Peters can afford to set several of her books in and around the tombs of Egypt — because she's been there and worked there. Why do you think horror writer Stephen King sets almost all his nerve-wracking novels in his home state of Maine?

Your job, if you have one other than writing, is of course a perfect source of fast stories; if not your job, then your hobbies. Information in trade journals in your field or specialized hobby publications can often be turned into stories for the general public. Here you already have the inside track on the necessary expertise. This kind of idea hunting has led me to sell stories on comic books and computers, both hobbies of mine.

The next step out in the circle of what's familiar and fast might be friends, neighbors or relatives, their vocations and avocations. I got the idea for a story on Tupperware, for example, from a neighbor who kept inviting my wife to her Tupperware parties; one night I accepted in my wife's stead, and wrote a man's-eye view of this mostly female institution. That was a lot easier, I might note, than pursuing the story the other way around: deciding to write about Tupperware and then trying to track down a party somewhere.

Finally, your own community is another good place to find workable ideas. If you live in a town of any size, you probably have a small army of people ready, willing and paid to supply you with story ideas: the public relations staffs at colleges and universities, hospitals and corporations. While many of their ideas will be dull or too obviously self-serving, these PR people do have a font of information and expertise at their fingertips that you can tap; the more experienced among them are savvy media professionals, used to pitching ideas to editors, who can help you identify salable stories. By making friends with your local PR staffs and by asking a few smart questions, you can benefit from their legwork and resources. Get on PR mailing lists. You'll throw out most of what you get, but what you cull from that chaff could be ready-made stories. The PR department of the university I used to work at, for example, produced an ongoing series of feature-idea "tip sheets" — capsule story descriptions, complete with phone numbers to call to follow up. Many of these could be instantly translated into queries: the campus ghostbusters, for example, or the world's top expert on how homing pigeons find their way home. Others needed only an infusion of a few other experts from around the country to round them out into major trend pieces: Is coal making a comeback? Should the terminally ill have the right to die? Can happy thoughts keep you healthier? Of course, such stories almost automatically qualify as fast, because the PR staff can give you a jump-start on researching and setting up interviews. Yes, they'll be happy to help — it's what they get paid for.

Other story starters will simply find you, once you know how to keep your eyes open in your community. Elizabeth Peters says she gets ideas from odd signs in shop windows, street names and fillers in her local paper. When I was writing my newspaper column, my wife used to scan the classified ads for me; that's how we found, for example, a woman whose business was raising canaries (in her home!). It also pays to follow the national media for tidbits about your community, that might not be known, right under your nose. For instance, the *New York Times* had an item about the growth of baseball in Australia, and happened to mention that the only Australian currently playing professionally in the U.S. was a Milwaukee Brewers farmhand. Bingo! There was a potential story for my city magazine. We soon discovered, in fact, that the Brewers have one of the major leagues' most active recruiting operations Down Under.

Finding your ideas close to home doesn't mean they have to be mundane or parochial (witness our leap to baseball in Australia). Even science fiction, that haven of far-out ideas and exotic locales, usually starts with the familiar: Roger Zelazny says he's used the Yellow Pages to generate ideas. He'll flip through the phone book, noting the first half-dozen or so entries he spots, then try to project those businesses into the future. Or he might shift some familiar enterprise to another planet, or make its customers aliens. A bait and tackle ad led to Zelazny's award-winning futuristic "fish story," "The Doors of His Face, the Lamps of His Mouth."

Starting from the known and projecting into the unknown is a lot easier than trying to imagine an utterly fictional reality with no grounding in the familiar. That's partly the secret of the science fiction writer's favorite question, "What if?" What if the South had won the Civil War (*Bring the Jubilee* by Ward Moore)? What if you could make yourself invisible (*The Invisible Man* by H.G. Wells, *The Murderer Invisible* by Philip Wylie)? What if an asteroid came too near the earth (*A Torrent of Faces* by James Blish and Norman L. Knight), or what if we earthlings ran out of room for our trash and began using asteroids as extraterrestrial landfills (*Garbage World* by Charles Platt)?

Once you get into the habit of looking around you for fast story ideas, you'll find them everywhere. You'll start to recognize that "fit" between an idea and your own abilities, interests and resources. Your mind will seem to work in overdrive, calculating the ways in which you and only you could put a particular spin on an idea. Instead of groping for stories you really can't write, and setting impossible goals for yourself, you'll discover a wealth of speedy, do-able stories virtually at your own front door.

That doesn't mean, of course, that you can't find fast ideas whenever you travel. Every weekend getaway, every vacation or business trip, is fodder for several stories. If you took the trip, after all, someone else might want to follow in your footsteps (or tire tracks) — and you can guide them. But travel doesn't have to be limited to ideas for travel articles per se: You can set a scene of your novel in your destination, or use examples from there in a round-up article.

The key to turning travel experiences into fast-story fodder is to be a pack rat. Grab every brochure, flier, handout, map, guidebook and pamphlet you can get your hands on. They're valuable not only for the written facts and figures, dates and names, but for the photographs that can jog your memory and add colorful descriptions to your copy. (You can also take photographs yourself, of course. It doesn't matter whether you're a terrific photographer or not, as long as your pictures are in focus. Always take *color* snapshots, so you'll know later whether that quaint old inn you're describing is red or blue.) Take an extra suitcase if you have to, just for your research goodies, or mail a package back home to yourself. Also tote a notebook, to supplement the published materials with insights and observations of your own. Don't count on remembering the details (addresses, prices, hours) of even the most memorable vacation; you might not use some of this raw material for months or even years. Then, once you get home, devote a file cabinet or a box in the closet to all your travel materials — labeled so you can find them when you need them. The result is a resource collection not even the biggest library can match, and a trove of story ideas almost as do-able as those found right around the corner.

NEXT, DON'T WRITE THAT STORY!

All right, let's assume you've got an idea, you know it's something you can handle, and — for the sake of example — it's for a magazine article. You've discovered a hot trend right in your hometown, and you know you can nationalize it with some library research (chapter five) and a few phone interviews (chapter six).

Stop right there. Whatever you do, don't write that story — at least, not yet. The final secret of finding fast stories, particularly in the nonfiction arena, is not to write them until you have a place that will print them. Otherwise you'll waste all the time you've saved, writing articles with the wrong slant for an audience that doesn't exist. You'll fill up your files with orphaned stories and have no time left to write for results.

If you want to write and sell nonfiction, you need to write query letters first. Don't go ahead and write the article, thinking that its sheer wonderfulness will sweep an editor off his feet; it might indeed be wonderful, but it still might not be right for the editor's publication. (If you're a beginner without a fistful of clips, you may have to write "on spec," without a guaranteed assignment, but you should still get an editor's interest and input before you write.) Don't go to the other extreme, either, and call the editor and put him on the spot: I've never assigned an article over the phone and I never will. At most, I'll grudgingly tell a telephoning writer to send me a query—which the writer could have done anyway, without interrupting my already hectic day. No, here are the three secrets to selling articles without wasting your time or the editor's: query, query, query.

Interestingly, successful query writing, like finding fast stories in the first place, has less to do with *finding* ideas than with evaluating them and applying your creativity to them. The key is the spin you put on an idea (the *angle*, in editor-ese), and how closely that approach fits the approach of the magazine. Obviously (though, trust me, it's not so obvious to many would-be writers), you shouldn't query an automotive magazine with an idea about politics, a city magazine with an idea set in some other city, or a children's magazine with tips on kitchen remodeling. But the fit between the query and the queried has to be much closer than just matching subject areas. Study the magazines you hope to sell to. Try to read the editor's mind. Photocopy or tear out the contents pages and save them—often the capsule descriptions of the stories are the best guides to what the editor wants out of his articles. Then try to imagine the stories you have in mind fitting into that contents page. If you can't, save your time and your stamps.

Querying thus becomes part of your whole idea-hunting process. Not only should you comb the vast universe of story ideas out there for ideas that *you* can readily write; you should further select only those stories that you can write *for somebody*. Think of what magazines you want to write for, markets you have a reasonable chance of cracking, and keep them in mind as you look for ideas. Play editor: If you were the editor of *Midwest Living*, would you be interested in a hard-hitting exposé of corruption in Kearney, Nebraska? After all, Nebraska is in the *Midwest*, and these corrupt guys are, well, *living*— right? Wrong. *Midwest Living* focuses on travel, home, food, gardening and other service topics—the good life in the Midwest, not the seamy underside of living there. What about a query on antiquing throughout Indiana, drawing on your own travels and on your own hobby of collecting antiques? It might be worth a shot.

There's no magic formula for writing winning query letters. It's a crapshoot. Maybe the editor's in a bad mood because his car's in the shop, or maybe she just bought a story almost identical to yours. All you can do is make sure your idea is in the ballpark, demonstrate its appeal in a few well-written paragraphs (and well proofread, for heaven's sake!), and show that you can handle the assignment. In other words, what should go into a query is what makes the idea a fast one: its congruence with the magazine's needs and your expertise and ability. If you approach every idea with those factors in mind, not only will you be able to speedily execute the assignments you get— you'll also increase your odds of getting assignments in the first place.

"Where do you get your ideas?" Now you can see why that's not the important question. The important question is, "What can you *do* with this idea?"

To fully answer *that* question, you need to be able to imagine an idea through the process of research and interviewing—to envision what you'll need to go through before getting an idea onto paper. You need to be able to formulate a fast battle plan for gathering the material for a story. You need, as we'll see in the next chapter, to become a good general.

CHAPTER FOUR

PLANNING YOUR RESEARCH AND INTERVIEWING

• • •

WINNING THE RESEARCH WAR

Efficiently gathering the material for a story — whether for a brief magazine article or a blockbuster novel — requires what West Point types might refer to as "good generalship." It's easy to get bogged down in research and interviewing; for a writer, these preparatory stages can be the authorial equivalent of a land war in Asia. You can expend all your mental matèriel on getting ready to write, and have little time or energy left for the real battle at the keyboard.

Remember those staff writers I talked about, who swore up and down that they'd have an assignment finished by the next day? Remember the commanders who kept promising "the light at the end of the tunnel" in Vietnam? Well, the dark at the end of the tunnel starts long before either the enemy or the lead sentence is engaged. Those writers not only tended to over-research and over-interview, but too often they approached their research and interviewing *without a strategy*. That's where the problem begins. That's the root of the jungle of notes (which must be slogged through, even though only a tiny fraction ever gets used) and the morass of taped interviews (which must be laboriously transcribed, even though only a few key comments will make it into the story). It's not bad writing; it's bad planning — bad generalship. And planning can spell the difference between a successful writing *blitzkrieg* and trench warfare in the library and with a tape recorder.

Like any general approaching a campaign, you need a strategy — and you need it before the first comma is fired. The strategy must grow out of your conception of the story: your angle, viewpoint, focus, audience. The research and interviewing strategy for a book-length project on, say, Hollywood special-effects artists would be very different from the strategy for a 2,500-word take on Industrial Light and Magic. But the difference is more than just a question of length and ambition. Your strategy for a *Premiere* magazine story on special-effects wizards ("Inside the ILM Workshop," for example) would be quite different from the research and interviewing plan for a special-effects story for *Inc.* magazine ("The Business of Movie Magic: How ILM Makes Special Effects Pay on the Bottom Line"). The strategy, like the query that got you the assignment in the first place, must spring from your unique understanding of the story you plan to tell.

Don't get the idea that I'm pooh-poohing the importance of thorough, enterprising research and interviewing. Quite the opposite: As Jim Bishop (*The Day Lincoln Was Shot*) has observed, "Assuming that all authors have a flair for a well-honed phrase, the difference between the winners and the losers is research, the digging of facts." Indeed, it's precisely because good research and savvy interviewing are so crucial that you must target your efforts and not fritter away your prewriting time. Let's face it: There are only so many hours in the day (twenty-four, last I looked), and every minute you waste on unnecessary or fruitless research is a minute you aren't getting good material — or honing your prose in actual writing. Over-researching is not good writing; it's busywork masquerading as good writing.

Nor am I saying that you can wave some magic wand and make the hard, often time-consuming work of research and interviewing disappear. *Roots* would not have been the same book, for example, if Alex Haley had researched the ocean-crossing ordeal of new slaves just by reading about it, or if he'd simply relied on his imagination. Instead, Haley caught a freighter from Africa to America and spent the nights of the voyage sleeping naked on a plank in the lightless hold of the ship. Only then could he write with feeling about how his ancestor must have felt. (The art of the possible comes into play here, however, along with the art of writing. If you don't have the time or resources to tackle a project as ambitious as *Roots*, don't get in over your head. Sure, retracing the journey of Marco Polo might make an interesting book, but unless you have a big bankroll and prior experience trekking across Asia, it might not be the book for you. Remember: Write only the stories you can write.)

Many of the most notable works of nonfiction in recent years are the result of prodigious feats of research. John McPhee's *Travels in Georgia*, which I've already discussed, sprang from traveling 1,100 miles of southern roads with his field-zoologist subject. For his book on Alaska, *Coming into the Country*, McPhee spent several months at a time over a two-year period touring that state's back country. Tracy Kidder spent eight months inside Digital Equipment Corp. to write his Pulitzer prizewinning *The Soul of a New Machine*. And of course the stories that broke the Watergate scandal resulted from a now-legendary interviewing dragnet; between them, *Washington Post* reporters Bob Woodward and Carl Bernstein interviewed more than 1,000 sources to get the story.

But it's not just nonfiction where research and even interviews are crucial to the success of a writing project; fiction, too, requires an infusion of facts to make credible those parts that you make up. Consider the novels of James Michener (*Hawaii, Iberia*, and many more) — rich, complex feats of research that just happen to take the form of fiction. Or Arthur Hailey, whose novels (*Airport, Wheels, Hotel*, and so on) require months of research before the writing.

Increasingly, in fact, the lines between nonfiction and fiction techniques have blurred. Tom Wolfe and others pioneered the "new journalism" in the 1960s, applying the techniques of fiction to reportage; more recently, Wolfe has applied his journalistic skills to the novel with *Bonfire of the Vanities*.

The point is, few works of writing can be simply made up out of whole cloth. Even (especially!) science fiction, which sets its sagas in imaginary worlds, requires research: Just how much of Jupiter *is* ammonia, anyway? It might be good to know before your hero tries to, er, land there.

So, no, the secret to speeding up your research and interviewing isn't simply to eliminate it, or even to do as little as possible. Indeed, doing too little advance work can actually slow you down once you start writing: If you don't have all the information you need, you can hit a roadblock far more serious than writer's block. By the time you've gone out and done the research you should have done in the first place, you'll have lost your "flow" — and you may have to trash some of what you've already written, to make it concur with the new-found facts.

Rather, to return to the military metaphor that you're probably hoping I forgot about several paragraphs back, the secret is developing a research and interviewing strategy that captures all the facts you need — and covers as little extraneous territory as possible. That requires thinking hard about your story right from the initial idea (as we started to do in the last chapter), developing efficient ways to record what you'll later use in writing your story (but not oodles of data you'll never need), approaching your research in a way that maximizes results, and preparing for your interviews so you get the most out of the least talking time.

In short, you need to read this chapter before setting foot in the library or asking your first question. Remember what they said about Wellington's defeat of Napoleon: The battle of Waterloo was won on the playing fields of Eton. So, first, some schooling; later, you'll be ready to take on the world.

MATCHING YOUR STRATEGY TO YOUR STORY

Part I: No Horsing Around

To show how to develop a research and interviewing strategy, and how that planning speeds up your work, let's look at two examples— one the researching of a "round-up" article and the other a personality profile. In both cases, I'll use stories I've written, not out of egotism, but because I know the story behind my own stories best.

The round-up article was an assignment for *Express*, a magazine published for Federal Express customers. The nature of the magazine made the roundup a little unusual and quite a bit more difficult: My job was to write 1,500 words on the horse-breeding industry— specifically, including how horse breeders and sellers rely on Federal Express to get their business done.

So this is what I had to start with: A very specific angle, which would guide and channel my research and interviews. A relatively brief word count, which meant I didn't have to learn everything there is to know about the thoroughbred world (but also that I'd have to be highly selective, since whole books have been written on this business). A few not-very-useful (as it turned out) leads on Federal Express customers in the horse trade. And, oh, by the way, a deadline only a couple of weeks away, since I was their second choice as the writer. (Writer number one, who lived closer to the heart of the horse business, had gotten a full-time job and dropped the assignment after frittering away most of the magazine's lead time. It was up to me to ride to the rescue.)

I quickly developed a handful of major goals for my research and interviewing, based on the kind of information I knew I'd have to gather to accomplish the assignment:

1. Get a quick general overview of the thoroughbred business.
2. Get some historical background and a feel for why the business is now so fast-paced and high-pressured that it needs Federal Express.

3. Find some specific examples of different ways in which horse breeders and sellers rely on overnight delivery.

4. Get some quotes from actual Federal Express customers, quotes that I could use to highlight points 1, 2 *and* 3. (I wouldn't have time to waste talking to generic experts for quotes relating to points 1 and 2; my interviews would have to concentrate on actual customers, once I found them, and get the overview material at the same time.)

With that basic strategy in mind, I started at the library with the *Encyclopedia of Associations*. There I found the Thoroughbred Owners and Breeders Association, to which I placed a quick call for help. Without going into a lot of detail, I simply asked for an introductory kit—brochures, back issues of their magazine, photocopies of news stories, or whatever they could send me—that would help give me an overview, as well as leads to potential Federal Express customers. At the library I also found a book, *The Horse Traders* by Steven Crist, that I scanned both for a feel of the business and (as it developed) three pages of specific notes. Sure, I could have checked out a dozen books on horses—but, remember, this was only a 1,500-word article. I didn't need to become an expert or to fill a dozen notebooks with information I'd never use. The most important part of my story (don't forget the angle!) wouldn't come from books, but from interviews.

I got another seven pages of notes from the materials sent by the Thoroughbred Owners and Breeders Association—including the addresses and phone numbers of the largest horse auction sales companies. I called Fasig-Tipton Co., the second-largest such firm, on the theory that number-two might be trying harder and thus more eager for publicity. Sure enough, eventually I got a phone interview with a charming senior vice president at Fasig-Tipton, who confessed (to my delight and relief) that the firm was "an extremely heavy user" of Federal Express. Thanks to my planning, I was able to get the Fasig-Tipton VP to talk quotably on the industry in general, why it was now so fast-paced, and, of course, how the firm uses overnight delivery for its sales catalogues and other key materials.

A few more interviews, following up on leads from Federal Express and on phone numbers found in the package from the association, and I was ready to write. In all, I took just twenty-one pages of tightly focused notes. And, yes, I turned in the story in time to make the tight deadline.

My fast thoroughbred story is an example of how to efficiently cut a specific slice out of a very big pie, how to cover a far-flung and distant subject without traveling except by phone lines, and how to maximize a minimum number of interviews. The approach fit the assignment—that's why it worked. If the task had been instead, say, a 5,000-word travel article celebrating the charms of Kentucky's thoroughbred country, the goals and strategy would have been entirely different. I still might have called the thoroughbred association and read a background book or two, but I would also have had to travel to get a notebook-full of visual details. I might still have interviewed the VP from Fasig-Tipton, but it would have been in the context of a walk-through of his operation.

More broadly, this example also shows some general tactical lessons you can apply to almost any story you undertake. Here are some key steps to keep in mind in your own projects:

1. Develop a list of major research goals, a list that flows directly from the specific focus of your story.

2. Break down your goals by likely sources of information. Wherever possible, combine your efforts to get the most out of a single library visit or interview.

3. Cast the widest net with the information sources that require the least effort on your part—like my simple phone call to the association. I didn't waste a lot of time making their job easier by narrowing my request.

4. As you tap each information source, be prepared. Make sure you get what you came for. *Then* explore whether this source might also be helpful in addressing any of your other research goals, and whether this source can in turn open doors to other efficient information resources.

5. Make your own luck. I called the number-two auction house because I figured they'd be more eager to talk. Lucky me, they also turned out to be a Federal Express customer. If I'd gone down the list to number 45, however, that firm might have proven too small to do much Federal Express business.

Part II: Capitalist Toolkit

Next let's look at another assignment I did for a sponsored magazine: a profile of publisher Malcolm Forbes for the Farmers Insurance Co.'s *Friendly Exchange*. Once again, the strategy had to fit the story—but it was a very different fit. Here I did travel and did interview face-to-face, gathering atmosphere and background details at the same time. My deadline wasn't so tight—but time was still of the essence, because I was allotted only half an hour with the great man. I had to prepare for the interview so as to get the most out of my time, and not to waste any of my minutes gathering facts I could get from secondary sources.

The story was for a special issue paying tribute to great Americans, so my job was to show Forbes as a personification of the American dream—a classic success story of a guy who, now that he's made it, enjoys life to the fullest by collecting, motorcycling, even ballooning. Gathering raw material in this case was no challenge: I quickly found or was sent by Forbes's PR man published stories from *Penthouse, Smithsonian, New York, New Jersey Monthly, Americana,* even *Printing News.* As I took notes from these stories and from Forbes's official bio, I kept track in the back of my mind what I *wasn't* finding. What questions did I still have about this unique American? What holes did I need to plug? In particular, I thought about what kind of quotes I would need from Forbes in person to support my American-dream angle.

Ultimately, I took into the interview my notebook and a single 5×8 index card on which I'd penned a very rough skeleton of my questions. Since I knew my time was limited, I planned to get right to the point and then back and fill from there. The first lines on my index card read:

Am. dream
inheritance — own start
own kids — handed to em?
anybody grow up to be MF?

Beside these starters I'd scribbled bits gleaned from previous Forbes interviews: "Sheer ability spelled inheritance" and "lucky." If I had trouble getting Forbes going, I figured I could toss these old quotes back at him to spark a reaction.

I also wanted to get at something crucial to my focus: Forbes's perception of himself as a self-made man versus his own modest inheritance and the more significant estate awaiting his children. And what about the American dream today—can anyone still grow up to be Malcolm Forbes?

"The American Dream in the hearts and minds of most people has probably rarely been more universally alive in this country," Forbes told me — good stuff, exactly what I needed for my assignment.

About his children, he told me: "They grew up understanding that these accoutrements [the magazine's yacht and so on] had a function in gathering information for the magazine. They knew darn well it wasn't theirs by divine right."

And his own secret for success, he said, was: "You can't be successful if you don't love what you're doing. . . . Psychic income is what real income is used for, anyway."

I asked him about capitalism ("No longer dirty word young?" my index card read, meaning, "Is capitalism no longer a dirty word to America's young people, as it was in the sixties?"), his "Capitalist Tool" slogan, and his role in the magazine. Then, with those indispensable inquiries under my belt, my questions went on through his career and his mania for collecting — seeking to add color to what I already knew about the man. Towards the bottom of my index card, finally, assuming I had the time, I planned to return to broader questions. I knew exactly how these answers, if I could get them, would provide an ending for my article:

What next?
• Retire?
• Regrets?
• Disappt?
• Epitaph?

Maybe that last was too stock a question, but it wound up giving me exactly what I needed for a close. In fact, it was a question Forbes had thought about.

My article concluded:

Not that he is about to step aside for his heirs any time soon.

"Retire? In no way, shape or form, till I'm called higher or—more likely—lower." He points and chuckles.

Though he's a man who has no intention of giving up his toys until he has to, Forbes has already written an epitaph for the day his time runs out. He grins and recites: "While alive, he lived."

Because I had a strategy, I got what I needed from my brief interview. Although I'd read a pile of previous articles about my subject, my story was fresh: Rather than getting bogged down in the huge amount of information readily available in my research, I plucked out of it only what I needed. My reading gave me background and raw facts and prepared me for an efficient interview, while the interview itself—hewing tightly to my angle—gave me most of the material that ultimately wound up in the story.

What generalizations can you draw from my "Capitalist Tool" encounter for your own projects? Here are four that occur to me:

1. Don't be afraid to get material the easy way, from secondary sources and PR people. Never plagiarize, but don't go out of your way to reinvent the wheel: Facts are facts, wherever and however you find them.

2. Use existing information—quotes, anecdotes—in an interview as fuel for new, original stuff: "You once said that. . . ." By feeding material back to a subject and forcing him to react to it, you can make it fresh—and your own.

3. Prioritize. Get the most important answers early on.

4. Choreograph your interviews in advance, but be prepared to go with—and redirect—the flow.

And, of course, fit the strategy to the story. From horses to heroes, the basics of efficient research and interviewing are the same: Get your angle. Develop a strategy that flows from your angle. Focus your efforts on achieving your strategic goals.

YOUR #1 WEAPON: THE NOTEBOOK

Okay, so you've got a strategy and you're ready to charge, armed to the teeth with . . . a pen and a notebook? Yes, even in these days of high-tech weaponry, the writer's most effective research and interviewing tools remain the humble pen and low-tech notebook. But bear with me: It's not as simple as it sounds. There are tricks to efficient notetaking, tricks only slightly less sophisticated than a Patriot missile or a $600 toilet seat.

Early in my career as a writer, I learned the hard way (notebooks scattered all over the room, and is that quote I want in the notebook on the chair or in the loose pile of photocopies atop the aquarium?) to take all the notes for one story in a single notebook, clearly labeled on the front. If your fact-gathering requires more pages, only then should you go to a second volume ("Malcolm Forbes Profile B"). Number the pages consecutively, from 1 to whatever it takes.

Your notebook isn't just for notes from interviews. Take the time to copy the salient points from any secondary sources into your notebook, rather than relying on marked-up photocopies or dog-ears in books. Not only does this save you from an unsightly and unworkable sprawl of information once you sit down to write, it actually aids the writing process in two ways. First, it forces you to begin distilling the data for your story; you will always have more facts than you can fit in an article, and the sooner you start boiling them down, the better. There's nothing like writer's cramp to force you to be selective. Second, taking notes from secondary sources places that selected information more firmly in your mind, where your subconscious can begin shaping it into original prose. Later, when you need a piece to fit the puzzle of your unfolding article, it will be in the back of your mind as well as in your notebook, ready to pop into place. A photocopier, by contrast, copies information only to another dead piece of paper, not into the lively confines of your creative brain.

Copying material into your notebook not only helps you remember the salient facts, but also why this information is important to your story. If you must copy it down, rather than simply slapping a book or article on the photocopier, you're forced to think about the reasons these facts are useful—how these notes advance the angle of your story. It might sound as though taking the time to copy research notes into your notebook is a waste of time, especially when high-tech alternatives like the photocopier are available. But, in fact, the time you invest at this stage will save far more time later, deeper in the writing process, when you must bring order out of a chaotic mass of information. That is the very heart of writing, and the sooner you begin this work, the better.

Whether copying from the printed page or recording interviews, you will, however, need a way of writing quickly. Some writers learn shorthand for this purpose; others develop their own personal shorthand of codes and abbreviations for common words. My own notes would be undecipherable to anyone else — and not just from the legacy of years of "U" for "Unsatisfactory" grade-school penmanship. I write "w/" for "with" and "&" for "and," of course, but other codes are more quirky: "cp" means "computer" and "×" (as in $4 \times 9 = 36$) stands for "time." You'll develop your own system as you go along; don't worry about deciding everything in advance—just remember what a notation means once you scribble it!

You can create other codes for an individual story, never to be used that way again. In the notebook for my horse-breeding story, for example, "thb" is short for "thoroughbred" and "h" means "horse"—though in a story about, say, a stage magician it might stand for "hypnosis." When profiling someone, it's surely not necessary to write the subject's full name every time it occurs in your notes: "Malcolm Forbes" could be just "MF" or "F." The same holds for a corporation—"R" for "Raytheon" or "W" for "Weyerhauser."

Here are some examples from my horse-breeding story notebook:

> ltd prtnerships—own pt int in sevl h rather than full in 1 (Limited partnerships means owning a part interest in several horses rather than a full interest in a single horse.)
>
> Gen Risk—1 of fw Ky Derby filly winners (Genuine Risk was one of the few Kentucky Derby filly winners.)
>
> most dram grwth as res of entr of Arab byers fr Gulf States fnnl huge amts cash 2 biz now most signif thb owners (The most dramatic growth came as a result of the entry of Arab buyers from the Gulf States, who funnelled huge amounts of cash into the business. They are now the most significant thoroughbred owners.)

You get the idea. An important point to note, however, is that I *can* still decipher my notes (though, given the scrawl of my handwriting, probably no one else could). The speediest shorthand system in the world won't help you if you get home and can't read what you wrote down.

We'll talk more about notetaking in a later chapter as it applies in particular to interviews. But first we'd better consider the steps for gathering notes in the first place: How do you start filling up that notebook?

BECOMING A GUIDED MISSILE IN THE INFORMATION EXPLOSION

For any story, article, novel, essay, screenplay or other work of writing that requires a grounding in facts, the information is out there if you know where to find it. Never before in history has so much information been so readily available. That's a blessing to writers, but it can also be a challenge. Part of the role of the writer, after all, is to become an "instant expert." That can pay rich dividends, or it can rob you of the time you should spend at the keyboard, putting words on paper. The key is not to become a casualty of the "information explosion." Think of yourself, instead, as a guided missile.

Your path to your information target begins right at your desk, within arm's reach: The fastest way to do research is to rely on your own collection of reference books. If you have to run to the library every time you need a smidgeon of knowledge, you'll put more mileage on your car than on your keyboard. Every writer needs a basic reference library, the contents of which will vary according to your areas of specialization and interest. In addition to almanacs, a dictionary, encyclopedias, a thesaurus, *Bartlett's Familiar Quotations*, and other general works, my shelves include specialized books on computers, movies, travel and other topics that I've often covered. The point here isn't to prescribe particular books for your home library — we'll mention some specific titles in the next chapter, on speedy research — but to suggest that fast fact-gathering begins at home.

For most stories, however, you'll eventually need to go to a library. Note that I said "*a* library" not "*the* library" — for indeed, there are many different kinds of libraries to choose from. In most larger cities, you'll find neighborhood public libraries, a main public library, a college or university library and often various specialty libraries. It's important for your research efficiency that you pick the right library for your story's needs.

Among public libraries, your neighborhood branch is clearly the best bet if you just need a simple fact or two, readily found in basic reference works. But generally you should head straight for the main branch, where you'll find a full line of reference books, periodicals and the databases and indexes needed to tap them quickly.

For anything technical, or if your local public library isn't large, you may want to go right to the nearest college or university library. Call ahead: Most will let you use their reference collection and periodicals even if you're not a student or faculty member; a few academic libraries have special arrangements under which the public can even check out books (sometimes you have to be a donor to the school, which is a tax-deductible investment worth considering). Large universities typically boast specialized libraries — in art, business, engineering, law or other areas of emphasis — in addition to their main collection; don't overlook these. The Association of College and Research Libraries of the American Library Association (50 Huron St., Chicago, IL 60611; (312) 944-6780) can help you identify academic libraries near you that specialize in your subject.

The next step would be to try one of the wide variety of specialty libraries dedicated to almost every subject. These include historical societies, museum libraries, newspaper libraries (call ahead, as public access is usually limited) and even corporate libraries (where you may have to explain your purpose to the librarian to wheedle your way in). The Special Libraries Association (1200 18th St. NW, Washington, D.C. 20009; (202) 234-4700) is a good place to start tracking down these resources.

Another useful guide to libraries, which can probably be found in your own public library, is the *American Library Directory*, which catalogs more than 30,000 U.S. and Canadian libraries.

Once you find the right library, it's important to use it right. You should cultivate a good relationship with the librarians, particularly the reference librarians. But don't expect them to read your mind — you have to learn to ask the right questions to elicit the answers you need. For example, suppose you're trying to track down the Thoroughbred Owners and Breeders Association. You might ask, "Do you have a phone book for Lexington, Kentucky?" Unless your library has an unusually good phone book collection, however, the answer will probably be *no* — and then you'll be at a dead end. But if you focus your question more exactly — "I need to find the address of the Thoroughbred Owners and Breeders Association" — the librarian could turn to a general reference such as *The Encyclopedia of Associations* and come up with an answer. (For single-shot questions like this, don't forget your library's "Ready Reference" telephone line, if it's got one. Why trek down there if a phone call can get the answer for you?)

In general, though librarians can be immensely helpful in pointing you in the right direction, answering ready-reference-type queries, or cracking tough research nuts, it's fastest to do most of your research yourself. You know what you're looking for, what angle the information must plug into. By doing it yourself, you'll avoid getting too much information or having to sort through lots of information that's not quite right. Again, here's a case where spending some time up front saves time in the long run.

But don't just wade right into the stacks and start grabbing anything that looks useful. By tackling the available research materials roughly in order of increasing complexity and specialization, you'll be able to learn about your subject in such a way that each new bit of knowledge builds on what came before; you won't stumble over unfamiliar concepts apart from a context in which they can be made useful to you. Every project will be different, but here's a rough outline of the order in which you might tap various resources:

1. Encyclopedias, almanacs and other general reference works for a lay audience
2. Periodicals for a general audience
3. General-interest books about the particular field
4. Specialized reference books
5. Specialized periodicals
6. Technical books in the field

For example, research about mathematics might start with reading the encyclopedia entries under "Mathematics" for an overall survey of the subject. Next, you might get a snapshot of current concerns in the field from magazine articles found using the *Reader's Guide to Periodical Literature*. Then you could check out a couple of books about mathematics written for lay persons, such as *Innumeracy* or *Journeys Through Genius*. That might be enough, and if so you should certainly quit right there—don't over-research. If not, however, only then (once you understand something of what you read) should you go on to mathematics-specific reference books, scholarly journals and books written for mathematicians.

Even within this rough order, you should try to tap similar, potentially overlapping resources in succession. Read all the articles you find on mathematics teaching one after another, for instance, before moving on to the articles about business and industrial applications of math. That way, the material will be fresh in your mind and you'll be less likely to waste time writing down duplicate information. You'll also be more likely to gain a quick, coherent understanding of a sub-topic—and to be able to gauge whether or not you need to go a level deeper in your research.

(As you take notes, of course, be sure to write down your sources and what library you found them in. After all, you know what they say about even the best-laid plans: You might have to make a second trip to the stacks, so leave the equivalent of a trail of breadcrumbs.)

Eventually, with most research projects, you'll reach a stage where you need a human being to interpret the information you've found, to put it in context and bring the facts to life. For nonfiction articles, these experts usually provide the heart of your story. But, as you've probably guessed by now, before you switch from library research to interviewing you need—yes, indeed—a plan.

PREPARING FOR THE INTERVIEW: WHAT TO DO BEFORE I-DAY

Whom should you interview? What should you ask?

Often at least part of that first question is obvious: For a profile of Malcolm Forbes, I needed to interview Malcolm Forbes. Depending on the angle, length and complexity of a profile, however, you may need to interview several, even dozens of friends, colleagues, relatives and foes of your subject to round out the story. Finding those people may be an important goal of your preliminary research: Who knows this guy? Who would be ready, willing and able to talk about him?

With other stories, whom to interview is less obvious. Typically, you need to find *experts*—those magical people who can be quoted about a subject with credibility. Again, you should comb your library resources for these crucial names and phone numbers. Who's quoted in other articles on this topic? Who's written books on this topic? What organizations or institutions might supply a spokesperson on this topic? Good sources of experts include government agencies, trade associations, chambers of commerce, corporations, and research and teaching hospitals.

College and university public relations offices can be gold mines of expertise; many publish "contacts" books and "media guides" that list their available experts by field. At the university where I worked, for example, we had experts available on almost every subject except for meteorology and agriculture. And Penn State, a phone call or a couple of hours on the highway away, had experts aplenty on both of those topics.

Another often-overlooked source of experts is other writers and editors—specifically, those at technical, professional and trade publications in the field you're investigating. If you're seen as a colleague rather than a competitor (make clear that you're writing for a lay audience), these fellow pros are usually happy to help. Because they know the field as well as knowing the ins and outs of writing, they may be more readily able to "translate" technical or specialized information than an expert who never gets his nose out of his subject. And these journalists' jobs give them instant credibility when you quote them in your story: "Joe Nerdnik, editor of *Cosmology Quarterly* magazine, says. . . ." If I hadn't gotten lucky in my horse-breeding story, I might have turned to the editor of *Thoroughbred* magazine for some quick expertise on how horse-breeding has become high-pressure and high-stakes.

Once you've begun to identify people to interview, you'll need to track them down. Most experts can be reached the same way you found them in the first place: through a PR department, at a particular organization, or via some association. Others can be found by checking *Who's Who in America* or any of the dozens of specialized Who's Who editions (see the next chapter). *The Address Book: How to Reach Anyone Who's Anyone* is another handy resource for doing just what its title describes. If you don't yet have an individual's name, but are trying to hunt down a subject through a company or an association, *The National Directory of Addresses and Telephone Numbers* is a terrific resource; it's like a national Yellow Pages of the numbers you're most likely to need, 120,000 listings in all. Authors can be contacted through their publishers, though it's usually faster to try to get their phone numbers from some reference book. And don't forget the simple expedient of checking the phone book or calling 555-1212 for directory assistance. Often if you can find where someone lives, you can easily get a phone number — even if it means calling all three people by that name and asking, "Is this Jane Doe, the biochemist?" Dust jackets of books are great resources for finding where authors live. I once tracked down a half-dozen science fiction writers for a story on future technology that way, with nothing more to go on than blurbs like "William Gibson lives in Portland, Oregon."

Your first successful interview can also start a snowball effect leading to other interviews. I often wind up an interview by asking, "Is there anyone else you can suggest that I ought to talk to on this subject?" Then I gently probe for phone numbers.

I keep emphasizing phone numbers here because almost every successful interview starts with a phone call. Never just drop in on somebody; always make an appointment. Even if you're just planning a phone interview, you may want to use the first call to introduce yourself and set up a mutually convenient time to call back.

When can you get by with just a phone interview — with what John Brady, in his invaluable *The Craft of Interviewing*, calls "the McDonald's of journalism"? Use the telephone interview for round-up stories, when you need a little bit from a lot of sources (like my horse-breeding and science fiction articles). Use it to gather background information and supporting quotes and anecdotes for a profile: Call the friends, relatives and archenemies, but go see the subject in person. Use the phone to gather specific, individual bits of information to fill out a story. But beware: As Brady notes, you must be even *better* prepared for a telephone interview than for an in-person encounter, because no winning smile or small talk can cover your gaffes over the phone.

Nonetheless, the telephone is almost always, by definition, faster than traveling to an in-person interview. So plan your in-person interviews carefully and sparingly, opt for subjects nearby before those several hours or days away, and try to package your interviews to minimize travel time. If you need to talk to three people in Manhattan, try to arrange to see at least two of them in a single excursion. (Of course, this saves money as well as time!)

Some stories by their nature demand that your eyes be on the scene; part of your research is going someplace and seeing or doing something. My horse-breeding story, because it was business-oriented and wide-ranging, could be done over the phone. By contrast, another assignment for the Federal Express magazine, about a historic art gallery in Gettysburg, demanded that I go there: I needed to see the art and the town, not just interview the owners.

Occasionally, merely traveling to an interview won't be enough; you'll have to physically pursue your subjects. With busy celebrities, you may want to avoid using the word "interview" at all, with its connotations of a long, static encounter. Try instead to arrange a "chat," or just to "talk" with a celebrity — even while he or she is doing something else. I've interviewed singers (Loretta Lynn, Gene Simmons of KISS) in their dressing rooms before a performance. John Brady got an interview with Jessica Mitford for *Writer's Digest* by driving her to the airport. Often these stolen slices of time can expand without the subject consciously agreeing: William Manchester's first interview with President Kennedy, Brady notes in *The Craft of Interviewing*, was supposed to last ten minutes, but stretched to more than three hours. Manchester got so much out of the president, he later said, because he'd done his homework. He'd prepared for the interview, so he was able to keep the conversation flowing — and JFK enjoyed it.

Another classic story of solid preparation is the time A.J. Liebling interviewed jockey Eddie Arcaro. Liebling's first question was, "How many holes longer do you keep your left stirrup than your right?" Clearly, the *New Yorker* reporter had done his research and knew something about racing. "That started him talking easily," Liebling later recalled, "and after an hour during which I had put in about twelve words, he said, 'I can see you've been around riders a lot.'"

Compare those encounters with the opening question a reporter once asked naturalist John Burroughs, "By the way, Mr. Burroughs, just what do you do? "

Yes, here's yet another instance where an investment of time beforehand will save time — or a total disaster! — in the actual interview. As author Cornelius Ryan once put it in "Ryan's Rules of Reportage": "Never interview anyone without knowing 60 percent of the answers."

This may sound like a waste of time, but it's not. Rather, it's a strategic apportionment of time. Learn the basics in the library; then use your interview time to get the color and quotes that can only be gained by talking to someone. Think of my Malcolm Forbes interview: I went in already knowing the details of his life story, the background of his magazine, and his history as a collector. I even knew, generally, how he might answer my questions about his career, the American dream and capitalism. What I needed from the interview was not a flash of revelation about Malcolm Forbes, but the fresh quotes to plug into a story that I'd already sketched out.

As with my Forbes interview, when you prepare for an interview you should scribble down a list of possible questions. You may not have to ask all of them, or you may not be able to ask everything; nor should you ask only those questions on your list if a more fruitful line of conversation develops. Write down your questions in a natural order, imagining how a conversation might run. At the same time, though, you should make sure that the questions most crucial to your angle are asked early on. What if your subject gets called away unexpectedly, or your interview takes longer than you've been allotted?

The unexpected does happen, and stories do take unanticipated turns. So your strategy needs to be flexible—a freewheeling Blitzkrieg, not a sitting-duck Maginot Line. Both for that reason and for simple time efficiency, you shouldn't *over*prepare for an interview any more than you should skimp on your pre-interview homework. You must strike a balance between impressing your subject as a sincere person who's thought about what questions to ask and pretending to know as much as your subject does. Don't bluff or lead your subject into pat answers. John McPhee says he likes to cultivate an "air of density" and to seem "as blank as the notebook pages" when he interviews, so not to limit his freedom to learn and to be surprised. If that seems contradictory to careful preparation, remember the rest of Liebling's experience with Eddie Arcaro: Once he won the jockey's confidence, Liebling knew enough to shut up and let Arcaro talk. Sometimes you have to know a lot to know when to say nothing.

It all comes down to "good generalship." Good generals never go into battle unprepared. But neither do good generals prepare and prepare and never engage the enemy. (As Lincoln, frustrated with General McClellan's inaction, once put it, "General, if you're not going to use your army, do you mind if I do?")

Now unsheathe your pens—we're ready to charge ahead.

CHAPTER FIVE

SECRETS OF SPEEDY RESEARCH

• • •

LOVE AND LOATHING IN THE STACKS

Some people — including most writers — love libraries. They could happily browse about them for hours, reveling in the aura of books and all that assembled information.

Other folks, perhaps shushed once too often by stereotypical old-maid librarians in their youth, would almost rather go to the dentist than to the library. Books piled upon books hold no allure for them, only terror. They'd sooner dash through a mine field than have to find a fact in the reference stacks.

Both types, alas, can run into problems when seeking to do speedy research. Library loathers, obviously, must overcome their trepidations long enough to venture into the stacks and come out with a successful harvest of information. But it's possible to be over fond of libraries, too — at least in your professional capacity as a working, time-conscious writer. Linger too long in the stacks, or get too easily distracted by this book or that, and your writing time will end up as nonproductive browsing time. These are the writers, too, who cart home biceps-building mountains of books for the simplest research chore. I've seen them, in their dens and offices, surrounded by research materials, seeking a slice of omniscience — and not getting word one actually written.

No, you can't afford either anxiety or amour when setting out to research a story. You've got to know what you're looking for (remember your plan from the last chapter?), go in and get it.

Whether your problem is library-phobia or -philia, the solution is the same: Know what research resources are available and how to use them — fast. That's what this chapter is all about. You'll find some resources here so useful for your particular specialties or areas of interest that you'll want to add them to your home library, skipping that trip to the stacks. You'll also learn how to tap a vast electronic library via your telephone — how to research without even getting up from your chair. Research has come a long way since you first learned how to write a term paper at the library. By learning a little bit more, you can write whatever you're writing now a lot more efficiently.

THE BASICS: YOU CAN LOOK IT UP

Your first research resource as a writer is a good dictionary. Well, of course! But the dictionary is useful not only for looking up your most fundamental tools — words themselves — but also thousands of small facts that searching for otherwise might slow you down. I've got a hefty unabridged *Webster's New Twentieth Century Dictionary*, second edition, that weighs in at over 2,000 pages. And in those 2,000-plus pages, in addition to spellings and definitions, I've got dictionaries of biography, geography, noted names and foreign phrases; abbreviations; weights and measures; presidents and vice presidents of the United States; the Constitution and Declaration of Independence; color plates of freshwater fish, insects, cats, cars, poisonous plants; sixteen pages of color maps . . . and much more. It's like a library in my lap (though my lap gets pretty weary under the weight after a while). The point is: Don't make research harder than it has to be. If you're writing a mystery story and need to toss in a few descriptions of poisonous plants, you might not need to consult a botany text in the library; your dictionary might have the answer. Try the obvious, easy resources *first*.

But what about questions of spelling, meaning and usage — the business of words so vital to writers? All the major dictionaries have their advocates among wordsmiths. In addition to *Webster's*, the *American Heritage Dictionary of the English Language* is handy because more of its listings are in a single A-Z chunk, saving you time in flipping through many separate sections. The *Random House Dictionary of the English Language* is a good choice if you want an emphasis on current usage. You'll also want a *Roget's International Thesaurus* and possibly *Webster's New Dictionary of Synonyms* — though you can probably replace both in everyday use with a faster, at-your-fingertips thesaurus that resides in your computer until you need it (WordFinder, for example). Either the *Dictionary of American Slang* or the *Dictionary of Slang and Unconventional English* can quickly answer your more offbeat word questions.

Dozens of books seek to resolve those usage questions (*who* or *whom*? *compose* or *comprise*?) that can bring your writing flow to a dead halt. But by far the best and most efficient is a slim black book by Roy

H. Copperud called *American Usage and Style: The Consensus*. Copperud surveyed seven of the most respected of those other usage handbooks and summarized their solutions in one straightforward, alphabetized volume. It will save you hours and win those grammatical debates with fussy editors. (Every copyeditor I've ever shown Copperud's book to has run out and bought his or her own copy.)

The other simple research gap that can turn into a black hole for your productivity is an inability to find or identify a quote. A well-turned phrase from the famous can give you an instant lead or punchy close, solve a transitional puzzle, or inspire a whole story—if you can find it somewhere more solid than the tip of your tongue. *Bartlett's Familiar Quotations* has long been the standard reference here; its 1980 revision, adding more contemporary material by such phrasemakers as Richard Nixon and Bob Dylan, made *Bartlett's* even more useful. To use it rapidly, you need to understand its format: Quotations are listed by author, and the authors are listed chronologically (plus an alphabetical index); most quote searches, unless you're positive of the author, should start in the fine-print keyword cross-reference in the back. If *Bartlett's* can't help you, the next best bet is "Stevenson," as Burton Stevenson's *Home Book of Quotations* is known to librarians. Turn to Stevenson if you're seeking a classical or historical phrase, or if you don't have a particular quotation in mind but need something about, say, war. Stevenson's tome is almost like *Bartlett's* turned inside-out, organized alphabetically by subject (with additional keyword and author indexes). More "pop" quotes can be found in Bergan Evans's *Dictionary of Quotations*, which is also organized by subject. Robert Byrne's quirky and amusing *The 637 Best Things Anybody Ever Said*, along with its similarly named sequels, is both a good inspiration (lots of fresh, not-overused quotations) and an excellent last resort for that elusive quote you can't find anywhere else. (For example, I stumped the Ready Reference librarians and exhausted my own library looking for the originator of that saying, a few chapters back, about staring at a blank page until drops of blood form on your forehead. Finally, I planted myself in the reference stacks at Waldenbooks, paging through quotation volumes. And there it was in one of Byrne's books. I guess I'd better break down and buy it now, huh?)

If you're looking for a specialized quote—a line from a movie, for example—it's fastest to go straight to a special-interest quotation reference, such as Harry Haun's wonderful *Movie Quote Book*. Other such resources include the *Macmillan Book of Business and Economic Quotes*, edited by Michael Jackman, and the *Morrow Book of Quotations in American History* by Joseph Conlin.

As these examples suggest, one of the secrets to speedy fact-finding is finding the right resource. That requires a balancing act: Never go to a more specialized, more technical resource than necessary (that's why simply looking things up in the dictionary is a good first choice), but, on the contrary, don't start your search for data in such a general resource that you'll likely have to look elsewhere. It's a balance that experience — and some of the tips in this chapter — will make it easier for you to strike.

Suppose you need to know the population of Ecuador. You could check an almanac, the back of an atlas, an encyclopedia, or even a good recent dictionary — all about equal on the general reference-to-technical tool spectrum. Or you could hunt down a book about Ecuador, order it through interlibrary loan from a distinguished university's Latin American collection, maybe have it translated from Spanish, and probably accomplish the same objective. Talk about breaking a butterfly on the wheel! On the other hand, an in-depth project on Ecuador might require just such a research endeavor — and looking up the country in the encyclopedia would be just a waste of time.

Most statistical research problems — like population figures — can be solved most efficiently just by consulting an almanac. The *Information Please Almanac* and *World Almanac and Book of Facts* are the two standard references; the latter is probably the most commonly consulted reference book in the United States. (If you need similar answers with a British slant, *Whitaker's Almanack* is the transatlantic equivalent.) *The Universal Almanac* is a newer entry with, despite its name, a somewhat quirkier selection of data. An intriguing adjunct to these basic almanacs is *The New York Public Library Desk Reference*, which contains the answers to the questions most asked of that mammoth library. Getting the book can save you time and phone calls of your own.

But these are only the start of the statistical research resources available — which shows why it's important that you define your problem first and try to pick the one source most likely to have an answer. Beyond almanacs, you should next turn to statistical references with a more specific focus. More complex questions relating to the U.S. population can be resolved with the *US Census Pocket Data Book* or its bigger cousin, the *Statistical Abstract of the United States*. International data can similarly be found in two United Nations publications, the *UNESCO Statistical Yearbook* and *UN Statistical Yearbook*.

Remember, too, that statistics aren't just useful the year they're produced. If, say, you're researching a historical novel, it's good to know that the *Statistical Abstract* goes back to 1878. Or you can consult *Historical Abstracts of the United States: Colonial Times to 1970*, also from the U.S. Department of Commerce. Similar information for Europe can be tracked down in Facts on File's *European Historical Statistics, 1750-1975*.

If these one-volume resources still fail you, the next step is to consult the three master indexes to statistics published by Congressional Information Service, Inc.: *American Statistics Index*, which covers state and federal agency-generated numbers from 1974 on; *Index to International Statistics*, which references UN agency data from 1983 on; and *Statistical Reference Index*, a guide to figures from commercial, association and university sources from 1980 to the present. Most large libraries have these handy, timesaving books. To use them, find the citation you want in the index volume, check the abstract volume for a summary to see if it's what you really want, and then ask the librarian for the actual reference. Another resource to try if you're researching a story with more of a business slant is *Gale's Encyclopedia of Business Information Sources*.

Atlases and gazetteers are other good sources of statistics — as well as being invaluable for the writer who's trying to write as though he's been there, but can't afford the airfare.The *Columbia Lippincott Gazetteer of the World* includes 130,000 place names, geography, history, population and other facts. The *Encyclopedia Britannica World Atlas International* is another good everyday reference. And for the U.S., the *Rand McNally Commercial Atlas and Marketing Guide* is a wonderful source of offbeat information you never dreamed existed.

For a more general overview of a subject than that afforded by either almanacs or atlases, you should turn to an encyclopedia. Not only are encyclopedia articles good fundamental research for almost any project; many of them also have citations and suggested readings at the end that can give you an instant bibliography for the rest of your research. Encyclopedias, like other references, run the range of complexity, from *World Book* on one end to *Britannica* on the other, with *Columbia, Americana* and others roughly in between. As always, try to fit the reference to the research chore.

In addition to using the encyclopedias at the library, you'll save time if you have access to a set all your own. But that doesn't have to mean one of those zillion-dollar bookshelf-breakers that shifty-eyed salesmen peddle door-to-door. I keep a three-volume, paperback *Concord* mini-encyclopedia on my desk for quick reference; more elaborate hardcover one-volume encyclopedias, about the size of an unabridged dictionary, are also available. Or, if you have a computer and a modem, you can use several of the on-line services I'll describe at the end of this chapter that include electronic encyclopedias. Use them heavily and you'll end up paying for a whole set one byte at a time, with nothing left to show for it, but such on-line references are certainly a quick—and up-to-date—way to tap an encyclopedia. Another high-tech solution is to invest in an encyclopedia on CD-ROM, which you can rapidly search from the comfort of your keyboard. The biggest investment here, if you already have a computer, is in the CD-ROM player; you'll be able to buy new (and no doubt better) encyclopedias on disk in the future for less than the cost of a new shelfload of books.

A few more thoughts on encyclopedias. With heavy-duty ones like the *Britannica*, it's speediest to check the index first: There might not be a separate entry under "R" for "Babe Ruth," for example, but he'd certainly be found under "Baseball"; the index will tell you, one way or the other. And don't forget to check the yearbooks that most encyclopedia publishers put out annually to keep their volumes up-to-date. The yearbooks often have more complete information on a given year's events than ever winds up in the actual encyclopedia. Old yearbooks, of course, provide a wonderful snapshot of the world and society in the past—fodder for fiction and nonfiction alike set back when.

Several other wide-ranging references—but with particular slants—are also worth keeping in mind. You're probably familiar with the *Guinness Book of World Records*. Another such useful book, focusing on primacy rather than superlatives of all sorts, is *Famous First Facts* by Joseph Nathan Kane. If it's names you're after, the *New Century Cyclopedia of Names*, edited by Clarence L. Barnhart and William D. Haley, is an interesting compilation of 100,000 people, places, works of art, fictional characters and other proper names, with spellings, pronunciations and essential facts. To get a quick overview of the past, try *What Happened When, The Timetables of History, The Timetables of American History* and *The Timetables of Science*, all of which are organized by date; it's a great way to get a sense of what was happening around the world, or in different fields, at about the same time. For writers in a hurry, such chronologies are good ways to get a date or a fact without having to wade through a whole history text.

Finally, city directories and telephone books represent a wealth of information beyond just phone numbers. The CIA and KGB use them; so do university sociologists. You might find a directory just the ticket if you need to drop some restaurant names into a story set in

Manhattan, or if your heroine needs to run down a street in Dallas. If you're trying to track down an association or organization and can't find it in the *Encyclopedia of Associations*, try the Manhattan or Washington, D.C., phone book. Most large libraries have a good phone book collection. If they lack the real things, they might have Phonefiche, a microfiche collection of more than 1,400 phone directories. (Or you can always call directory assistance at 1 + the area code [800 for toll-free numbers]-555-1212. Keep that number on you.) And don't forget the *National Directory of Addresses and Telephone Numbers*, plugged in the previous chapter.

PEOPLE WHO NEED PEOPLE: FINDING OUT WHO'S WHO IN A HURRY

Just as much of your writing will focus on people, so will much of your research. People may be subjects of your profiles or sources of expertise for your articles and books. But first you have to find them, or find out about them. Fortunately, there's a whole set of research resources to help you find out who's who in a hurry.

The key distinction to make before tackling the stacks is whether your subject is alive or dead. For the living, a good place to start for basic information — such as the biographical data you might not have to waste time asking in an interview — is the Marquis Who's Who series. You're probably familiar with *Who's Who in America*, but there are more than a dozen Who's Who volumes in all, including specialized books on finance and industry, regions of the country and well-known women. To find your quarry, use the *Index to Who's Who Books*.

If your subject is an author like yourself, turn first to Gale's *Contemporary Authors*. People currently in the news can be found in Wilson's *Current Biography*, a monthly update on newsmakers. And Wilson's *Biography Index* is a more comprehensive index to magazine articles about people than the old green *Reader's Guide* you probably used in school.

For quick reference to the dead, a terrific source is the *New York Times Obituaries Index*, which covers 1858-1978. (Those who died after 1978 can be found under "Deaths" in the regular *New York Times Index*.) *Times* obituary writers cover their subjects much like the authors of good profiles — including interviewing them while they're still alive.

Other handy guides that focus mostly or exclusively on the late famous are: Scribner's *Dictionary of American Biography* ("D.A.B." to librarians), a guide to every American who's "made a significant contribution" to his or her field; the British equivalent, Oxford's *Dictionary of National Biography*; *Webster's Biographical Dictionary*, a quick guide to 45,000 of the former famous; *A Dictionary of Universal Biography* by Albert M. Hyamson, which adds a bibliography of more complete information on each person; and of course *Who Was Who in America*, which is where famous folks go when they die.

If you've gone through the appropriate resources and still can't get all you need on an individual, don't despair. But don't wade into the stacks and just start searching for specialized directories, either. The most efficient way to do in-depth research on people is to tap a directory of directories. Still with me? Yes, there are actually master indexes that cross-reference ("interfile" in librarian-speak) dozens of different biographical reference books — reference books to reference books, if you will. Among the many such indexes are: *Index to Literary Biography*, which interfiles 100 directories, and *Author Biographies Master Index*, which references 140; *Historical Biographical Dictionaries Master Index* to 36 directories; *Journalist Biographies Master Index* to 200 volumes; *Performing Arts Biography Index* to 100 volumes . . . you get the idea. The point is to use reference works to help figure out which reference works to consult. That two-step process may save you a hundred-step wild-goose chase.

THE JOY OF REFERENCE BOOKS: FROM VIENNA TO CHISHOLM, MINNESOTA

Just as there are specialized resources that can speed up your research on people, other special-focus references can make your investigations in particular fields more efficient. The secret is knowing where to look — and when to turn to these special references. If all you need to know is when Mozart lived, for example, there's no need to seek out the massive *Grove's Dictionary of Music and Musicians*. But if you're writing a novel, say, set in Mozart's time and need to know details of not only Mozart but also his lesser-known contemporaries, well, *Grove's* — which covers all music since 1450 in nine basic volumes — might be just the ticket. Or you could turn to the *Oxford Companion to Music*, with its 10,000 entries, or *Baker's Biographical Dictionary of Musicians*.

Similar references exist for almost any field on which you need quick and accurate answers. In the arts, for example, you can tap the *Oxford Companion to the Theatre*, the *Dance Encyclopedia*, the *Encyclopedia of Jazz*, the *Encyclopedia of World Art*, and the *Oxford Companion to Art*. Most writers probably already know the good guides to literature, but if not you should make friends with the *Oxford Companion to English Literature*, *Oxford Companion to American Literature*, and *The Reader's Encyclopedia*. A useful one-volume, paperback resource on all things cultural in this century is Alan Bullock and R.B. Woodings's biographically oriented *20th Century Culture*.

When I was a film critic, I found I couldn't work without Leslie Halliwell's handy *Filmgoer's Companion* (which lists films by director, actor, actress and key themes) and the complementary *Halliwell's Film Guide* (which is alphabetical by movie). I also liked Pauline Kael's *5001 Nights at the Movies*, for recent films, and such even-more-specialized guides as Brian Garfield's *Western Films*. If your field is TV — or if you just need a tidbit of TV information to drop into a story — the single best one-volume reference is *The Complete Directory to Prime Time Network TV Shows*.

Even really highbrow subjects have their handy guides. You can find everything but the meaning of life (and there will be some pretty good stabs at that one) in the *Encyclopedia of Religion and Ethics* and the *Encyclopedia of Philosophy*. Higher learning itself can be quickly researched in *American Universities and Colleges*, the *College Blue Book*, Macmillan's *Encyclopedia of Education*, *Peterson's Guide*, and similar books.

Science writing of any sort, from popular science articles to science fiction novels, requires an unusually hefty grounding in research; fortunately, every branch of science also has its reference books that can facilitate your basic research. First, you might start with the *McGraw-Hill Encyclopedia of Science and Technology*, which is to science what the *Encyclopedia Britannica* is to the world in general: It was the first contemporary, multivolume reference devoted to the sciences. A useful companion is *Van Nostrand's Scientific Encyclopedia*, which explains more than 16,000 scientific terms. And then you get into references on particular sciences: Patrick Moore's handsome *Atlas of the Universe* and McGraw-Hill's *Encyclopedia of Space* in astronomy, *A Dictionary of Geology*, the *Encyclopedia of Oceanography*, the *International Dictionary of Applied Mathematics*, the *Dictionary of Physics*, the *Condensed Chemical Dictionary*, the *Encyclopedia of the Biological Sciences*, *Gray's Manual of Botany*, the *Psychiatric Dictionary*, the *Encyclopedia of Psychology*, *Stedman's Medical Dictionary*. You name it, there's a reference book that can help you. If you can name the science but not a specific book, don't hesitate to ask the reference librarian for help.

Or suppose you need to know whether your crime-novel hero really can get off scot-free with that clever ruse you've cooked up: *Black's Law Dictionary* is the standard reference.

For another slant on the law, what if you need to know about our lawmakers? I once had to track down specific congressmen across the country for an article on the importance of voting—congressmen who'd been elected by extremely narrow margins. Not only did the *Almanac of American Politics* tell me who'd won razor-thin victories, it also gave me their office numbers and key facts about their districts. Other useful volumes on politics include *Congressional Quarterly Almanac*, *Facts About the Presidents*, and *Who's Who in American Politics*.

Business is another area chockablock with reference works. Just tracking down stock market and other investment-related data could give you information overload. But here are a few places to look first: *Encyclopedia of Banking and Finance*, *Moody's Manual of Investments*, and the invaluable *Poor's Register of Corporations, Directors, and Executives*.

One last example, in case you think all specialized references have to be gray and serious. What if you need to know something about sports? Specialized references can answer your questions about everything from archery to windsurfing, but let's just consider baseball. There's Macmillan's multithousand-page *Baseball Encyclopedia*, with statistics on everyone who ever played the game, even for a single inning. (Yes, fans of *Field of Dreams*—and *Shoeless Joe*, the book the movie was based on—the *Baseball Encyclopedia* reveals that there really was a Moonlight Graham, who appeared in only one game, no at-bats, for the New York Giants in 1905 and died in Chisholm, Minnesota, in 1965. Where do you think *Shoeless Joe* author W.P. Kinsella got the facts for his fable?) But that's barely the first inning when it comes to baseball resources. For a different statistical slant on the game, you could try *The Bill James Historical Baseball Abstract*—which, despite the fondness for statistics that brought James to prominence, is actually more a font of fascinating anecdotes. No, Moonlight Graham's not in here, but you will learn the uniform colors of the 1882 Detroit Wolverines (different for each position on the field) and who was the fattest player of the 1930s (295-pound hurler Jumbo Brown).

This is just the tip of a very large reference iceberg. For more specifics, you can consult, yes, a reference book to reference books—the 1,000-page *Guide to Reference Books*, issued and regularly updated by the American Library Association.

INTO THE STACKS: CARD CATALOG TRICKS

So far, we've mostly stuck to the books in the library with an "R" for "reference" on their spines. For many research projects, that's as deep as you'll need to go into the shelves.

Sometimes, though, the fastest way to get the facts you need is to wade into the card catalog and check out a (small) pile of books on your subject. For example, my horse-breeding story required an overview of the subject, rather than just a collection of specific facts. The specifics I would get from my interviews; what I needed was the broad familiarity, the sense of trends and historical background, that could only be gotten from in-depth reading.

That's a good rule of thumb, in fact, for judging whether to concentrate on reference books or regular books: If you need facts, go to the reference shelf. If you need a feel for a subject (in addition, of course, to whatever specific facts might wind up in your notebook), head for the card catalog.

Suppose that you're still working on that historical blockbuster set in Mozart's Vienna. To find out the population of Vienna in the latter half of the eighteenth century, or pictures of what the people wore, or what they called their money (pounds? ducats? moolah?), rely on reference books. But to immerse yourself in the times, to get a sense of how the people lived, you'll need a book or two (not twenty, or you'll never get your own book written!) from the 900 section of the general stacks.

If that "900" reference threw you, then you also need a quick refresher course in how to use the library beyond the reference desk. And, yes, there are faster, more efficient ways to find what you need in the stacks.

The "900" comes from the Dewey Decimal System that you probably learned in grade school (see following chart). Many libraries, however, have switched to the less-familiar Library of Congress classification scheme listed on the next page.

It's useful to know these broad classification schemes, but unless you're prepared to memorize the zillions of subcategories (let's see, is "PN" French literature or Russian literature?), your best bet is to start with the card catalog. Whether in rows and rows of index cards or the more high-tech versions that use a computer terminal linked to an electronic database, card catalogs generally let you search for books by author, title and subject. Suppose you don't know the specific book you're looking for — as is frequently the case when doing research for writing. You can search by subject, of course, but that may yield more titles than you can readily make sense out of. Research expert William L. Rivers, author of the excellent *Finding Facts*, suggests deciding what the title of the perfect book you need would be — *if* someone had written it. Then look up the title you've invented; in a large library, Rivers says, you'll hit the jackpot about half the time.

THE DEWEY DECIMAL SYSTEM

000s	General Works
100s	Philosophy
200s	Religion
300s	Social Sciences
400s	Language
500s	Natural Sciences
600s	Applied Arts
700s	Fine Arts
800s	Literature
900s	History and Biography

LIBRARY OF CONGRESS CLASSIFICATION SYSTEM

A	General Works
B	Philosophy, Psychology, Religion
C	Auxiliary Sciences of History (archeology, for example)
D	History: General and Old World
E, F	History: America
G	Geography, Anthropology, Recreation
H	Social Sciences
K	Law
L	Education
M	Music
N	Fine Arts
P	Language and Literature
Q	Science
R	Medicine
S	Agriculture
T	Technology
U	Military Science
V	Naval Science
Z	Bibliography, Library Science

Another trick I use is to search by subject, or by the one appropriate title that I *do* know, to find the specific code—either Dewey decimal or Library of Congress—for the section of the stacks that has the books that I need. Then I go there and browse almost as I would in a bookstore. It's usually much faster to figure out from the actual book whether it's useful than by deciphering the card catalog entry; this also saves me from having to write down a long list of book titles and numbers for specific books that may already be checked out anyway. There in the stacks, I can tell at a glance or a quick flip what books are clearly too old and out-of-date, too scholarly, not detailed enough. Librarians would probably shudder at this method, but it works. It's also a strong reason to shun those prisonlike libraries where they don't let you back into the actual stacks, but make you fill out little slips of paper for every book you want to see.

Still another shortcut to the books you need is the *Subject Guide to Books in Print*. This multivolume reference is aimed at bookstores and library book buyers, but it also makes a handy bibliography for researchers. The *Subject Guide* lists more than 600,000 current titles, cross-referenced under more than 60,000 headings. If the book you want exists but isn't in your local library, you can probably get it through inter-library loan.

Once you've found books that might be useful, how many should you check out? There's probably a good reason that God gave us only two arms and the ability to carry no more than the weight of a sack of potatoes or two. But even if you've been pumping iron and can cart home a whole shelfload of books, control yourself. Remember that eventually you have to quit researching and start writing, and that this is a story, not a PhD thesis. I've seldom checked out more than a half-dozen books for even a complex magazine article—and then I *scanned* the books, not read them cover to cover! Go much beyond ten books, unless you're tackling a book-length project, and you're crossing the line into research as an excuse not to do the hard work of writing.

KEEPING UP WITH NEWSPAPERS AND MAGAZINES

Reference books and other books can be a gold mine of information, but even the best of them can't always keep up with a fast-changing world. Because they're meant to last, books must shun the ephemeral and the transient—exactly the stuff that often makes good stories. Reference books, printed and bound with tender loving care, are also hard-pressed simply to keep up with the swift changes in our high-tech society, where encyclopedia entries can be out-of-date almost before the ink is dry.

Newspapers make an ideal antidote to the datedness of reference books. Printed every day and packed with information, they can be a banquet to a writer hungry for current facts. Newspapers also make a superb historical resource, both for culling details that didn't make it into the history books (and thus are fresh fodder for your story) and for getting a sense of how people lived and thought way back whenever.

Unfortunately, because of their throwaway nature – more newspapers wind up at the bottom of bird cages than on reference shelves – newspapers are hard to use efficiently for research. You're likely to find yourself bleary-eyed in front of a scratched microfilm screen, scrolling through page after page of old department store sale ads in search of a single nugget of information. Not enough newspapers are indexed and not all major metropolitan dailies allow nonstaff writers access to their morgues. (Check with your local paper, though, to see. Befriend the newspaper's librarians. Their painstakingly maintained files, whether clips in envelopes or in some more high-tech storage, are one of the quickest ways to get a lot of current information quickly. How else do you think newspaper reporters keep up with their daily deadlines?)

Fortunately, though, some newspapers *are* readily accessible to researchers. The best bet, and most likely to be found in your local library, is the hardbound *New York Times Index*. These marvelous volumes not only index each day's *Times*, but provide a brief precis with each entry. If all you really need is a nugget of information – a date, a name, a statistic – you may find it in the precis, sparing you the time and trouble of consulting the microfilmed newspaper at all. The *Times* is not only the nation's newspaper of record, but by far the most complete source of information on global events. Other newspapers whose indexes may be available include the *Washington Post* (your best bet for political happenings), the *Wall Street Journal* (first stop for business and financial facts), the *Christian Science Monitor*, and the *Los Angeles Times*. All of these papers, plus the *New York Times*, are jointly indexed in the National Newspaper Index (Information Access Corp.). For more complete coverage across the nation, you can turn to NewsBank, a microfiche of 200 newspapers dating from 1970 on what's available in many major libraries. NewsBank clips and arranges stories according to fourteen topic areas, plus provides a printed subject and name index. It's a handy way to get a perspective from around the country on national trends and topics. If an even more selective index will satisfy you, *Facts on File* — a loose-leaf compilation of current events found in major newspapers, with cumulative indexes — might be a suitable shortcut.

Overall, however, you'll probably find magazines more fruitful and useful than newspapers for speedy research. Magazines fall into a nice middle ground between the daily flux of newspapers and the stately pace of books. Most do a pretty good job of keeping current — weekly newsmagazines will often do just as well as newspapers for your purposes — and they are more likely to be indexed, bound and shelved. Because magazines exist for almost every conceivable trade or special interest, from *Garbage* to *Sailing*, they're also an excellent resource for information too specialized to make its way into the daily papers. (Often your own stories can serve as a bridge between the specialized information found in narrow-audience magazines and those magazines that represent the next step out toward general interest. Just add fresh quotes from experts, their names uncovered in those same specialized magazines, and serve.)

How to tap magazines without paging through a pile of periodicals? You're no doubt familiar with the *Reader's Guide to Periodical Literature*. But that's only one of more than 100 different periodical indexes, each filling a particular niche. The trick is figuring out which niche, and thus which index, your research mostly falls into.

For general-interest magazines, the trusty *Reader's Guide* is certainly a place to start. But don't neglect *Access*, which indexes some 150 popular magazines not found in the *Reader's Guide*. (Getting listed in the *Reader's Guide* is the magazine equivalent of sainthood, and about as difficult; it's a status not granted lightly or quickly, which means a lot of excellent magazines never make it and some no-longer-very-useful magazines remain listed for all eternity.) If your library has it, you can do one-stop shopping with the *Magazine Index*, a guide to more than 400 magazines since 1977 — including all of those listed in both the *Reader's Guide* and *Access*. Periodicals from the nineteenth century are indexed in *Poole's Index to Periodical Literature*, which is virtually the only tool to tap these historical resources.

Beyond those general-interest guides, there's a periodical guide for every slice of society. The *Alternative Press Index* lists about 200 liberal, New Age, and what used to be called "counterculture" magazines from 1969 onward. Way on the other hand, the *Business Index* covers some 350 capitalist tools, plus the *New York Times* business section. Depending on your subject, you may also want to try: *Art Index* (140 magazines from 1929 on), *Applied Science and Technology Index* (180 periodicals starting way back in 1913), *Criminal Justice Abstracts* (160 publications from 1968 on), *Film Literature Index* (135 magazines from 1973 on), *Engineering Index* (a whopping 1,400 journals from 1884 to the present), *Education Index* (200 publications dating from 1929), *Music Index* (260 journals from 1949 onward), *Psychological Abstracts* (850 periodicals from around the world, from 1927), *Public Affairs Information Service Bulletin* (425 publications from 1915), *Writings on American History* (400 journals starting in 1903), *Sociological Abstracts* (1,300 worldwide periodicals from 1953 on), or some of the many other, even more specialized guides. H.H. Wilson Co. produces many of these volumes on scientific subject areas; it also publishes the *General Science Index*, a sampling of ninety periodicals from the other Wilson indexes, which may be just what you need without getting too specialized and technical.

Don't forget the periodicals published by the U.S. government, which altogether is the largest publisher in the country. The *Index to U.S. Government Periodicals* is a useful guide to some 170 federal-government publications from 1970 to the present. A complete bibliography to government periodicals, as well as books, pamphlets, brochures and other publications, is the *Monthly Catalog* issued since 1895 by the Superintendent of Documents. You can tap all the *Catalogs* from 1900-1971 in one 15-volume source by checking the government's *Cumulative Subject Index*, found in many libraries. (The documents themselves can be accessed in the 1,300 libraries designated as official U.S. depository libraries. Note that the books and brochures found here are *not* classified in the library's Dewey decimal or Library of Congress system, so unless you check these special indexes you'll miss them.) Another useful resource for tapping the vast trove of data churned out by Uncle Sam is a book by Matthew Lesko, *Information U.S.A.*

INFORMATION THAT'S JUST A PHONE CALL AWAY

A few years ago, this chapter would have ended right here. But the personal computer, linked by telephone to massive mainframe computer databases, has created a whole new and extremely fast way of researching. To access this electronic world of on-line information, you need a personal computer (almost any brand will do), basic communications software, and a modem (*mo*dulator-*dem*odulator) that hooks up to your phone line and lets your computer talk to other computers. If you already have a computer for word processing, the rest of what you need can be bought for as little as $200; there are even shareware programs (honor-system software you pay for after you get it and try it, usually just ten to twenty-five dollars) that will meet all your communications needs. Some large libraries also have on-line access capabilities, usually for a fee.

Before I wax enthusiastic about the brave new world of on-line databases, however, there's a caveat, and it has to do with those fees. If you don't know what you're doing, or get in over your head, you can wander around on-line for a long time and run up enormous charges from the on-line service. The really serious databases like Dialog can cost you hundreds of dollars before you know it. So, yes, on-line services can certainly be your fastest research solution—but start slowly, get your feet wet before plunging into the deep end, and keep an eye on the meter.

The biggest service in number of subscribers, and probably the best place to explore on-line information without spending your life's savings, is CompuServe (call 614-457-8600 for sign-up information). CompuServe offers everything from an electronic shopping mall in which you can place orders right from your computer to special-interest forums on scuba diving, all makes of computers, comic books and dozens of other subjects. *How to Get the Most Out of CompuServe*, a book by Charles Bowen and David Peyton, is an excellent get-acquainted guide to these on-line wonders.

For quick research, however, there are a couple of key CompuServe features you'll want to know about. Almost everything you'd expect to find in the reference section of a library is here in electronic, up-to-date form: *Grolier's Academic Encyclopedia*, a magazine index, access to stories from major newspapers. Plus you can tap the Associated Press wire service, extensive travel data through such sources as the Official Airline Guide and the Eaasy Sabre reservations system used by travel agents, and, through a subset of CompuServe called IQuest, all the database riches of most of the big guys like Dialog, BRS and SDC (for an additional charge). IQuest will even pick the database for you—you just have to feed it the key words to search for.

Think hard about your selection of words, because the right key words can make the difference between retrieving just the right few articles and winding up with an unmanageable (and expensive) several hundred. When I was researching an article on mathematics, for example, I used CompuServe to cast a wide research net quickly. But if I'd searched IQuest using just "mathematics" as my keyword, I'd have been deluged. Instead I tried such combinations as "mathematics and teaching" and "mathematics and employment or jobs." You can also narrow your search *too* much: Lest I miss something, I ended up using a "wild-card" feature that let me search for articles with the words "math," "mathematics" or "mathematicians" simply by typing "math*" (that is, search for "math" followed by any other characters). If hunting for articles on computers, I might employ "comput*" to retrieve mentions of "computer," "computers" and "computing." Most articles you'll get through this "gateway" are "full text" — avoid those that are abstracts only, requiring a trip to the library anyway.

To give you a more mundane example of CompuServe's rapid-fire utility, let me tell you how I bought a car. I needed to pick a new car fast because I had to drive it to a new job that began in about a week — leaving the rest of my family and our regular car temporarily behind. So I fired up CompuServe, turned to the magazine database, and searched by key word for the names of the cars I was interested in. Almost instantly I had what I needed from *Consumer Reports* and *Car and Driver*. By "downloading" the articles from CompuServe to my computer, I could get the information at cost-efficient high speed, and read the articles or print them out later, at my leisure and "off the clock."

But CompuServe is hardly the only game in town. Several other general-interest services offer much the same array of features: GEnie (301-340-4005), Delphi from General Videotex Corp. (800-365-4636) and Prodigy (914-993-8789) are among the most popular. (A word of caution about Prodigy, which has been growing rapidly since its introduction: It's great if you don't mind ads on your computer screen along with the information.) Delphi, for example, has two encyclopedias, an international database, a medical reference maintained by licensed physicians, a gateway to Dialog, and much more. Most of these services offer electronic mail for instant communication with fellow users, special-interest forums, some sort of current news service, and business and financial facts. Rates run about four to twelve dollars for every hour that you're connected.

A few other, more specialized services are also worth singling out. Dow Jones News/Retrieval (609-520-4632), one of the pioneers in the on-line industry, is the best source for business and financial news, including access to back issues of the *Wall Street Journal*. Almost anything you need to know about a corporation or its stock can be found here, either in one of the many statistical databases or by a keyword search. Also useful, though pretty expensive, is DataTimes (800-642-2525), which works like a giant electronic newspaper morgue — for not just one newspaper, but dailies all across the country. Many newspapers, in fact, are jettisoning their traditional morgues and relying on DataTimes for their own in-house use. Like most databases, Data-

Times lets you search by keyword for fast fact retrieval. Finally, News-Net (800-345-1301) is an electronic compilation of dozens of specialized newsletters—publications that you'd never see otherwise, that would cost a fortune to subscribe to. You can even set up an electronic "clipping service" that culls stories as they come in according to keywords of interest to you. You might set up a clipping file for anything mentioning your hometown, for example, to get a jump on stories of local interest and easy access—before your hometown newspaper covers them. (CompuServe's Executive Information Service, a pricier service tier, offers a similar clipping service, as does Dow Jones News/Retrieval.) Since you pay by the "clip," a too-broad choice of keywords can run into serious money, but a smart selection can save you connect time and money reading through whole newsletters on-line.

These examples are merely the tip of the on-line iceberg. For a complete list, consult a multithousand-page tome called *Computer-Readable Databases: A Directory and Data Sourcebook*, published by Gale. And to keep up-to-date on the latest developments in on-line resources, you can subscribe to *Link-Up*, published by Learned Information, Inc. (143 Old Marlton Pike, Medford, NJ; [609] 654-6266). This bimonthly newspaper covers the field in a way that's accessible to the lay user and the novice.

One last warning about these cutting-edge research resources: They're fun. That means they can be addictive, which means it's easy to spend an awful lot of time fooling around on-line.

Eventually, you're going to have to get out of the house and do some interviewing. So "log off" and turn to the next chapter. . . .

EFFICIENT INTERVIEWING

• • •

OF FACTS AND CHARACTER

Though the term "interview" goes back to Old French, when it meant "to meet, to visit" and had rather courtly connotations ("Yes, sir knight, I shall grant you an interview"), its application to the writer's craft is relatively recent. By some accounts, the first interview in the modern journalistic sense was in 1859, when an anonymous reporter for the *New York Herald* quizzed abolitionist Gerrit Smits in the wake of John Brown's raid on Harper's Ferry. A few years later, beginning in 1868, a series of interviews by historian and writer James Redpath for the *Boston Advertiser* newspaper established the interview as a fixture of American journalism.

Today, of course, the interview is a staple—the raw material of everything from scholarly books to tabloids. Andy Warhol founded a whole publication named *Interview,* and the *Playboy* Interview has uncovered the secrets of subjects from movie stars to presidents (remember Jimmy Carter's lust in his heart?). Even if they don't use the "Q&A" format, many nonfiction assignments are at their core interviews wrapped in reporter's prose. "I want you to do a profile on Suzy Celebrity," says an editor, meaning essentially, *interview* her. Without the interview—without a good interview—you have no story.

And, as I've already alluded, not only nonfiction profiles depend heavily on successful interviewing. My horse-breeding story, for example, drew almost as much on phone interviews as my Malcolm Forbes profile depended on my interview with the great man. Novelists, too, from Zola to Tom Wolfe have used interviews to create their settings, flesh out their details, and give voice to their characters.

Interviews can be great fun to do, or they can be as agonizing as root canal work. More to the point of this particular book, they can also be huge time wasters—not only in the hours spent doing actual interviewing, but equally so in the effort of organizing and utilizing the fruits of your conversations.

The first challenge inherent in interviewing is that, fundamentally, an interview is a quest for information, for truth—but a quest that must twist through the convolutions of the human character. That's a mission that would have caused Don Quixote to hang up his lance and go home. Psychologists David Weiss and Rene Davis, quoted in the book *Finding Facts*, state flatly, "It is indefensible to assume the validity of purportedly factual data obtained by interviews." Or, as journalist Thomas Morgan said of his subjects, "*I* want the truth; *they* want to be beautiful."

The second chore facing most interviewers is the search for more than just data; it's the need to collect facts clothed in personality. That same human element that makes it so hard to get straight information is also the key to making the information interesting. It's not enough to get just the facts, ma'am; you want them colorfully spoken, delivered from the heart, wrapped in amusing anecdotes.

Finally, you don't want just any old information or whatever anecdotes please your subject to pass along. No, you want—you must have—material that fits the particular angle of your story. When *TWA Ambassador* sent me to interview author Paul Erdman about his doomsday novel, *The Crash of '79*, I was supposed to bring back his thoughts on the economy and the saga of how he'd turned from banker into writer. If he'd instead spent the afternoon regaling me with charming tales of boyhood adventures with his pet collie, I wouldn't have had a story—at any rate, not the right story. This challenge is stiffest, of course, when your assignment is to interview someone about something they'd really rather not talk about: "So what about that sex scandal, Mister Mayor?" "Did I ever tell you about the time Mrs. Mayor and I built a treehouse for our children? It's a terrific anecdote. There was this tree, see. . . ."

To get the facts, to get character, and to get the *right* facts and character—now there's a set of hurdles to daunt the would-be efficient interviewer. For many writers, the response is to try to get *everything*: interview for hours on end, talk with anybody who'll hold still long enough, and then spend more hours back at your office or den transcribing the interview tapes, so not to miss a revealing "uh-huh." This approach, born out of anxiety or lack of focus, is like dropping an H-bomb on your house to kill an invading mosquito. Better to get a good flyswatter and learn to use it—*swat!*—right.

THE GREAT DEBATE: TAPE RECORDER VS. NOTEBOOK

For many writers, the key ingredient in their H-bomb interviewing arsenal—the plutonium, if you will—is the tape recorder. Capture everything, goes this line of thought, and you're bound to get the good stuff. These writers forget (to extend a metaphor past the snapping point) that plutonium can be as dangerous to the bomber as to the bombee.

I'm getting into controversial territory here, I know. Opinions about whether interviewers should use tape recorders run as fierce as the debate over whether martinis should be shaken or stirred. As you've already deduced, I come down adamantly on the "agin it" side. Part of this is a legacy from the very first cover assignment I got for *TWA Ambassador* magazine: that interview with Paul Erdman. I still remember the thrill of jetting out to the California wine country, sitting by Erdman's pool, and listening to him discourse into my tape recorder on the future of the world's economy. It's a good thing my memory of that encounter was so vivid, because when I got back to the office I found that my tape recorder, like the economy in Erdman's best-seller, had crashed. After a few minutes of the splash-and-whirr of Erdman's pool skimmer, the tape was a blank. If my memory hadn't been in high gear—and if I hadn't also been taking some notes—my cover story would have been a blank as well.

But my prejudice against tape recorders isn't just a lingering suspicion about the cussedness of machines. Rather, it stems from a lesson I learned the hard way from my Erdman story: Only the most vivid and memorable quotes should wind up in your story, anyway. *Nobody* is so quotable that every word from his or her mouth must be recorded.

This lesson was reinforced, again rather vigorously, during my three-year stint as a newspaper columnist. During this time, I was interviewing for and writing three feature stories a week. If I'd tried to keep up that pace while painstakingly transcribing taped interviews before writing each column, I'd have quickly turned into one of the oddballs I sometimes wrote about ("Burned-Out Ex-Columnist Listens to Tapes All Day While Giggling Maniacally").

John Brady, a sometime-advocate of the tape recorder in his superb *The Craft of Interviewing*, concedes, "A tape must be transcribed, and a transcription must be boiled down and ironed out for publication, and in the process, the tape's fidelity becomes tedious and exasperating. You will play a barely audible passage, rewind, play it again, rewind, play it again, pummel the typewriter, and wish to God that you had, after all, resorted to notetaking—a hasty and inventive enterprise that, through sheer panic, boils down and irons out a man's remarks almost as he remarks them."

If this sounds like laziness, it's not—just the opposite. As Pulitzer prizewinner Tracy Kidder (*The Soul of a New Machine, House, Among Schoolchildren*) once told a *Writer's Digest* interviewer after echoing Brady's point about the frustrating time-wastingness of transcribing, "A tape recorder tends to make me lazy, so I might stop taking notes and miss a lot." Kidder believes that his notetaking is actually *more* accurate than the results of tape recording. The machine, he insists, fails to catch the subtleties of an interview. In recording *what* people say, it misses *how* they say it: the gestures, the facial expressions, the relationship of speaker to setting.

As you scribble, you should concentrate on capturing the "true" voice of your subjects, so that later when you turn your compressed notes into a story it's like adding water to dehydrated food (only tastier). If you can capture the voice and personality of your subjects, your story will be much more "true" than if you transcribe every word accurately but miss the person behind the words. The author with a tape recorder tries to cheat his way around the challenges of interviewing, and so winds up tilting at windmills. You and your humble notebook must grapple with a writer's real dragons.

Another argument against relying on the tape recorder goes back to Brady's point about boiling down and ironing out remarks almost as they are remarked—and to my revelation in writing the Erdman story mostly from my head. Just as taking notes from your secondary sources forces you to distill the material, taking notes in an interview makes you edit while listening. You'll soon learn to scribble down only what's essential while politely nodding and mumbling "Uh-huh" as your subject rambles on. Don't worry: You'll still have four times as much raw material as you can or should use in an article. "If you fall behind," journalist Max Gunther once advised, "the reason probably is that you are trying to take down the subject's words too fully." Only about 10 percent of the words uttered in an average interview, Gunther guessed, are genuinely meaningful.

It's this boiling-down effect that is so important to efficient interviewing and, ultimately, writing quickly—and why I've spent so much space here annoying the manufacturers of tape recorders and dictaphones. Obviously, it's a time waster to sit and transcribe taped interviews. (So much so, in fact, that I've written whole stories—from my notebook—in less time than it's taken writers down the hall just to transcribe their tapes.) But the greatest time-saver in taking notes is the way it forces you to focus on what's important in the interview: *Will you use this quote? Is this information what you're really after?* If the answer is *no*, then don't write it down so you won't have to deal with it again later! Writer's cramp is a terrific disciplinarian.

This is time saved in the writing process itself; it's the decision-making and selecting that is the hardest, most time-consuming part of writing. Taking notes on the fly demands that you think about your story as it is unfolding in the interview. You begin to shape and select your material in the back of your mind, even as most of your brain is formulating the next question. And that's a highly effective synergy. The ongoing editing of your material begins to affect the direction of your questioning. You know what gaps must be filled with answers or anecdotes, what areas have been covered and needn't be queried again. As you gain experience, the story (or parts of it, in longer assignments) will begin to write itself in your head during the interview: *Here's the lead. Here's a perfect transition from this subject to that. Here's a quote that coincides perfectly with that previous phone interview with the subject's college roommate.*

Of course, to successfully rely on your notebook rather than a tape recorder requires highly adept and efficient notetaking. You'll need to know shorthand or to develop your own system of notetaking shortcuts, as we discussed in chapter four. (In England, by the way, it's almost unheard-of for a journalist not to know shorthand.) You'll need, ultimately, to be able to decipher—to decompress, if you will—your own notes. Don't be like humorist Robert Benchley, who once wrote a piece on the impossibility of decoding his own notes—presumably because he couldn't understand his notes for the piece he'd originally intended to write!

But beyond those basics, there are a few notetaking tricks you can adopt to ease the process of not just writing down an interview as it happens but editing it as you go. I single out good material, the stuff I know will fit the story I've envisioned, even as I'm interviewing: Immediately after scribbling down something particularly useful, I'll draw a rough slash, or line, beside it in my notebook. When I'm reviewing my notes and organizing my story, that's my signal to pay particular attention to this section of scribbling. I'll also put crude brackets—[ ]—around material that represents my own observations, either about what the subject is saying or about his surroundings. While the subject is babbling on about something less than germane to my story, I'll use the time not only to catch up with my notetaking but to write down the colorful details that help bring the story alive: trinkets on the person's desk, little signs on her wall, how he's dressed, characteristic actions like tenting one's fingers or leaning back in one's chair, habits of voice, even the view out the subject's window. All these things I set off by brackets, so I know instantly that this isn't direct quotation; no need, then, to put quotation marks around everything else I take down.

In my Malcolm Forbes interview, for example, I took notes—while he was talking—that wound up this way in the story: "Forbes declaims, as usual, in a pose of hands knitted in back of his white-haired head, the eyes in his owlish black-rimmed glasses closed for concentration. His mahogany desk is like a miniature of his gallery: jade Fabergé push buttons on the intercom and a gilt writing portfolio with the crowned double monogram of Nicholas and Alexandra."

This sort of material, incidentally, can be as crucial to your story as the quotes you gather. I once asked a writer why, in the profile article he'd written for me, there was not a single nugget of visual or other sensory detail about his subject or his subject's surroundings. "That sort of thing doesn't interest me," the writer replied. Well, you'd better *get* interested—unless you want your stories to read like glorified transcriptions.

Your notebook, remember, is your repository for everything—from research notes to quotes to observations made on the fly. Part of the trick of really effective in-person interviewing is to capture this kind of telling, specific detail, even while getting what you need direct from the source's mouth. "*Show* us, don't tell us," an editor will often admonish—and such notes become an important part of the "showing." If you're going to go to the time and trouble of a face-to-face interview, after all, you might as well make the most of it; otherwise you should have stayed home and used the phone.

Now, if you're *still* daunted by the prospect of entering an interview without the security blanket of a tape recorder, let me just add a few words about the ultimate in interviewing-without-a-net: relying on memory alone. Truman Capote, fearful that even the presence of a simple notebook would prove off-putting to his subjects for *In Cold Blood*, practiced memorizing an interview by having a friend talk to him. He'd tape the conversation, for checking purposes, and then write up the interview strictly from memory. When the write-up matched the tape with 97 percent accuracy, Capote figured he was ready to go to work on *In Cold Blood*.

While I'm a long way from a Capote in either writing ability or memory skills, I know from experience that it is indeed possible for a writer to fly solo, without even a notebook. When *TWA Ambassador* sent me out to a California chess tournament to interview chess champion and jack-of-all-games Walter Browne, I found myself hounding the great gamesman for interview time. Every moment, it seemed, he was either actually playing chess or preparing for his next match. I finally got the time I needed by going to dinner with him—but the restaurant Browne picked was too dark to take notes, even if I'd been able to wield a pencil along with my knife and fork. So we talked—more of a dinner conversation than a formal interview, the casual atmosphere seeming to put him more at ease. And then, after I bade Browne good night, I raced back to my tiny motel room. Frantically, I wrote down all I could recall of the evening's several hours of revealing conversation. Much to my amazement, I remembered almost everything of importance (just as I had, with a few more notes, reconstructed my Erdman interview).

The point is not to urge you to throw your notebook in the trash heap with your tape recorder, but to underscore the point: Yes, you can get what you really need with notebook alone. Yes, you will remember what is truly important for your story, with or without a notebook. And it's only the most memorable material that belongs in your writing, anyway. If you couldn't remember it (with a little help from your notes), it's probably not good enough or central enough to put in the story.

Daniel Lang of *The New Yorker*, for example, takes notes during his interviews—but seldom refers to his notes when writing. He'll check his notes only for specific facts like a date or a number, and then again after his first draft, to make certain his facts are correct. Your own memory, you see, is the most efficient recording device available to you—because it's hard-wired to your "output device," the part of your brain that does the writing. As Lang understands, the best and fastest way to write is to let the hardest parts happen mostly inside your head.

GETTING OFF TO A FAST START

Your first question sets the tone and pace for the entire interview. Whether your subject is friendly or adversarial, whether you're playing cuddly Charles Kuralt or go-get-'em Mike Wallace, your subject is bound to be a bit apprehensive just about the strange process of Being Interviewed. How you start the process can make the difference between a productive conversation and a tough, time-wasting battle of wills.

So, even if you're really planning to nail this subject, it's usually best to launch the interview on an easygoing note. Don't lob your dynamite question first; save it for later—otherwise there might not be a later. Instead, you might simply ask how your subject got started in whatever it is you're interviewing him about. Or you might ask what her typical day is like. Your first question can be surprising, even fresh (à la Liebling's opener to Eddie Arcaro), as long as it works to open up the communication rather than bring down the wall. Associated Press reporter Saul Pett once started an interview with New York Mayor John Lindsay by asking, "Would you want your daughter to marry a mayor of New York?" (Presumably in these more enlightened times he would have asked, "Would you want your daughter to grow up to be mayor of New York?") When I interviewed Gene Simmons, the masked and jackbooted lead singer of the KISS rock group, in his dressing room, I was admittedly intimidated—not so much by his fame as by his steel-and-leather costume and fierce demeanor. This was a guy who breathed fire on stage, after all! My first question served as much to set me at ease as my subject: "What does your mother think of what you do?" (As it turned out, Simmons had used some of his KISS earnings to buy a very nice home for his mom, and she thought his rock-and-rollin' was just dandy. That tidbit proved to be my lead.)

"The object," author John Gunther once observed of interviewing, "is to get the interviewee relaxed, to make him really *talk* instead of just answering questions." Keep that in mind as your interviews unfold. It's important for rapid writing not just in the obvious sense that you want to get as much out of a free-talking subject as quickly as possible, but in the broader implications of an effective interview for your writing. Good quotes and colorful facts make writing easy—and therefore fast. Yes and no answers, grunts and evasions make for agony at the word processor.

Practice is the best teacher of a productive interviewing technique, but there are some simple tricks that can immediately make your interviews flow better. As I've already suggested, it's best to start on a friendly note and seek to establish empathy with your subject. Follow his or her lead—a little small talk at this stage is not necessarily a waste of time. Besides, you can use the small talk time to take notes on your subject's surroundings, appearance and mannerisms. Not only in the beginning but throughout the interview, you should avoid questions that invite yes-or-no answers. You're looking for telling quotes, after all—not monosyllables. And don't waste time on questions that merely confirm what you already know from your research:

"So, you graduated from Harvard in 1957?" On the other hand, don't lob questions that really have no answers, or that are so broad that they generate useless generalities: "How do you feel about the country these days?" or "How do you feel about being a songwriter?" To get results, you've got to strike a happy medium between the too specific and the blandly general.

The aim is to get momentum going, to establish a natural conversational rhythm. As Robert Louis Stevenson once put it, "You start a question, and it's like starting a stone. You sit quietly on the top of a hill, and away the stone goes, starting others."

Once you've started the interview rolling, except for an occasional question to keep it rolling or steer it in the right direction, the most efficient thing you can do is shut up and listen. Never get so caught up in the conversation, so overly empathic or so argumentative, that you wind up talking as much as your subject. Never, even more seriously, get so full of yourself that you forget who's the interviewer and who's the interviewee. Talk about wasting time! "The worst thing an interviewer can do is talk a lot himself," Liebling advised. "Just listen to reporters in a barroom. You can tell the ones who go out and impress their powerful personalities on their subject and then come back and make up what they think he would have said if he had had a chance to say anything."

When I was writing my column in Dubuque, I used to get a bit upset when (it being a smallish town) I'd later run into my former interview subjects on the street — and they didn't remember or recognize me! Here we'd spent several hours in intense conversation, my picture ran with the story about them, and they acted as though I were invisible. Later, I came to realize this was not an insult but a point of pride: It showed I had succeeded in fading into the background, in letting my subjects talk rather than taking over the interview. I was as neutral and faceless to them as a tape recorder, which was just perfect for the work I had to do.

THE POWER OF "UH-HUH"

So if you're not supposed to waste time chitchatting once an interview gets rolling, what *are* you supposed to say? Probably the best thing an efficient interviewer can contribute to the dialogue in an interview is: "Uh-huh." When your subject is pouring his heart out, say "uh-huh." When your subject is spilling her guts, say "uh-huh." It's the interviewer's universal solvent, guaranteed to keep the interview going without taking it over yourself. If "uh-huh" gets too repetitious, you can really go wild and try "Yes" or "I see." John Brady calls this principle "the sympathetic noise." Not only is the sympathetic noise useful in stalling for time while you scribble the really interesting response to your previous question, Brady says, it's also a highly effective follow-up "question."

A variant on the sympathetic noise is simply to feed back to the subject what he or she has just said. This can serve the interests of clarity, in making certain that you understand what you're hearing; it can also, by reinforcing and slightly rephrasing the subject's words, spark the next round of good stuff. Such a follow-up, Brady advises, "can unleash a torrent of anecdotes and naked quotes."

Of course, efficient interviewing sometimes requires that you do more than merely keep your subject talking; even in the most productive interview, you'll occasionally need to steer that talk toward the lines of your story. Certainly, for example, you should pursue the details of a topic if your subject seems to be skimming the surface — but not at the expense of the conversational flow of the interview. "If you make a man stop to explain everything," Liebling advised, "he will soon quit on you, like a horse that you alternately spur and curb." Better, generally, to gently steer the talk back to subjects still vague or unclear to you: "Getting back for a moment to what you said about. . . ."

Be firmer, though, when your subject veers completely off the track that your story must follow. Don't hesitate to take the talk back to your area of interest — and as quickly as possible. If you let your subject wander too far and too long astray, it may be hard to steer him back without seeming rude: "Enough about your little dog Checkers, already, Mr. Nixon. What about this scandal?"

To successfully keep an interview on track, it's necessary to have a clear idea of where you want it to go and what you need out of it. This means more than just having a list of questions: It demands a sense of the story you're after, the key parts you need to get your writing contraption in gear.

Sometimes, when time is extremely short, it means having a handle on the bare minimum — quotes, facts, color, anecdotes — necessary to write your story at all. That was the case with my Malcolm Forbes interview. It was also true when I profiled renowned transplant surgeon Dr. Thomas Starzl: I actually felt guilty about taking up *any* of his time, which surely could be better spent saving lives. Once I got into his office, I was intimidated still further by the sheaf of pink "While You Were Out" telephone messages taped all over his door, almost completely obscuring the wood with notes from people who wanted a bit of Starzl's precious time. From the moment I asked my first question, I was acutely aware that I was (not unlike his patients) on borrowed time; at any instant, a medical emergency or the arrival of a donor organ could sweep Starzl away, never to return to the interview. In this extreme situation, I almost completely abandoned the sympathetic noise in favor of a quick barrage of questions designed to generate answers I could plug into my story:

How do you feel about the fame your work has brought you? "I haven't paid too much attention. I never have time to watch TV, so I don't get into that. That's probably best; you can get your feelings hurt pretty quick otherwise."

What kind of risk did you take, professionally, when you started doing transplants? "That was terra incognita back then. If it hadn't worked, it would have been professionally ruinous. . . ."

What does it take to make a good transplant surgeon? "It requires creative people above all. It requires curiosity and inventiveness, because transplantation isn't perfected yet. . . ."

And so on—not much more than a dozen key questions in all. I added Starzl's responses—before he was, indeed, called away—to what I'd already read about him and what he said at a press conference I attended, and produced a story that ran four magazine pages. I had my angle clearly in mind—Starzl as legend, as a sort of medical icon—and knew exactly what ground I'd cover, so the actual writing was a snap. I even managed to use the difficulty of interviewing him in my lead:

If you have a call in to Tom Starzl, don't worry: You're up there on his door, along with everyone else who wants to talk to Pitt's most famous transplant surgeon. Pink Scotch-taped "While You Were Out" slips mosaic the inside of Starzl's office door. The trouble is, there are only twenty-four hours in a day—no matter how hard the doctor tries to squeeze in twenty-six or twenty-seven.

Lean, almost gaunt in his surgical greens and white lab coat, Starzl shuts his door for a little uninterrupted time with his visitor. Immediately, he's interrupted by probably the four millionth phone call of the day. Somebody from overseas, so Starzl takes it. Waiting on a sofa made almost comfortable for catnaps with the addition of a papery hospital pillow, the visitor feels guilty: Could Starzl be out saving lives instead of talking to me?

Can you see what I was busily writing down, in brackets, while the famous physician took his transatlantic phone call? Instead of just fretting about my precious interview time slipping away (though I did that, too), I took notes on my subject and his surroundings. And the minute he was off the phone, I was off and interviewing!

If you're ever in a similar super-time-pressured situation, the lesson is simple: Know in advance the bare minimum you need to write your story and get it first, no matter what.

Starzl was at least cooperative, for the brief time I commanded his attention. But how do you productively steer an interview with a tough subject — with the interviewee who'd really rather be somewhere else, doing almost anything else?

The classic tough interview is one in which, despite your carefully calculated queries, you get nothing but "Yes," "No" and "*grunt*" responses. Hard to write much of a story out of monosyllables. You can try rephrasing your questions so they're impossible to answer in a single word: "Why?" is an excellent such nudge. Or you can quickly cast around for a question that will break the logjam. John Gunther once suggested, "One thing I have found out is that almost any person will talk freely — such is human frailty — if you will ask him the measure of his own accomplishment." Ace inquisitor Barbara Walters once revealed to the *New York Times* her five "foolproof questions for the over-interviewed":

1. If you were recuperating in a hospital, who would you want in the bed next to you, excluding relatives?
2. What was your first job?
3. When was the last time you cried?
4. Who was the first person you ever loved?
5. What has given you the most pleasure in the last year?

Be wary, though, of asking too grand a question of the wrong person — it can have exactly the opposite effect as desired. I was once part of an incredibly awkward press conference to which philosopher and author Mortimer Adler had been shanghaied to promote a lecture at a local campus. An enterprising but utterly ill-prepared reporter for a TV station, aware only that Adler had written a recent book with "God" in the title, made the mistake of asking, "Mr. Adler, what is your theory about God?" Adler responded with a stare that could have frozen the TV lights, then icily informed the eager interrogator that he did not have a "theory" about God. He followed with a brief but stern lecture on the impossibility of understanding theology when you are an ignorant young TV reporter from a hick town.

Well, at least my TV colleague didn't get a yes-or-no answer. And,

I'll admit, I turned the tongue-lashing he received into the basis for my lead — something to the effect that Mortimer Adler doesn't suffer fools gladly.

FINDING THE MAGIC ANECDOTE — AND THE DOOR

In several examples, I've mentioned a detail or anecdote that made an ideal lead; other times in interviews you'll be lucky enough to chance upon a bit that makes a perfect closer, a dynamite "hook" for your story, or a sort of epiphany, summing up your subject in a way no fancy words of yours could do. Usually such gems are anecdotes, and usually a skilled writer/interviewer will recognize them the moment they are uttered. *Yes*, you'll say to yourself, hand trembling a bit with excitement as you strive to get this jewel down in your notebook, *that says it all*.

If this "magic anecdote" doesn't appear of its own accord early on in an interview, it's easy to get frustrated and try to force it. There's no magic formula, alas, for eliciting the truly telling stuff. All an efficient interviewer can do is be alert — don't miss it! — from the very start of the interview to the last words out of your subject's mouth, even after you've flipped your notebook closed.

Most of the examples I've already cited came early in an interview, or sprang from some detail in the interview's circumstances or setting. Others — think back to the telling, devastating anecdote about rehearsing in the cafeteria that Dubuque's maestro told me — come well into the heart of an interview.

The trickiest revelations come at the end, after the interview is apparently concluded. By this point, your subject may well be at his or her least guarded; you will have had your maximum opportunity to establish empathy. The nuggets dropped here, as you conversationally collect your coat and amble toward the door, epitomize the importance of squeezing the most out of every instant of time with your subject. In my story on the problems facing math educators, for example, I was almost out the door when one of the faculty members I was interviewing told me the anecdote that gave me my lead:

> When asked about the chasm between his work and the comprehension of most nonmathematicians, Charles Hall likes to tell about the time he was hiring a computer programmer for Pitt's Institute for Computational Mathematics and Applications. He had to review the job description with an administrator, for

whom the technical terminology might as well have been Martian. Finally, the puzzled administrator interjected, "I have to ask you about this 'math research.' What's math research? After all, aren't all the numbers already known?"

Hall, a professor in the Department of Mathematics and Statistics, cocks an eyebrow at his punchline and adds, "As a matter of fact, all the numbers *aren't* already known."

This little anecdote got my story off to a fast start. It introduced Hall, one of my major characters, and his institute. It fed readily into my "hook," which went on about the myths that most of us have about math. And it was a perfect example of the popular math ignorance expressed in the story's subhead: "Mathematics is entering a new era, powered by the computer, in which it may change the world around us. But most of us still can't do fractions."

But I never would have gotten it if I hadn't kept my ears open and my mind churning as I headed out of Hall's office—and if I hadn't whipped open my notebook again the second I was politely out of sight, to scribble down the story he'd just related. I've taken some of my best notes after the interview is over and I'm on my way home. It's like the "spirit of the back stair"—you always come up with the perfect line just as you're slipping down the back stairway. The writer's advantage is that, for you, the conversation doesn't have to end as long as you can open your notebook again. So keep alert during every second you're with your subject, even as you're heading out the door—and be prepared to take some more notes the instant you're alone.

The opposite extreme is the interview that never seems to end because your subject won't shut up, or you're too reluctant—*Have I got enough yet? Or should we go on for another ten hours?*—to bring it to a close. How do you know when to *stop* interviewing, when you've got a magic hatful of anecdotes and it's time to go home to your keyboard? The question may sound frivolous, but it's linked to a lot of time wasting. People *like* to talk about themselves; once you get somebody rolling, he or she might happily bend your ear until all your notebook pages, front and back both, are full—and then some. Or, if you're doing many interviews for a single story, there's always that temptation (or feeling of inadequacy): *Maybe I need just one more.* Because, face it, sitting down at the keyboard and putting one word after another is hard, lonely work, yet another interview can be a way of putting off your real writing.

The ideal, of course, is to know in advance exactly what you want from each interview—as I've already prescribed—and to sit down to write as soon as you've got it all. Life isn't always that tidy, unfortunately, so you'll have to develop an intuitive feel for when your notebook is full. John McPhee says that his rule of thumb is that when he starts hearing the same information a third time, he knows he's done interviewing. Without the resources of the *New Yorker* behind you, you might want to stop one iteration earlier. If you feel like you've heard it all before, it's time to get on with your story.

Similarly, in any given interview there's no advantage in continuing to chat once all your bases are covered, or when you start to hear the same answers over again. William Manchester once said he figured that he'd gotten all he could out of an interview if he'd elicited ten good anecdotes. (But keep alert for the unexpected pearl once the chemistry has changed and you're headed out the door!) Or, if you've clearly outstayed your welcome — say, a friendly subject starts to clip his answers and look at his watch — ask your most crucial remaining questions and make a graceful exit. "One last question," you might say, as a signal that: a) you need to wrap up this marathon and get on with your life, or b) this ordeal is almost over, if the subject will humor you just a smidge longer. "I don't want to take up too much of your time . . ." is another of my favorite getting-ready-to-exit lines. (Which, admittedly, gives my subject a chance to reply, "No, no, I've got plenty of time. Have I told you yet about my cat's hernia operation back in '54 . . . ?") Manchester said he used to like to wrap things up with, "Is there anything you think is important which I haven't asked?" If the reply is negative, you can hardly be judged rude for leaving, right?

Close your notebook — but not your ears — and head slowly for the door. Make any last-minute notations as the door swings shut behind you, then head for home. Put on a fresh pot of coffee. It's time to get down to the real business of writing.

CHAPTER SEVEN

PUT IT ALL TOGETHER TO BEAT WRITER'S BLOCK

• • •

PROCRASTINATORS R US

Writers aren't the world's only procrastinators, but we're among the very best at it. For all the glamour and appeal of the writer's life, we know the hard truth that sitting down at the keyboard and actually putting one word after another is just about the toughest activity ever attempted by humankind. And so we invent excuses — writers are good at inventing things, remember — to stay away from the real work of authorship. We'll do anything rather than write: *Honey, the lawn needs mowing — I think I'd better do it before I tackle that next chapter. In fact, gosh, the neighbors' yard needs mowing, too. What do you know? The median strip over on the freeway is looking a little shaggy, now that I think of it. . . .*

Many of the time-wasters I've already talked about in previous chapters — over-researching, endless interviewing — are essentially devices to avoid real writing. (An afternoon in the reference stacks beats mowing the lawn, right?) You could probably speed up your writing production significantly without reading another sentence in this book if only you could master the willpower to make yourself simply sit down and *write*.

Wait, come back! It's not as easy as it sounds, this willpower stuff. We humans are weak creatures; otherwise there'd be no market for chocolate or nacho corn chips. The best tactic for building up your willingness to write is not relying on some neo-Nietzschean willpower exercise (like quitting cigarettes, only much harder), but rather removing some of the fear and loathing that accompanies staring at the blank page and trying to make one word follow the next. In short, don't try to go *through* your writer's block; instead, undermine and ultimately dismantle it.

For here's the plain truth: Except perhaps for a few truly psychologically disturbed cases, there's no such thing as writer's block. There are only disorganized writers—writers who don't know where their next sentence is going. If you don't know where your writing is going—if, like Columbus's sailors, for all you know the next instant may take you off the edge of the world—it's no wonder you're fearful of writing. In that case, writer's block is only a logical defense mechanism. It may even be your mind's quite rational effort to save you from yourself, to keep you from writing until you know what the heck you're doing.

This chapter will show you how to conquer writer's block once and for all one brick at a time. Ladies and gentlemen, start chipping away.

GETTING DOWN TO WORK BY GOOFING OFF

It probably seems impossibly contrary for me to follow that stirring speech by proclaiming that your first step in dismantling writer's block, once all your research and interviews are done, is to do nothing. But that's the way the mind works best, and if you're going to write faster you'd better learn to go with, not against, your own brain.

Whether they knew it consciously or not, most great writers worked this way. Ernest Hemingway, for example, used to sharpen twenty pencils each day before he could settle down to write. The pencils weren't the point; what mattered most, I suspect, was the routine that allowed Hemingway's unconscious to get a head start on his conscious writing. Similarly, Thomas Wolfe had to wander the streets all night before he could work, sleepier but wiser, the next morning. Thornton Wilder took long walks to prepare for writing.

Even when I was under the gun as a newspaper columnist, I tried to schedule my interviews far enough in advance of my deadlines to allow a few days' rumination on what I'd heard. Your unconscious is a marvelous organizer and problem solver, even when (especially when) you're not aware it's at work. While you're sharpening pencils or ambling on a long walk, taking a shower or mowing the lawn, your unconscious will be sorting the pieces that must fall into place and make a story for you. Rushing the process will only slow you down in the long run.

This is the work, as Kenneth Atchity notes in *A Writer's Time*, that only time can do. "Percolation," he calls it—and you know what they say about a watched pot. Put your story away, even if only for an afternoon, in a pile or a file drawer or just the back of your mind. "Start things down the track," Atchity advises, "and let time's engineering do most of the work."

Your percolating or gestation period may vary from task to task, or as you gain greater experience (and your mind begins to recognize the patterns a story might fit). Certainly, it varies from writer to writer: Georges Simenon, the prolific French mystery writer, took just two days to be ready to write the next of his 400 novels; William Faulkner required six months.

Soon, however, you will find yourself feeling as James Thurber did. "I never quite know when I'm not writing," Thurber once said, half in complaint. "Sometimes my wife comes up to me at a dinner party and says, 'Dammit, Thurber, stop writing.' She usually catches me in the middle of a paragraph. Or my daughter will look up from the dinner table and ask, 'Is he sick?' 'No,' my wife says. 'He's writing.'" Thurber wrote mostly in his head because his eyes were too poor for staring at the page; you'll find that letting your head lay the foundation before you start writing will keep you, too, from having to stare at an empty page.

FINDING THE *DAVID*: OUTLINING A-B-C'S

This "head work," as opposed to paperwork, is so important because it begins the organizing, the shaping and the molding of your mass of material. Your subconscious is expert at spotting patterns, at connecting the dots. Once your material is organized — first in your head and then on paper or floppy disk — the rest is just carpentry. The real art lies in developing the blueprint; the writing is mere craft.

Consider Michelangelo, who was once asked whether carving his statue of David was difficult. Carving the *David* wasn't the hard part, the great sculptor is said to have replied. The great challenge was finding the block of marble that contained the *David* within it. Once that was accomplished, he simply carved away everything that wasn't the *David*.

How do you find the *David* that is the best story that lies within your material? The answer's not nearly so grand as my Renaissance metaphor might lead you to expect. In fact, it goes back to a simple skill you probably learned in grade school: outlining.

Yes, Mrs. Griswold back in fifth grade was right about outlines. Though your outlines need not conform to the strict I-A-a format she preached at the blackboard, outlines are indeed the surest and easiest way to speed your story from scribbled notes to polished manuscript. Sure, you can just haul off and hack away at that chunk of marble (metaphorically speaking again), but without an outline you're likely to wind up with a pile of hard-won dust. Once again (and, I promise, this is the last time I'll say this), an investment of a little time up front will pay you big-time dividends at the keyboard. So outline, outline, outline!

I'll confess, I learned the writing benefits of outlining long after fifth grade, and sort of backwards. As a fledgling associate editor at *TWA Ambassador* magazine, I was lucky enough to work under a great editor, Jim Morgan (later of *Playboy* and *Southern* magazines), who taught me that stories don't always go straight from a writer's manuscript into a magazine's pages. Sometimes an editor's scissors and tape intervene. (Yes, this was back in the pre-word processor Stone Age, when dinosaurs roamed the earth.) Frankly, I was amazed at the cutting and pasting that were often necessary, even when "big-name writers" were behind the typewriter. To keep the patchwork straight, I fell back on my fifth-grade lessons and began outlining stories *after the fact*—creating the logical structure the writer should have used in the first place. Remember the "big-name" financial writer (who shall remain nameless here) whose story I had to assemble, in effect, paragraph by paragraph over the phone? My outline told me what pieces of the puzzle he had yet to supply for the story to hold together; I would then call and badger him into fleshing out the structure I'd crafted for him.

Computers, of course, have simplified the harried editor's cut-and-paste operation, but you can still save yourself and your editor time and grief by outlining your story *before* it's written. Your outline can be as crude as scrawls on a notepad or as sophisticated as a neatly numbered computer document that would make Mrs. Griswold beam. Many popular word processing programs, such as WordPerfect and Microsoft Word, offer built-in outlining, from which you can easily spring to the actual writing of your article. (Sometimes, indeed, the outline simply grows seamlessly into the story, as you add to it and refine it.) Other outlining programs operate as "stand-alones" (More, for example) or as "desk accessories" (such as Acta) you can use while running your regular word processing program.

But you don't have to know a floppy disk from a flapjack to outline your work and speed up your writing. (In fact, too much time spent fiddling around on your computer can wind up being yet another time waster. I speak from experience here.) Index cards, yellow legal pads, manila folders, envelopes, and other low-tech tools can work just fine to transform your morass of notes into marching orders for your writing.

One of the best and most inspiring systems for organizing a writer's work that I've ever read about, for example, is John McPhee's — using nothing more high-tech than a pair of scissors. McPhee's approach is notable not only for the elegance of its simple yet effective organization, but also for what it illustrates about a writer's thought processes.

After percolating on his story for a while, McPhee will develop a basic outline using index cards. (According to *The John McPhee Reader*, McPhee was inspired by — you guessed it — Mrs. Olive McKee, an old English teacher.) He uses one card for each broad topic area he intends to cover, then shuffles and re-sorts the cards until he arrives at an order that works. (Remember the examples of his organizational *architectonics* back in chapter two?) Once satisfied with his story structure, McPhee tacks the index cards on the wall, in order. Next he photocopies his notes, files one set in a notebook for permanent reference, and cuts apart the second set. Each chunk of information or quotation becomes a sliver of paper. The pieces of notes are then filed into big envelopes — one for each index card. As McPhee writes his way through each envelope, he tracks his progress through the topics with a steel dart through the index cards on his wall.

One envelope, one topic at a time — that's the secret of this approach. Each section of the story becomes like a ministory in itself. McPhee tackles the writing challenges of what's before him, then moves on. He doesn't need to worry about the long stretch of writing that may lie ahead; he just writes what's in each envelope, and worries about each one in turn.

Such an approach — whether mimicking McPhee's, or the simple legal pad technique I'll describe later in this chapter, or some polished program on your computer — is basic to beating writer's block. Outlining forces you to break a story down into its component parts and put them in order. Even the most keyboard-phobic can usually manage to write one paragraph, as long as you know exactly what's supposed to happen in that paragraph. Great. Write the paragraph — dealing with no more than two or three chunks of notes — and then move on to the next. Paragraph by paragraph, even one sentence at a time, your outline holds your hand through the whole writing process. Don't fret about tomorrow or even the next chunk; do the job at hand and let your outline tell you what to do then.

Peace of mind is what you're buying with an outline — not to mention the time saved by being free to plow straight through your story, without backtracking and rewriting. Outlining may have seemed like a straitjacket back in Mrs. Griswold's class. In truth, it's the key to liberation.

Growing an Outline

All right, already — you're sold, right? But how do you turn your glob of notes into a ready-to-write outline? How do you figure out what goes where?

You've already started this process (back in chapter two) by thinking about the organization of your story. Your outline should grow, first, from the overall theme of your story and, more specifically, from your organizational plan. What's your "hook"? Plug it into the outline. Do you have a thematic metaphor that winds through your story (remember my cafeteria scene with the Dubuque maestro)? Great — your outline is almost done for you. If you've thought hard about what your story is really about, and gathered material that fits the points you intend to make, building and filling in an outline should be a snap.

Or, if it's fiction you're writing, the march of your story becomes your outline. Now is the time to decide whether the scene in the revolving restaurant comes before or after the scene at the farm. Once those parts are placed in order, your notes on character and setting and plot detail can be sorted by scene and section, outlining what will be revealed when.

Whatever you're outlining, that movement from general to particular is the way to work. Begin with the broadest strokes — the main topics that Mrs. Griswold might label "I-II-III" — and then fill in the "A-B-C" and "1-2-3" and even the "a-b-c." For my Malcolm Forbes profile, for example, my broad topics ran like this:

Lead set in Forbes museum
Capitalism can be fun
Forbes's other fruits of capitalism
Describe office at magazine
Opinions expressed in magazine, other opinions
Brush with politics in the 1950s
Instead, wound up at magazine
Founded by father
Took helm
His own offspring/their inheritance
But he's not ready to retire

That's hardly a work of art or anything to aspire to, architectonically speaking, but it helped get my thoughts on the story flowing.

And, ultimately, a good outline will begin to grow organically; you'll find yourself filling in the gaps here and there, making connections, seeing transitions, structuring themes. Outlining will be easier if you're already familiar with your material—as you will be by now if you've followed the chapters on research and interviewing. Here's where that notetaking begins to pay off. As your outline grows, ideas and elements from your notes will spring from the back of your mind into your working brain. It's probably best not to even refer to your notes at this preliminary outlining stage; if it's an important enough thread to belong in your story, you should remember it by now. (Things you nonetheless forget can be scribbled in later—neatness doesn't count at this stage, Mrs. Griswold notwithstanding.)

Developing my Forbes outline, for example, was not the sterile, step-by-step process that the bare bones above might suggest. As I scribbled (the real thing is on an oversized index card), transitions suggested themselves; one idea led to the next. The item on the "fruits of capitalism," for instance, gave me a way to get from Forbes's collection to the magazine's airplane (christened *Capitalist Tool*) to Forbes's office itself (placing him in it) with its Rubens painting and the Fabergé folder on his desk that once belonged to the Czar. And the folder, well, I remembered from my notes that it held ideas for Forbes's own magazine editorials. From the editorials in the folder I could go to Forbes's strongly held opinions . . . and so on.

This business of building transitions is absolutely crucial to speeding up your actual writing. Your outline should give you links from one thought or topic to the next. Sometimes these can be obvious and direct—like the transition from Forbes's inheritance to his children's—or they can be subtle, almost sneaky—like the link between the folder and Forbes's opinions. Transitions can be physical, visual or simply verbal. But, however you accomplish them, if you know before you start writing that you can get from here to there (and how you'll do it), you can hit the keyboard without fear that you'll write a section and then not know how to begin the next one. As an editor, I check for transitions to make certain the reader is carried smoothly along from the lead to the close; as a writer, you'll find your work goes much faster if you, like your ultimate audience, are swept along in logical, seamless sequence.

So try to make each specific item under the general headings link somehow not only to the overall topic but also to the item before and the item after. You can use the principle of similarity: If I'm talking about Forbes's collection of toys, it's easy to go from a section on toy soldiers to a section on toy boats; it's only a bit more of a stretch from such literal toys to a section on grown-up "toys" like Forbes's hot-air balloons and motorcycles. For greater logical leaps, you can also use the trick of contrast—those handy paragraphs that often begin with "But . . .": I went from a litany of Forbes's more serious collectibles (Paul Revere's expense account, the diary of the *Enola Gay*) to the aforementioned toys with a simple contrast. In my outline, it reads:

Serious stuff
Not so serious—toys

You don't have to have every transition nailed down to the last comma before you're ready to write, but your outline should provide a basic guide to getting there from here. As long as the items in your outline flow smoothly, you can approach the actual writing with confidence that the transitions will work. For one thing, it's a lot easier to write transitions between topics in logical sequence than it is to craft labored, awkward links between subjects that don't belong together.

As your outline grows from trunk and branches to finer twigs, as you fill in the finer details where they belong, the outline will begin to reflect your whole story. Ultimately, your outline should be detailed enough that no more than two or three items from your notes will wind up under each outline subheading. I like to write my outlines for magazine articles on yellow legal pads: The plan for a typical magazine feature should fill a page or two of a legal pad.

Once you've sketched in your outline, the next step is to link it to your notes. You can take the McPhee approach, scissoring apart a copy of your notes. But for a simple feature story (rather than a booklength project such as those McPhee usually undertakes) with no more than, say, sixty pages of notes, I prefer to simply annotate my outline. First I number all the pages in my notebook. Then I go through my notebook with a red pen, highlighting (with a simple line along the side or by underlining) quotes and facts I'm pretty sure I want to use in my story—things that fit into the outline I've already developed. At the same time, I write the page number of each key quote or fact at the place in the outline where this item will go.

The outline, it's important to note, isn't cast in stone. As I study my notes and the material comes alive for me again, I'll mark additions and changes in my outline to better reflect how the story should proceed. (Resist, though, the temptation to tinker with your outline just to squeeze in a favorite fact or anecdote if it doesn't really fit the focus of your story.)

My Forbes outline wound up looking like this:

Describe office 23, 24
Rubens etc. 30
Fabergé folder 31

And so on. Just as, when McPhee opens a new envelope, all the relevant material is right before him, my annotated outline takes me straight to what I need to write each chunk.

Don't fret too much over whether your plan is perfect at this stage. When you actually sit down to write, you may change it or drop some parts entirely. That's all right: The important thing is to have a plan for getting from point A to point Z, and thus to be able to start at point A without writer's block.

By now you've developed the trunk, filled in the branches and figured out where the twigs should go. It's going to be a lot easier now to add the leaves—the words that bring your story alive.

Before we talk about the details of rapidly putting words on paper, however, I'd like to share two case studies that show the growing and the greening of an outline. It's important that you see not only how it works but that, yes, it really *does* work—because if you shortcut or short shrift this process, you'll find yourself back in the slow-writing bog, battling writer's block.

As you've probably guessed by now, both case studies come from one of my favorite writers—me.

CASE STUDY #1: THE SHY SPEAKER

One of my favorite assignments when I was a newspaper columnist—at least it started off as one of my favorites—was covering a speech by Garrison Keillor. The then-host of "A Prairie Home Companion" was giving the commencement address at a little Lutheran college on the fringe of our coverage area. I was going to get to drive up and hear him speak and then interview him afterwards.

Anyway, that was the plan. As it turned out, the day was so hot and the auditorium so sweltering that by the time it was Keillor's turn to speak he cut his talk down to a few sentences. Then the interview turned out to be a "press conference," at which the sweaty and only semicooperative radio star fielded questions from not just me but also reporters from every weekly paper for miles around.

This was a less-than-ideal start for a story. Worse, I had to drive ninety minutes back to the newspaper and write my column that night, for the next day's paper. No chance to mull things over, as I preferred to do, and figure out at some leisure what the heck to make of this experience. I had to write fast, with not much to go on. But I still took the time to scratch out an outline — and it was my outline that made the story work.

I sketched the situation in my lead, which was outlined like this:

most famous shy person
sweaty grads
most Norwegian outpost this side of Oslo
if bachelor Norwegian farmers who make Powdermilk Biscuits
    ("give strength") to college, to Luther
Powdermilk Biscuits, other sponsors
Lake Wobegon
credit not fictional sponsor's biscuits
but myopia for strength to go on

When I sat down to write, this plus my notes became these opening paragraphs:

DECORAH, Iowa — Where else would the most famous shy person in America spend a sultry summer Sunday but in front of a crowd of sweating graduates and their relatives, their programs fanning like tethered seagulls, at Luther College in Decorah?

Garrison Keillor, of course, is known to two million listeners as the host of American Public Radio's "A Prairie Home Companion," broadcast live every Saturday night from St. Paul, Minn. His fans know Keillor despite the fact that he never announces his name on the air and despite his renowned shyness. He is the author of a manifesto, "Shy Rights: Why Not Pretty Soon?"

Luther College, of course, is known as the most Norwegian outpost of academia this side of Oslo. If the "bachelor Norwegian farmers" who grow the whole wheat for Powdermilk Biscuits went to college, they'd go to Luther.

Powdermilk Biscuits, of course, sponsor "A Prairie Home Companion." In company with Bertha's Kitty Boutique, Minnesota Language Systems, Ralph's Pretty Good Grocery ("If you can't find it at Ralph's, you can probably get along without it"), Raw Bits cereal, the Fearmonger's Shop and the Chatterbox Cafe, Powdermilk Biscuits brings America the weekly news from Lake Wobegon, Minn.

Lake Wobegon, of course, is "the little town that time forgot and the decades cannot improve." With the addition of a college and a few thousand people and a move to Iowa, it could be Decorah.

Keillor denied downing a big blue box of Powdermilk Biscuits, "the biscuits that give shy people the strength to get up and do what has to be done," before speaking in Decorah. Instead he credited his courage to myopia.

"What I do is take my glasses off," he said in an interview after the commencement ceremony, doing just that. "Without my glasses I really can't see beyond the first row. It's a wonderful advantage to be nearsighted when you have to stand up in front of people. I don't know what people with 20/20 vision do."

Notice how much territory I managed to cover in just seven paragraphs. I think one of the key characteristics of good writing is that it conveys a lot of information quickly yet palatably; in short, that it not be fluff or empty verbiage. An outline helps you achieve this, by making you concentrate and focus your notes. If you don't have anything to say, an outline won't let you say it.

Here I managed to set the scene, introduce Keillor and his creations to the uninitiated, make a link between Keillor and the setting, and set my whole "shyness" theme in motion. That contrast between Keillor's self-proclaimed shyness, his genuine reluctance to be a celebrity, and his undeniable fame (epitomized by his presence at this graduation ceremony) would make the basic yin-yang of my story.

Notice, too, the "movement" of the narrative, which I laid out in highly abbreviated format in my outline. If I'd had more time and wanted to waste it making a pretty outline instead of getting my story written, I might have traced the narrative movement something like this:

```
Shy speaker/sweaty setting
        Speaker: Keillor, of course
        Setting: Luther College, of course
      > Powdermilk Biscuits
    > Speaker: Powdermilk Biscuits, of course
     > Lake Wobegon
        Speaker: Lake Wobegon, of course
    could be   > Setting: Decorah
        Speaker: Not Powdermilk Biscuits
  > Shy speaker/sweaty setting: Overcoming shyness-
    myopia
```

HOW TO WRITE FAST

Okay, in retrospect I think I overdid the "of course" device—hey, I was on deadline. But otherwise the various threads—from speaker to setting, from Lake Wobegon to Decorah and back, and the "courage" setup and pay-off with Powdermilk Biscuits—move the opening along and convey a lot of basic information at the same time. My actual outline didn't spell this out quite as literally, but behind the shorthand I pretty much knew that this was how the story would flow.

From here, I finished the myopia gag, quickly elaborated on why Keillor came to Luther College (*"L gave K degree"*), and quoted the brief commencement talk (*"K gave commencement address—abbrev cuz heat—pithy advice"*).

Now I had to find a way to smoothly flash back to how Keillor got to this point, how a shy guy became a celebrity. I seized on a line in his short speech: "There is something for you to do in the world that you can do almost better than anybody else and I hope you find it. When you do, don't tell anyone else and they'll be amazed and delighted." My outline took it from there:

Not till 1974 K find something do better than anybody else: tell
  stories—amazed and delighted

And from that point I was off into Keillor's rise to fame:

Dishwasher & parking lot attendant till job U of Minn radio
Wrote stories—trip to Grand Ole Opry—idea for own show
Show born—natl 1980

On this last bit I wrote: " 'A Prairie Home Companion' went on the air in 1974. Enough listeners were amazed and delighted that it went national in 1980." And, yes, I knew I was going to make that "amazed and delighted" reference again; my outline had an arrow from "amazed and delighted" in the line beginning *"Not till 1974 . . ."* down to between *"Show born"* and *"natl 1980."*

Once I got him on national radio, the story flowed fast:

Success unexpected
Lake W born from youth in Anoka
People think recognize, don't
Real? Bristles

It was easy to go from Keillor's radio success to his creation of Lake Wobegon, and from his fictional town to people's reactions to it. You'll reach points in almost any story where the pieces just naturally fall into place. The real thing read:

"We didn't worry about success and fame when the show started," Keillor said. "We had other things to worry about, like whether we'd be able to continue for another three months. One of the beauties of a weekly deadline is it helps keep your mind off a lot of things you're probably better off not thinking about anyway."

He drew Lake Wobegon, his most famous creation, from his memories of growing up in Anoka, Minn., where he was born in 1942. Some folks back home think they recognize facts in his fictions about Lake Wobegon, but Keillor shook his head: "I don't think they do. They're better disguised than that."

Still, he bristled when asked whether his fans often wonder if Lake Wobegon is real. "No, I don't get that. People naturally assume there is a Lake Wobegon and of course they'd be right, *wouldn't they?*"

Each quote I used was carefully noted by page number right on the outline, so it was right at hand when I needed it. Notice, by the way, that each outline entry needn't equal a paragraph—but that, by and large, particularly in the short-paragraph world of newspapers, it works out pretty close to that.

What you *won't* notice is a sentence on the AAA motor club listing Lake Wobegon in some information about Minnesota: I originally had "*AAA lists—7*" scrawled along the side of my outline about this point, but that bit didn't fit into the actual writing of my story. I also may have noticed by this time that the story was running a tad long, and decided to axe that little detour. The point is, your outline should act as a guide—not a mindless conveyor belt. When you're writing, you should feel free to change course as the inspiration strikes you or (preferably) to cut something short if the story as outlined is running long.

From Lake Wobegon it was logical to move to how Keillor writes his radio stories about Lake Wobegon and next to his comments on radio as a medium. By contrast, then, I could introduce a few quotes about TV:

the stories—how he develops (no script)
radio ideal
spurned TV—about TV, David Letterman

With another contrast, I could zip from TV and radio to the medium Keillor had now shown himself willing to grapple with: the novel. His *Lake Wobegon Days* was due out, and I was thus able to complete the circle by using the novel to bring the narrative back to Lake Wobegon:

novel — not 100% happy
will tell things can't on radio

These two points became a single paragraph:

But radio is fleeting, novels endure. So Keillor has struggled to bring Lake Wobegon to life on the printed page, a struggle he's not entirely sure he won. He does tell some stories in the forthcoming book he couldn't on radio, historical stuff like the truth about the Unitarian missionaries and about the expedition to the North Dakota ocean that turned out to be prehistoric.

Time to wrap it up now. I'd brought the chronology back to the present and I'd almost run out of good stuff from my difficult interview. Quickly I tacked on, in orderly sequence, what else Keillor had had to say about his work and Lake Wobegon:

not tired of Lake W
still stories to tell, get it right
lost touch with material
danger of success

Here, with Keillor's concerns about losing touch with his material, with his success perhaps taking him away from what had made him so successful, I began to make the full turn into the homestretch. As the outline grew, I knew I'd have to bring it back around to the paradox of "the most famous shy person in America," to what seemed to me the gist of the story. Keillor hadn't really wanted to be there, in that small, hot town, any more than he really wanted to be the sort of celebrity who got invited to give commencement talks to hordes of sweaty graduates. Yet the path I traced had brought him, inexorably it seemed, to this sweltering day and this fame so strange and alien for a boy from "Lake Wobegon, Minnesota." My outline concluded:

but couldn't live there — sad

Which became:

And yet Garrison Keillor knows he can't go home again to Lake Wobegon, not to stay. "Maybe ten years ago I could have. Not now."

His voice dropped to a throaty whisper. "It's because of me. I don't think I would fit in. I wish I thought otherwise, but I don't. I think I am too ambitious to live up there."

I knew this was how the story would end before I actually started writing it, and that gave me the confidence to plow through it (even better than a box of Powdermilk Biscuits!). This story was going somewhere, I knew. Moreover, because I was familiar with the path ahead, I could make decisions en route that strengthened and supported my overall theme.

In your own stories, the same basic lessons apply:

1. Resist the temptation to skip outlining to "save time." It is precisely the process of outlining, however crudely, that will save you that precious time — just as it helped me meet my late-night deadline here.

2. Use your outline to compress and distill your story, packing it with facts and events. "Dense" stories turn out to be much faster to write than fluffy ones with the facts far between, since you don't have to make up so much on the fly.

3. Employ comparison and contrast to impart "movement" to your narrative and to smooth your transitions. If your story's pace zips right along, so will the writing.

4. Don't be afraid to jettison material, even notes carefully marked in your outline, if they don't fit into the actual writing of your story.

As for my own Keillor story, it's hardly a classic — that's not the point. The point is, I was done and on my way home from the paper before the last sports stringers had finished filing their stories. And my story, when it appeared in the paper the very next day, didn't read like something dashed off on deadline: Unlike most time-pressured newspaper stories, it had a narrative flow more elegant than the "inverted pyramid," and the points I made worked together to support an overall thesis about my subject.

Because I took a few minutes to outline, and then to link my notes to the outline, I was able to write it faster. And better. You can start doing the same, if you'll trust me on this.

CASE STUDY #2: THE AMAZING AMISH

A few years before, I'd tackled an entirely different sort of assignment for *AAA World*, a magazine for motor-club members. This time the challenge wasn't making the most out of scant information, but rather wrapping up a huge subject in just a few words. Oh, and by the way, I had just three weeks to do it in.

The subject was . . . well, I'll let the editor tell you: "We're looking for 750-1,000 words . . . to help dad answer the burning question, 'What's that?' when the family car drives by the familiar wagon," then-national editor Dick Schaaf wrote me. He went on to ask for "a look at a unique and tradition-laden American lifestyle, focusing on south-eastern Pennsylvania, but also making note of Amish communities in other parts of the country."

Never mind that I was living in Iowa at the time, or that 750 to 1,000 words wasn't much room in which to capture a whole culture. Heck, I needed a freelance paycheck the same as the next guy: "No problem," I told Dick.

Following many of the research and interviewing tricks I've already shared with you, I managed to gather a nice notebook full of informa-tion. And, thank goodness, I realized that Iowa, too, has a thriving Amish community that I could also draw on for the story (while keep-ing the editor's command about Pennsylvania firmly in mind). Now I just had to write this thing. Fast.

Out came the yellow pad. My outline—pretty detailed for a manu-script that ran less than four full pages—covered most of one sheet of 8½-by-11-inch lined paper (mostly ignoring the lines). I annotated the outline and my notebook in red; my outline had thirty-four sepa-rate page-number citations, which was probably more information than I could fit into 1,000 words. But it was better to begin winnowing my notes now rather than after I'd wasted a lot of time actually writing them up.

My outline opened on exactly the note my editor had asked for:

Buggy seems to have rolled out of the past—describe
Penn. Dutch, though, not Dutch—a corruption of Deutsch, G or
 Sw
Live in X [for number, which I'd fill in from my notes] states &
 prov. as well as PA
#s and location
only in PA, tho . . . Amish Mnnites
food and crafts
"Not actors"
Don't take pix

In the actual story, that opening became:

The horse-and-buggy seems to have clip-clopped out of the past onto a Pennsylvania turnpike. The buggy is hand-hewn of hickory, topped with canvas. Its occupants are just as simply clad: The bearded men wear wide-brimmed hats, coats without collars fastened by hooks instead of buttons, tight trousers, high-topped shoes, all in black. The women wear black coats over high-necked dresses in solid colors—no gaudy prints or patterns—and black bonnets over white prayer caps. The children look like miniatures of their parents.

They are among those people called "Pennsylvania Dutch," though they are not Dutch (a corruption of *Deutsch*) but German and Swiss in ancestry, and they live in nineteen states and one Canadian province as well as in Pennsylvania. Only in Pennsylvania, though, do the numbers and location of "Amish Mennonites" (as they're properly called) make them a tourist attraction. Visitors flock to Lancaster County, Penn., home of 14,000 Amish. But a brochure for Pennsylvania Dutch country cautions, "Please keep in mind that the Amish are not actors; they are ordinary people who choose a simpler way of life." And, please, do not photograph the Amish as you might snap Mickey Mouse at Disneyland. They believe photographs in which they can be recognized violate the Biblical commandment against graven images.

Notice that, while the first outline item turned into a single paragraph, all the next seven are packed into the following paragraph; typically, one outline item here equals one sentence. (Contrast this pace to my Keillor story.) That's not just the frantic compression of a writer who realizes that his story is already almost one-fourth expired. Rather, it's typical of the structure of this kind of story: The lead establishes a mood and makes a single point or two; then the "hook" packs in a bunch of points important to both reader interest and understanding. You've got only so much room in which to grab the reader, after all—never mind the editor's length restrictions—so you'd better be zipping through those outline points pretty early on.

The outline made it fast and simple for me to make tracks once my "mood" paragraph was done. One after another, my outline items fed into each other in logical sequence. The whole second paragraph, really, hangs on my introduction of the phrase "Pennsylvania Dutch": They're not *Dutch* and they don't all live in *Pennsylvania*. Here's where they do live. Only in *Pennsylvania* are they numerous enough to be a *tourist* attraction. But, please, *tourists*, they're people and not actors, so don't take their pictures.

I had no idea, at the outline stage, that the actual paragraph would end there and another thought take off from *"Don't take pix."* But when you put your points in sequence they just naturally tend to gather themselves into paragraphs—making the subsequent writing much faster and smoother. So it was a breeze to pick up on the photo theme (and the horse-and-buggy and old-fashioned clothes from the first paragraph) for the next paragraph, and extend it to the other aspects of modern technology shunned by the Amish:

Auto & camera & designer jeans not only trappings of "English" world shun
No phones, electricity, TV, zippers, plumbing
no more than 1 mirror—straighten bonnet only
church services by old hymnal

Once I'd established how "old-fashioned" Amish life is today, it was a swift segue into the origins of this Amish way of living: "Little of Amish life has changed since the seventeenth century, when the sect was founded by Jacob Ammen, the Mennonite bishop of Bern, Switzerland. . . ." That transition accomplished, my historical notes about the Amish snapped into place:

persecuted thru Europe
came to New World same reason so many: fleeing religious persec.
Wm Penn offer sanctuary = "PA Dutch"

That got the Amish to Pennsylvania. Next I spread them out across the country and talked about their population trends:

all over country, largest now Ohio
pop #s
predict demise—actually growing

After quoting a social scientist and Amish expert on how the Amish are thriving, even growing in numbers, I had a spot for some intriguing information I'd found on outsiders joining the Amish:

p join—"seekers"
attraction of way of life for seekers—extreme simplicity

Here's how the copy went:

In fact, people from the "English" outside world occasionally join the Amish, who call such converts "seekers." David Luthy, who heads the Amish library in Aylmer, Ont., abandoned the posh life of a banking family. He says, "None of us are born Amish. We all choose to become Amish."
Why would someone turn his back on the 20th century and choose a life rooted in the past? [Sociologist Thomas] Foster explains, "Their way of life grows out of their religious belief that

a true follower of Christ has to be separated from the world. To be yoked to unbelievers would be to compromise a Christ-like life-style."

The interesting, even startling nugget that some people actually convert to the simple Amish way might have been difficult to plug into the story — it *is* a bit of a detour — if not for my outline. The outline gave me confidence that I could go down that road and still get back to my main story. From Foster's quote about separation from the world (carefully noted in my outline as being on page 16 of my notebook), I could launch into my main body of information about the Amish lifestyle — the *Ordnung*, or written rules by which they live so strictly yet simply — and their ways of keeping apart from "English" society:

communities — how run — Ordnung — close-knit
Amish children school only thru 8th grade
take care of own — no insurance, Social Security exemption

By this point I knew I'd be running out of space, so I had to make some more fast moves. It was important to note that economics have forced some young Amish out of this separate life-style, and yet that in many ways traditional Amish agriculture is "state-of-the-art" in its productivity and reliance on ecologically sound techniques. So I zigged:

work in factories

Simple contrast got me from the traditional, *Ordnung* life to this departure from it: "Though an increasing number of young Amish have been forced into factory jobs by the high price of farm land. . . ." And then another contrast got me back to:

small farms, highly productive
model?

Which turned into:

. . . agriculture remains the backbone of Amish life. Amish farms are rarely more than 150 acres; bigger farms would require the displacement of others in the community. The farmers rely on Belgian horses rather than tractors, manure instead of commercial fertilizer. They are more concerned with soil conservation than crop yield. As one Amish writer put it, "We didn't inherit the land from our fathers; we are borrowing it from our children."

Yet Amish farms are highly productive. They can grow a bushel of corn for one-sixth the cost of a bushel grown the "modern" way. "In the 1800s, they were looked on as progressive because their agriculture was so efficient," Foster notes. He believes the Amish might be a model for our energy-scarce era, likening it to the "frugal community" E.F. Schumacher described in *Small Is Beautiful*.

"They more or less instinctively adopted 'alternative technology' before anyone coined the phrase," Foster adds. "They are in the forefront of the conservation movement today."

I shamelessly seized on this irony—that the "backward" and "old-fashioned" Amish might in fact be *ahead* of all of us—to bring the story to a quick close, winding back rapidly to my opening:

future—horse-and-buggy

Is how I outlined it, which became:

So listen well to the clip-clop of the horse-and-buggy. That steady rhythm of the past might be the beat for the future.

And I was done. On time, within my length limit. Oh, sure, I could have done it without outlining the story first. I could have written twice as many words as the editor needed, some of them not quite connecting to the paragraphs before or after, and then cut and cut and pasted until I arrived at pretty much the same place. But creating my outline and attaching my notes to it took less than an hour "extra." How long do you think the alternative would have wasted? Right—much more time.

In addition to further proving that yes, by golly, it works, this second "case study" highlights several more key points to remember about outlining, whatever kind of story you're writing:

1. Your outline should grow directly from the focus of your story—whether that comes in turn from an editor's assignment or your query or sheer inner inspiration. Here's where you start to deliver the goods!

2. Particularly if space is precious, use your outline to winnow your notes; don't write for the trash can.

3. Don't worry at this stage about where your paragraphs will begin and end; that will work itself out in the actual writing.

4. Outline even your detours and asides, to make sure you have a route back to your main narrative.

What you *can't* tell from either of these case studies, of course, is how little time I wasted agonizing over "writer's block." So you'll just have to take my word for it: *zilch*.

Once my outlines were done and my notes all sorted, the hard work was over. Then the lead and the rest of the first draft flowed out of my fingers as fast as I could type, with only occasional interruptions to fetch a cup of coffee (and subsequent interruptions to go to the bathroom).

Trust me. It really is all downhill from here.

CHAPTER EIGHT

GETTING A HEAD START ON WRITING

• • •

THOSE ELUSIVE FIRST WORDS

Henry Adams made it sound almost appealing: "The fascination of the silent midnight, the veiled lamp, the smouldering fire, the white paper asking to be covered with elusive words; the thoughts grouping themselves into architectural forms, and slowly rising into dreamy structures, constantly changing, shifting, beautifying their outlines — this is the subtlest of solitary temptations, and the loftiest of all the intoxications of genius."

As my third-grade daughter would say, "Yeah, right." It's that "white paper asking to be covered with elusive words" that stops most writers, particularly the "elusive words" part. Becoming a writer seemed like a good idea at the time, but there comes a point where you actually have to follow Hemingway's first rule for writers: Apply the seat of your pants to the seat of a chair. And then you've really no choice but to apply your fingers to the keyboard and, well, *write*. Commit authorship. Pick words out of nowhere and put them down for all the world to see. Or, as Peter DeVries put it, a bit less gushingly than Mr. Adams, "I love being a writer. What I can't stand is the paperwork."

Starting, that's the hardest, slowest part. Breathes there a writer who actually *enjoys* writing that first sentence, the opener, the lead? (Or "lede," as some spell it, thinking perhaps that a trick of orthography will make the problem go away.)

As long as there have been writers, there has been agony over the lead. Plato supposedly rewrote the first sentence of his *The Republic* fifty times. Authors of all stripes have tried everything to get their creative juices flowing, confronting the blank page from almost every imaginable vantage point: Hemingway, Lewis Carroll and Virginia Woolf all wrote standing up. Truman Capote, Robert Louis Stevenson and Mark Twain tried it lying down. Willa Cather read a passage from the Bible, more for prose style than for divine inspiration. Edgar Allan Poe sat his Siamese cat on his shoulder before starting a new poem. Even the bathtub has been a popular balm for writers seeking to wash the kinks out of their starting sentences; Ben Franklin and Edmond Rostand were among those who attempted to drown their lead sorrows. And Robin Moore, the tough-minded writer of *The Green Berets*, combined elements of the first and last methods listed here: He wrote standing up, but naked.

Why all the agony? Why not just start writing?

If you really had to ask those questions, you're obviously a non-writer — an accountant in disguise, maybe — who's somehow sneaked all the way to chapter eight. The lead, my friends, is not merely the beginning. Write it wrong, and it can also be the *end* for turned-off editors and readers.

As editor Brian Vachon once put it, "If that first and most important paragraph does not slap and sparkle like the sun in water, then we editors can't bother unduly with the rest."

With so much riding on the lead, such a weight bearing down on a few frail sentences, you'd do better to wonder how anything ever gets written at all.

BEYOND GRABBING THE READER: AIMING YOUR STORY FROM THE HEART

As if that's not enough pressure, I'm about to add some more: Properly written, your lead should point the way for you to write the whole rest of your story. The hard work of crafting your opening should be like climbing to the top of rollercoaster track: From here on there will be ups and downs, but there's nowhere else to go but forward. Just hang on and enjoy the ride.

Or, to saddle up a different metaphor, you can think of your lead like getting the right golf stance or developing the proper tennis stroke. A good lead makes your follow-through — the rest of your story — both more natural and more powerful.

Before this latest load piled on the humble lead makes you decide to give up writing and take up something sane, like Hollywood stunt work, let me quickly add: Don't panic. If you've come this far along the path to writing faster, you'll find that writing leads is suddenly much less awful — and much quicker — than it used to be.

The reason for this is the same reason that your leads will now function like loading the gun to fire off your entire story: By now, you really and truly understand what your story is about. You've focused on the idea and the angle, and religiously kept that focus through research and interviewing. You've outlined your story from start (gee, your lead is already in the works, isn't it?) to finish.

What this means is that your lead is no longer like some alien organism, grafted onto the body of your story from afar to grab readers' attention. Forget the artificial, unnatural, souped-up opener. No need to start your story like somebody with a cranky car, pouring a capful of gasoline straight into the carburetor. You know the sort of lead I mean: When he was just starting out as a reporter, for example, James Thurber was instructed by his editor to make his leads brief, dramatic and crammed full of the facts. So one day Thurber turned in a story that began: "Dead. That's what the man was, when they found him with a knife in his back at 4 P.M. in front of Riley's Saloon at the corner of 52nd and 12th streets."

No, what I'm suggesting is that by now you know what your story's about, and that you let your leads spring from that focus. Forget the capful of gas into the carburetor; just turn the key in the ignition and your story will roll.

I'm not saying that your leads can or should be dull. Just the opposite: By loading your opening with the best, truest, most telling material from your notebook, you'll write leads that are compelling without resorting to gimmicks or trickery.

Look at the Greeks, who knew a good lead when they saw one. Remember back in chapter two when we talked about beginning *in medias res*? By starting the story in the middle, in the very heart of the action, and then filling in the reader on what has gone before, Greek authors from Homer to Sophocles succeeded in encapsulating their stories in their openings. They took their best stuff and led with it, confident that the reader, once hooked, would hang on for the ride. If Homer had started with, say, Odysseus's childhood or his wooing and wedding of Penelope, we might never have stayed with the story until the action got good.

Starting *in medias res* is also faster for the writer. You get to write the easiest, most dramatic material first. If you can't write the heart of the story, even sitting there staring at a blank screen, maybe you should take up something easier, like brain surgery. Lead with the part of the story that almost tells itself; the rest will follow, and fast.

Your outline can help here. The outline of a story that starts *in medias res* is pretty basic, but awfully useful. Much condensed, it's always going to follow this fundamental pattern:

Open at a dramatic highpoint, preclimax
Exposition on opening scene
"Hook" or other pivotal paragraph
Flashback: How we got to this point
Catch up to the main flow of the narrative at the point of the lead
Continue to climax and conclusion

Once you develop a sense of what moment—not too early, not too late—to lead with, this becomes an almost foolproof scheme for a story. I've used it for tales of everything from science to romance, animal husbandry to art. For example, when I was doing my newspaper column I set out to do a yarn on "turtle tapping"—guys who hunt snapping turtles by tapping for them in the mud with long metal poles. (Go figure.) Now, I could have started with my protagonist setting out for the creek, gathering his gear; I could even have led with how he learned this arcane practice. But I knew the fastest way in and through the story was to start with the turtle tapping itself:

> Turtles love mud. At the first snap of fall, they burrow into the ooze and sleep like the dead, safe as babes—they think—in the dank, gooey, lightless cradle of a creekbank. Turtle paradise.
>
> Wayne Olson probes the mud with a steel pole as tall as he is and slender as a finger, flaked with rust. He pecks out a pattern as precisely as a maestro with a baton, orchestrating a symphony in the muck: *Pocketa-squish. Pocketa-squish.*
>
> *Thunk.*
>
> The sound of pole striking turtle—a hollow, anybody-home? kind of sound—stands out like a bass-drum beat in a tinkly piano concerto, once you know what to listen for. . . .

By starting with the "thunk" of finding a turtle, not only was I able to get the story quickly underway and hook the reader, I was also able to convey a lot of information fast, here and in the subsequent paragraphs. I set the scene, started the explanation of what was going on, and introduced my main character. The lead itself was easy to write, because I had real, solid material to weave into it; then, with that much territory already covered, I was able to approach the rest of the tale with much less trepidation. I soon backtracked to the background leading up to this actual tapping of a turtle, then (flashback complete and main thread rejoined) I zipped forward to the conclusion, which had Olson eating his catch (of course!).

The *in medias res* lead works, but it's hardly the only way to get a story off to a fast start. The important thing to remember is the principle of starting from strength—from good, solid stuff that you can build the rest of your story on, not a jerrybuilt lead that's going to topple under the weight of subsequent paragraphs.

It's probably worth noting, by the way, that this approach also leads to better storytelling. Just ask the Greeks.

GETTING SPECIFIC

In learning about leads, you've probably heard something like this: "Don't give too much away. Keep the reader guessing!" Well, forget it. That's the prescription for forced, cutesy-wootsy leads better suited to joke books than serious writing. "Keeping the reader guessing" is a sure way to make readers flip the page in search of less obtuse writing, and to make even comparatively young editors sigh like senior citizens.

Good leads spring from the material, not guesswork. They telegraph to the reader what's to come, so he or she can make an informed decision of whether to read on. They don't try to trick readers into turning the page; that way lies books and magazines hurled across the library in disgust.

Great leads don't just emerge from the material; they focus it, encapsulate it, and somehow sum it all up. They keep the reader reading, deliver what they promise, and mean even more in light of the whole story.

Best of all from the standpoint of the time-conscious writer, great leads carry the author inexorably into and through the story. Because they in some way sum up the entire story, great leads light the way to the final sentence at the end of the writing tunnel.

A simple example—maybe not the stuff of great leads, but good and useful—is the lead that flows from the specific to the general. By quickly dramatizing a piece of the whole, you catch the readers' attention (particulars are always more interesting than generalizations) and create almost a miniature of the larger story. Properly chosen, the specific-example lead forces you to focus on what your story is really about. Like the *in medias res* opening, it lends itself to a cyclical sort of structure:

Opening: Specific example
"Hook" or pivotal paragraph tying specific to larger whole
Elaboration on larger picture
Back to specific example to amplify

And so on, continuing with more examples or more general points.

I used this approach for a story on international adoption I wrote for *American Way*, the American Airlines inflight magazine. I could have started like this:

Holt International Children's Services, based in Eugene, Ore., is a $2 million nonprofit corporation with seven regional offices and affiliates worldwide. In addition to adoption services, Holt provides parent counseling, emergency care and housing for homeless children, clinics and medical care, physical and speech therapy, foster-parent training and educational support for children who otherwise would have to leave school to support their families. It operates Il San, an orphanage near Seoul that's home for 240 handicapped orphans unlikely to find another home.

But that general introduction to Holt was actually my sixth paragraph instead of my first. I decided it was more dramatic and compelling to start with a specific example of a family built by Holt:

Every year, nearly 900 American couples like Van and Shirley Waggoner wait for their new baby to arrive at an airport instead of at a hospital. The Waggoners, who live in Asbury, Iowa, adopted their daughter, Amanda, from Korea in 1982. Shirley remembers, "Both of us went through the 'labor pains' of adoption. When we went to get Amanda, there were six babies on the plane. They had little armbands so not to get mixed up. An escort went on and brought them off one by one: 'This is the Waggoner baby.' It was a really neat feeling."

Of course this lead worked better. By using the element of surprise (on which I'll talk more later) — contrasting the airport delivery of the Waggoners' baby with more traditional labor pains — it managed to grab the readers' attention. Then it went straight for their heartstrings.

But this approach wasn't simply more interesting and reader-friendly; it also helped propel me into the rest of the story, speeding me along in my writing. Where could I have gone from that general paragraph about Holt? It doesn't hold out many little coat hooks for me to hang subsequent paragraphs on. The specific-example lead, by contrast, fed logically into a "big picture" paragraph that set the Waggoners in a broader context:

The Waggoners, like so many couples, couldn't have a baby the hospital way. They looked into adopting an American child, but learned they might have to wait as long as ten years. That's when they turned to Holt International Children's Services, which, with its affiliate agency in Korea, is the world's largest international adoption organization. Holt's mission is as simple as its motto: "Every child deserves a home of his own."

Specific to general—it's a natural movement that speeds up your writing. But I wasn't stranded here, either: Now that I'd set the Waggoners in context, I could go back and finish their story (though I'd later bring them in again to illustrate some of the complexities of international adoption). And from the Waggoners' wait at the airport for their new child, I segued smoothly to founder Bertha Holt's airport wait for her husband and their *eight* Korean adoptees back in 1955—the adoption that started the whole enterprise. (Yes, by the way, I could have started the story with *this* specific scene and then moved to Holt today; there's no single right way to lead off any story.) Then I wrote: "They were the first of nearly 50,000 children the Holts and the agencies they founded have brought from Asia and Latin America to new homes all over the world." Only after that did I unfurl my general paragraph about the Eugene-based organization. By that time, I'd already established Bertha Holt as a character, so I could jump from the general paragraph about Holt today back to Bertha Holt today, and my quotes from her.

By leading with the specific, you can build a nice little path leading through the key initial elements of your story—instead of erecting writing roadblocks for yourself. Comb your notes for your best examples: The specifics that have lead potential are those that are not only dramatic (getting a baby at the airport) but also give you somewhere else to go (Holt helps would-be parents like this all over the country). Find those specifics that let you make an easy hop to your most important general points, and you may have found your lead!

THE "TELLING" LEAD: SUMMING IT UP AT THE START

For the efficient writer, the advantages of starting *in medias res* or leading with a specific example are pretty much the same: You jump-start your story, beginning not necessarily at the beginning but with the good stuff that gives you somewhere to go. An even better approach is to take that philosophy one step further and try to find some "telling" anecdote, scene or metaphor that starts the story rolling *and* (remember what I said about *great* leads) somehow encapsulates, focuses and sums up the essence of your story.

That's not as tall an order as it might sound. After all, you've been working all along toward just this goal: *What's your story really about?* Okay, now you just have to sort through your material and find the item that best epitomizes what your story's about. Bingo! Not only have you got an almost instant lead (instead of agonizing for hours and filling your wastebasket in frustration), but you've made the job of writing the rest of your story infinitely easier.

Remember the anecdote I got, at the very last minute, that perfectly expressed the point of my math story? Once I had it, and once I recognized it as my lead, I was off to the races with the remaining writing.

Anecdotes are ideal for this kind of lead. The "telling anecdote," if you will, typically introduces at least one of your characters, contains some sort of irony or drama, and makes the point that you plan to spend the rest of the story proving, explaining and elaborating. Plus, of course, all that I've said about starting with specifics also applies.

Here's how I started yet another story about math teaching, this from my days as a newspaper columnist:

> The school bus drummed along the highway and its teenaged passengers, in the giggling harmony that comes only on a day free of pencils and books, sang with the beat of the wheels. After "Ninety-nine Bottles of Beer on the Wall," the students joined in a chorus of "The Pythagorean Theorem":
> 'The square of the hypotenuse/ Of a right triangle/ Is equal to the sum of the squares of the two adjacent sides.'

I knew that would be my lead the minute I scribbled it in my notebook. Aside from the element of surprise (yes, yes, more on that later)—students *singing* about math?—the anecdote immediately communicated that music was being linked to math and that it seemed to be making teens feel amazingly positive about the subject. It captured what my story was really about: a high school math teacher who'd found a novel way to use music to teach math better.

Generally, your own "telling anecdotes" will follow a similar pattern. Many stories can be summarized as the bringing together of two seemingly disparate elements—in this case, music and math teaching. When scouting for your own leads, study your notes for anecdotes that combine the key factors in your story. In a personality profile, for example, one of those elements is almost always the thing that makes your subject noteworthy or newsworthy; the other is often some fact in ironic or surprising juxtaposition to that noteworthy element. (Remember the glamorous maggot farmer from a few chapters back?) Your telling anecdote, then, will be a minisaga that dramatizes this contrast. (The contrast or surprise, of course, is also what gives the anecdote its punch.)

For example, *Savvy* magazine once asked me to profile Kay Sexton, the book-buying maven for the huge B. Dalton bookstore chain. The story turned on the fact that here was one of the most powerful people in the publishing industry—but she was hidden away in the Twin Cities, and almost no one in Manhattan publishing circles knew who she was. So when she told me this anecdote, I spotted it immediately as lead material:

> Kay Sexton, vice president for merchandise, communications and publications for B. Dalton Bookseller, likes to tell of her arrival at a publication party in New York for Bruce Jay Friedman's *The Lonely Guy's Book of Life*. One of the hosts promptly took her to the author, saying Friedman was "just dying to meet you, Kay." Upon being introduced to the chief best-seller-spotter for the nation's largest bookselling chain, Friedman responded with a befuddled, "Kay who?"

When you think you've got a lead anecdote, the way to test it is to play with your outline and see if, indeed, the anecdote opens the way for the rest of the story to zip logically along. That's what I did here—and, sure enough, the anecdote made for a natural progression into Sexton's ironic obscurity, the details of her importance to the book trade, how she got to this point, and the details of how she does her important but nearly anonymous job.

Can you take it and run with it? If the answer's yes, you've likely found your lead.

SETTING THE SCENE

Sometimes, of course, stories don't cooperate and fall together as neatly as you might like. Maybe there *is* no telling anecdote, or at least none presents itself. What then? For one thing, you can fall back on what we might call the "telling scene"—usually some scene that you've observed in the course of your research and interviewing, the description of which sets the stage for all that is to come. Here's how I started a story on high-tech advances in air safety, for Honeywell's corporate magazine:

> John Riley stabs an index finger at a small black screen. "That's a flat-panel display, the latest LCD technology—only

four inches deep." He taps a button and the screen comes to life, portraying a 12-mile-long-by-9-mile-wide slice of the sky. In the center is a blue chevron encircled by a dozen blue dots marking a two-mile range. "That's you in the center," Riley says. Another few taps and the screen fills with triangles: A lot of traffic out there.

Not to worry: The TCAS II system, under development by the Air Transport Systems Division of Honeywell's Sperry Commercial Flight Systems Group in Phoenix, can track forty aircraft at once. Riley, manager of airline sales, says, "It requires the most complex software ever developed in our building, including all our flight management software."

Brilliant stuff this was not, but it suited the story and got it off to a fast start. The scene came right out of my notebook (here's a place for the detail you scribbled down while murmuring "uh-huh" in your interviews); the lead actually begins to get into the meat of my quotes from my interviews. What made me select this chunk to start the story was simple: It had a dramatic, you-are-there feel ("That's you in the center"), it dramatized one of the sexier pieces of new hardware I was writing about, and it brought together the two key elements of my story, high technology and air safety.

The telling scene can even be your chance to get colorful in your writing, a place to unsheathe those turns of phrase you've been longing to use. But beware: The lead must *grab* the reader, not merely mesmerize him with its poetry. Adjectives and adverbs should be used sparingly, if at all, and only in the service of fleshing out specific, five-senses detail; instead, opt for strong nouns and verbs wherever possible.

That caveat out of the way, yes, sometimes a scene that you observe and note can be artfully written into a lead — without benefit of quotes or anecdotes. Here, for example, is how I launched a newspaper story on a guy who raised buffalo in rural Wisconsin:

GAYS MILLS, Wis. — Penned by wooden fences and blue hills bristled with trees, forty buffalo snort steam into the winter air. They pad and shudder like captive locomotives. A big bull lumbers into profile against the silver-bright sky — an old nickel come to life.

This descriptive lead worked because the premise of the story was so straightforward: What the heck are *buffalo* doing in Wisconsin? Thus, the lead really just had to present this startling image as powerfully, vividly and briefly as possible. It set up the rest of the story, of course, as an explanation of what the reader has just "seen," and so also met the test of clearing the way for what's to come.

A telling anecdote is almost always better than a telling scene to start a story, just because an anecdote is usually more interesting and more evocative than a description. But if you don't get the anecdote you need, and particularly if the underlying concept of your story is fairly simple, you can often start by describing the most vivid scene you encountered. If it grabbed your attention, it will probably interest readers, too.

WRITING YOUR OWN: WHAT A METAPHOR'S FOR

More complicated and more subtle than either the telling anecdote or the telling scene is what we might call the "telling metaphor." Now, cooking up a metaphorical scheme for your story is a hazardous undertaking. But, done properly, it can add a depth and finesse to your writing that makes it more than just the sum of your words. I've already talked a bit about how metaphors and symbols can aid in the structuring of your work (remember the *chop-chop* that became a running theme in my maestro story?). If you're going to go this route, it's almost an absolute that you start it with your lead.

But you don't have to have a complex metaphorical scheme in mind to lead with a "telling metaphor." Sometimes a metaphorical approach simply works in the same way that a good anecdote or vivid scene does—encapsulating your theme and getting things going with a bang. Think of it as making up your *own* "telling" lead, when unadorned reality has declined to cooperate and provide you with one. Or it may be that no "straight" lead can quite do the job as elegantly as your metaphor. The great A.J. Liebling, for example, started a lengthy *New Yorker* profile of the Longs of Louisiana political infamy like this:

> Southern political personalities, like sweet corn, travel badly. They lose flavor with every hundred yards away from the patch. By the time they reach New York, they are like Golden Bantam that has been trucked up from Texas—stale and unprofitable. The consumer forgets that the corn tastes different where it grows. That, I suppose, is why for twenty-five years I underrated Huey Pierce Long. . . .

That notion of "traveling badly," like "sweet corn," (I know, it's actually a simile rather than a metaphor) launched Liebling into his thesis: "the corn tastes different where it grows." For New Yorkers, baffled by the enduring appeal of the Long dynasty, Liebling proposed to go down "where it grows" and see why the "corn" tasted so sweet to Louisiana voters.

Like anecdotes and scenes, your "telling metaphor" can also arise from the material itself—once again, a piece of the story is thrust into the lead, where it's made to stand for the whole. I started a story on an exhibition of Grant Wood paintings this way, by letting one lesser-known painting act as a metaphor for the artist's entire life:

> In "Death on the Ridge Road," Grant Wood poised a low-slung sedan near the top of a hill. The sedan, in the left lane, has just passed a pokey Ford. But a blood-red truck looms in the storm clouds atop the hill, about to deliver tragedy.
>
> That painting might have been a map of Grant Wood's career. When the Iowa artist painted it in 1935, Wood was zooming toward the top of the artistic world, fueled by the phenomenal success of his "American Gothic."

Two paragraphs further on, I completed the metaphor: "Seven years later, Grant Wood was dead, his reputation a wreck." (Note the "wreck" allusion to the impending crash of the painting.)

At the story's end I subtly reintroduced my lead metaphor. (Frequently you'll find your lead metaphors also solve the tricky problem of how to end the tale.) I concluded with Wood's actual death:

> On his deathbed, Grant Wood told his friend and fellow regionalist artist, Thomas Hart Benton, that when he got well he was going to change his name. He would move where no one knew him. He would start all over again in a new style, take a different route. But it was too late.

Another example of how a metaphor can give you not only a lead but an ending, and in the process add a thematic unity to your work, is one of my favorite stories from my newspaper days. It was also one of the hardest to write: an on-deadline report of the funeral of a young man in a tiny northeast Iowa town who was one of the few casualties of the Grenada invasion. Obviously this was a tragedy. But how could I make it more than just a stock war-victim story—how could I make it uniquely about this particular young man? As in the Grant Wood story, I used a small piece of knowledge about the subject to epitomize the whole:

HARPERS FERRY, Iowa—The morning opened leaden and low, wind whispering of cold rain.

Lousy weather for baseball, Rusty Robinson might have said.

Pvt. Russell L. Robinson, 22, was an outfielder, a son of Harpers Ferry and a gung-ho Army Ranger. Last week, on the sunny Caribbean island of Grenada, somebody pitched him one he couldn't handle. . . .

Here, really, I combined the lead scene with the lead metaphor, contrasting the metaphor with the reality. Notice how quickly, however, I segued from the metaphorical to the hard facts. The story went on: "A few hours after he parachuted in with U.S. invasion forces on Oct. 25, a rocket struck his jeep."

After the details of the funeral, my lead metaphor provided a framework in which to pour the final facts. I closed the story on a note reminiscent of how I'd begun:

As the mourners drifted away, the last rifle report seemed still to echo in the wounded air, like the crack of a bat driving one deep to the outfield wall, very deep indeed.

In a sense, one of the most famous leads of literature—the opening of Herman Melville's *Moby Dick*—falls into this same "telling metaphor" category. After his well-known "Call me Ishmael" first line, Melville soon launched into the imagery of death and funerals:

. . . Whenever I find myself growing grim about the mouth; whenever it is a damp, drizzly November in my soul; whenever I find myself involuntarily pausing before coffin warehouses, and bringing up the rear of every funeral I meet . . . then, I account it high time to get to sea as soon as I can.

In the end, of course, Ishmael watches Ahab go down with his ship, and the sea and the image of death come together in a final metaphorical flourish: ". . . then all collapsed, and the great shroud of the sea rolled on as it rolled five thousand years ago."

As Melville certainly knew, the telling metaphor can be the most powerful of these devices, because it gives your story a thematic structure at the same time that it lifts your work to a more thoughtful plane. And it almost always sets you up for at least one possible ending. But be careful! Not for nothing does the *New Yorker* run groaning little clips headed "Block That Metaphor!" A lead metaphor run amok, or overly labored, can turn a good story into ludicrous dreck.

So when should you use a telling anecdote or a scene or a metaphor to get your story off to a fast start? Let your material dictate. If you've got one, the telling anecdote is the closest thing to a sure-fire lead. The scene is probably the weakest of this lot, but it's a good fallback if you lack a terrific anecdote and the story doesn't lend itself to metaphor. Stories with an inherent drama — and most serious fiction — can support a metaphorical lead. The key, in every case, is to find a lead that's truly "telling" — that captures the heart of what's to come.

BUILDING YOUR LEAD OUT OF A COLLISION

Think about what makes a good story, whether fact or fiction. The essence of many good stories is conflict: two forces, two ideas, two trends in opposition or in contrast. If the real focus of your story is some sort of collision, that ought to be reflected in your lead. And by starting your story with two opposing notions, of course, you make it easy to organize and write the rest.

We've already looked at several leads built on conflict or contrast. Remember the contrast of airport-delivered babies vs. hospital delivery in the international-adoption story, or of Kay Sexton's importance vs. her anonymity? As these examples suggest, the "conflict" in your lead (and in your story) need not be a violent one; you don't have to be writing about war or good vs. evil or even William F. Buckley vs. Gore Vidal. Sometimes the collision is as quiet and simple as the past vs. the present, as in this column I wrote about a small-town grocery store time seemed to have bypassed:

> LIVINGSTON, Wis. — Two blocks east of Joe F. Allen's Store, Wisconsin 80 winds from Livingston to Platteville, where you can squeeze kiwi fruit and pluck three-course turkey dinners from the fog of freezers and browse the *National Enquirer* by the fluorescent glow of a modern supermarket. From there, freeways flow to Madison, to Milwaukee, to New York City, where the twentieth century is as tangible as the smog.
>
> But in Joe F. Allen's Store, dust coats the boxes of Mistol Drops — still 65 cents — like that on an old maid's hope chest, embalming them against the years as surely as a scarab in amber.

Certainly, this approach does work as well for stories that do contain real conflict, real violence. For example, *Rolling Stone* reporters David Felton and David Dalton used this lead to launch a story on the Charles Manson trial — contrasting the childlike innocence of some of Manson's fans with the brutal crime:

Three young girls dance down the hallway of the Superior Court Building in Los Angeles, holding hands and singing one of Charlie's songs. They might be on their way to a birthday party in their short, crisp cotton dresses, but actually they are attending a preliminary hearing to a murder trial.

That's a much more gripping, startling lead than merely recounting Manson's crimes. It's the contrast—the collision between birthday-party appearances and murder-trial reality—that gives this lead its power and its motive force.

What's your story fundamentally about? If some sort of conflict lies at its core, you can use that X vs. Y to find your lead. Boil it down to its essentials, then use the techniques we've already discussed—anecdotes, scenes, metaphors—to dramatize the conflict or collision of opposites. Find an anecdote that captures the contrast. Paint a scene—like the girls in their cotton dresses—that vividly brings the opposites together. Develop a metaphor that symbolizes the fundamental conflict. Suddenly you'll have the start of a story.

SURPRISING STARTS

A similar, even overlapping way to start a story quickly is the surprise lead. I don't mean a lead that's out of character with the rest of the story, but rather one that expresses the essence of a story in a startling way. Girls in party dresses . . . going to a *murder trial*? That gets the story going with a bang, a *frisson* of surprise and curiosity.

In another *Rolling Stone* story, a profile of the then-extremely spacey Marlon Brando, writer Chris Hodenfield started with this grabber:

Marlon Brando's body was going through the motions, awaiting the return of his personality. It was miles away. He was reeling it in like a dancing sailfish.

Makes you want to read on, doesn't it? More important from the speedy-writing standpoint, this surprising lead compels the writer to explain it—and thus immediately invites the writing of the rest of the story.

I used a much milder form of the surprise lead, in the guise of a telling scene, to start a story for *Databar* magazine on business games:

Like any struggle out of the jungle or the pages of the *Wall Street Journal*, the competition between Apex Co. and Evergreen Corp. is tooth-and-nail. At stake is survival. A single misstep in the forest of decisions about pricing, capacity, inventory, promotion and research-and-development can prove fatal. Executives of both firms lose sleep, pondering their choices in smoky conference rooms over bitter coffee. They know the fate of the losers: A sea of blood-red ink.

But no heads will roll, whatever the outcome. The top executives of Apex and Evergreen and similar imaginary firms all hold secure jobs at Boeing Co. The only thing these thirty-six middle and senior managers risk by playing "Topexec," a sophisticated training game, is their pride. . . .

The surprise here is admittedly a pretty cheap one—not unlike Bobby Ewing coming back to life in "Dallas" because "it was all a dream." Top executives in cut-throat competition—but, surprise!, it's only a computer game. Nonetheless, it gets the story going, dramatizes a pretty undramatic subject, and does indeed capture the essence of the story: business training by computer simulation.

The point is, you don't have to have a huge, stunning surprise to use the element of surprise to start your story. If there is indeed something unexpected or unusual at the heart of your story (Marlon Brando's a space cadet, computers can create realistic business simulations), the surprise lead can bring it to the fore and catch the reader's attention.

Surprise leads can even (surprisingly) feed into your endings. Ayn Rand fans can probably quote the startling opening of her novel *The Fountainhead* from memory:

> Howard Roark laughed.
> He stood naked at the edge of a cliff. The lake lay far below him. . . .

Now, immediately the reader wants to know why this guy is outside, naked, and what the heck he has to laugh about. Or is he just crazy? We're hooked, and the story zips along for nearly 700 pages from there.

But, 695 pages later, we come back to the undaunted figure of our hero, still poised by a large body of water: "Then there was only the ocean and the sky and the figure of Howard Roark."

When should you try a surprise lead? It sounds facile to answer, "Whenever you have a surprise you can start with," but that's essentially the best approach. Some element of surprise or the unexpected, whenever you can identify it in your raw material, makes a natural grabber for the reader's attention. So you can hardly go wrong with a bit of surprise at the start—as long as it isn't forced, but fits naturally with the focus of your story. And, don't forget that, because a surprise lead compels you to explain it, it can't help but get your story off to a fast start and give you plenty of clues as to where to go next with your narrative.

PACING YOURSELF RIGHT FROM THE START

I keep talking about leads that are "fast starts." Primarily I mean openings whose material naturally tends to lead you (not to mention the reader) into the meat of the story: leads, if you will, that don't give writer's block a chance to catch up.

But there's another sense in which you can get off to a "fast start," and that has to do with the actual pace of the writing. Your lead not only sets the tone and the stage for what's ahead, but also begins the rhythm of words, sentences and paragraphs that will have to take you and your readers through to the end. It's like a conductor with a baton; the rest of the story is like the orchestra. If you can get yourself going with a good rhythm, the story will be more likely to "write itself." Start awkwardly and you're like a marathoner with an irregular heartbeat, unlikely to reach the finish line.

Your pace in the lead depends on the nature of the story. You can be breathless or lyrical, smooth as a river or staccato as gunfire. Just as in music, a clever combination of rhythms in your lead can create marvelous and subtle effects, which in turn set an intriguing pace for what's ahead.

Raymond Chandler was a master of this verbal pacing; it's what makes his copy so often imitated and even parodied. That command of rhythm got Chandler's stories started with a bang, like this classic from *The Big Sleep*:

> It was about eleven o'clock in the morning, mid October, with the sun not shining and a look of hard wet rain in the clearness of the foothills. I was wearing my powder-blue suit, with dark blue shirt, tie and display handkerchief, black brogues, black wool socks with dark blue clocks on them. I was neat, clean, shaved and sober, and I didn't care who knew it. I was everything the well-dressed private detective ought to be. I was calling on four million dollars.

The whole first paragraph serves as a setup, if you will, for the last-sentence punch line. Then he's got us hooked. Imagine if instead

Chandler had been deaf to the niceties of pace and written the opener this way:

> It was about eleven o'clock in the morning in mid-October and the sun was not shining. There was a look of hard wet rain in the clearness of the foothills. I was wearing my powder-blue suit. I also was wearing a dark blue shirt, tie and display handkerchief. I had on black brogues and black wool socks with dark blue clocks on them, and I was neat and clean. I was shaved and sober. Furthermore, I did not care who knew it. I was well dressed because I was calling on a client who was worth four million dollars.

You might as well stop the story right there, because readers sure will. But the point isn't just readability; it's what pace — right or wrong — can do to the writing of the story. The right tempo can set you up for success. The wrong rhythm — well, how could any writer keep going after the paragraph above?

But proper pacing isn't something you just graft onto a lead, like a heart transplant that makes your story beat right. Like any other element of your lead, your pace must spring naturally from the fundamentals of the story. Faster isn't always better; stop-and-go sometimes fits better than smooth.

For example, I once did a story on Dubuque's only old-fashioned tailor — a dramatic sort of fellow with a parrot in his shop and a fondness for opera records. The tempo of my first few paragraphs had to reflect his colorful personality:

> Dubuque's only tailor seizes a baby-blue suit coat from the iron bar overhead and squashes its lapels between leathery hands.
>
> "Most of the clothes today are glued. Feel the lapel — it's stiff like cardboard," says Rocco Buda, offering the offending jacket for inspection.
>
> "Garments are just put together, mass-produced, no shape to them. They invent everything today to make clothes cheaper, cheaper, cheaper."
>
> He roams his corner shop on the seventh floor of the American Trust building.
>
> He sits beside his old, jet-black sewing machine, nudging the outermost of two dozen rainbow spools of thread.
>
> He alights on the cutting table. All the while, Rocco Buda's tan polo shirt and matching slacks fit him like the skin on a cougar.

Seizing, roaming, alighting — the tempo of the lead has to match.

And that's the secret to establishing a successful tempo, really: listening to your story. It has a natural, innate pace in which it wants to come out, if only you'll pay attention. If you've been keeping tightly to the focus of your story all along, that shouldn't be difficult. By this point, you should be "hearing" your story in your head. (It's almost like all those books a few years ago, on "Inner Tennis" and "Inner Golf" and "the Zen of Archery": Relax and let it happen.)

Ideally, in fact, you won't quite know where your lead ends and the body of your story begins. Both structurally and rhythmically, your opening lines should carry you into the next paragraph, and the next, and so on.

Before you know it, you'll be writing your first draft.

CHAPTER NINE

WRITING A FIRST DRAFT RIGHT FROM THE START

• • •

WRESTLING WITH THE MUSE

Too many writers simply can't write a solid first draft straight through. It's agony to them, a psychological and sometimes physical war within that they keep losing. Their first drafts are a chaotic mess of starts and stops, backtracking and second-guessing. Not until many time-wasting drafts down the line, with 90 percent of the hard-won first draft tossed out, do these writers begin to create a manuscript they can show anyone.

Such writers think they are being quite noble, of course — wrestling with the muse, looking writer's block straight in the eye hour after hour. They think this kind of inefficient stewing is the essence, the very bitter heart and soul of the writer's art. They may never finish anything, but by golly they sure do suffer like writers! And they've got the bleary eyes, caffeine stains and pencil nubs to prove it.

If that sounds all too familiar, by now I trust you've begun to realize that it doesn't have to be that way. You can be organized, efficient and systematic and still be a good writer — in fact, you'll be a *better* writer.

You know by this point that moods and nobility and the muse have nothing to do with the real work of writing. "A professional can write even when he doesn't feel like it," is how literary agent Scott Meredith once put it. "An amateur can't — even when he *does*." Author Ray Bradbury, arguably one of the most lyrical and inspired popular authors of this century, was even more hard-nosed in his advice to struggling writers: "Start writing more. It'll get rid of all those moods you're having."

People who let their inner demons get the better of their writing, whose first drafts must be painfully squeezed out through the chinks in their psyches, don't have a *writing* problem. They have an organizational problem, a willpower problem, a self-discipline problem. "Writer's block," Norman Mailer once observed, "is a failure of the ego—it's a matter of not being in charge of your own mind."

If you've been following along, chapter by chapter, you've already come further than you may realize toward taking charge of your own writer's mind. You'll find that the next time you sit down to compose a first draft, it will be less of a struggle. Instead of trying to assemble a thousand-piece jigsaw puzzle, you'll be solving simple, finite problems, one step at a time. You're in charge, and your first drafts—the first of many fewer—will show it.

CREATING—AND GOING WITH—THE FLOW

You know that feeling when your brain seems to be working in overdrive, when the words spill out effortlessly onto the page? Hours speed by, the pages pile up, and the next thing you know it's 4 A.M. and you can't believe how much work you've done. The heck with "no pain, no gain"—this was so painless, yet productive, that you can hardly believe it was you doing the work.

As we mentioned back in chapter two, psychologists who study creativity call this mental process "flow." It's a sense of being vividly alive, plugged in and productive. The creative work—whether it's writing a novel, crafting a sculpture, or cooking up a new recipe—just seems to happen, to *flow*.

Most of the groundwork we've already laid has been designed in part to help you achieve a sense of "flow" in your writing, virtually on command. We've scuttled all the roadblocks between you and sitting down to write your heart out. Achieving this "flow" in your writing sessions is, in turn, the key to writing faster and better—really *writing*, the putting-one-word-after-another part of the task. As the words come flowing out of you, as all your preparatory labors come into play exactly as planned, you will write faster than you ever thought possible.

To reach that point of "flow" when you write, it's important not to rush the process. This isn't like a mystery novel, where you can skip ahead and read the ending. The *process* is how you put the stuff into your head so it will be there when you need it. Nothing makes it harder for the words to flow effortlessly out than if you have to stop in mid-stream to figure out where you're going, or what luggage you should have packed.

The process is a way of building what Kenneth Atchity calls "creative pressure." In effect, you've been putting off that first draft as long as possible — doing worthwhile work in the meantime, of course. You've been putting it off until you can hardly stand it anymore, until you're just itching to get to that keyboard and let off some of that creative steam.

Writers who get frustrated over their first drafts are writers who try to short-circuit the process. Every time they begin to build up a head of creativity, they unleash it by blowing off partial drafts, pieces of leads, fragments of dialogue. A couple of pages of that and they're spent.

You should never sit down to write a first draft until you've gone through the whole process, until you know what you're about to write and you can almost read it off the backs of your eyeballs. Build that creative pressure till the bursting point. "When your mind wants to come up with something to write," Atchity observes in *A Writer's Time*, "it draws from storehouses of ideas and images. You can't pry an idea from a flat piece of paper."

The worst thing about trying to write without building up creative pressure is that when you fail — and you will — you will be teaching yourself an unfortunate and inaccurate lesson: *You can't write. Writing is painful and frustrating and slow.*

Those are lies. You *can* write. Writing is joyful and liberating and fast.

If you think you spot a contradiction in all this, me trying to pull a fast one, hang on. Whatever happened to "A professional can write even when he doesn't feel like it"? How can you write on demand and yet build creative pressure? Is this the sound of one hand clapping?

Don't forget the *process*. A professional, in my book, is a writer who goes about the mundane, step-by-step details of writing: focusing, researching, interviewing, organizing and outlining, crafting a lead. If you go through that process for every writing project, when the time comes to punch out sentences you'll find the creative pressure is right there waiting for you. That mysterious and ordinarily elusive sense of "flow" will be at your fingertips.

Summoning the muse? This is all about having the muse bound and padlocked and filed under "M" in your desk drawer. Open it up and say, "Get to work."

KEEPING THE LARD OUT

Once you're ready to unleash your "creative pressure," success in writing a first draft right from the start depends on striking a happy medium between writing well and writing perfectly. The former is well within reach on your first draft; the latter is impossible, of course, and trying to achieve perfection will only bog you down. Yes, you should write a "keeper" of a first draft, one that requires an absolute minimum of revision — and you'll be able to accomplish that, thanks to the process you've already gone through. But, no, you won't be able to write a first draft that's absolutely flawless. The secret is not to let that keep you from writing as good and as clean a draft as you can. (Or, as is too often the case, to keep you from writing anything at all. Perfectionists typically can never get any work done, because to take even the first step requires bringing something from the ideal world of your imagination into the inevitably flawed world of reality.)

Let's tackle first the problem of sloppy first drafts — the "it doesn't really matter, because this is only a first draft and I'll fix it later" syndrome. Of course it matters! Why waste time and creative energy writing something second-rate when, with a little more discipline and concentration, you can write 95 percent of your final draft on the first try? The "I'll fix it later" mind-set fritters away your time in two ways: in useless first drafts and in endless rewriting. Rewriting and revising is the number one time waster for most writers, often consuming more precious hours than the whole rest of the writing process put together. Far better and faster to make your first draft almost your final draft.

So avoid what Scott Meredith calls "first draft-itis" — writing loosely and carelessly, figuring you'll get it right a couple drafts down the line. As Meredith notes in his *Writing to Sell*, this kind of thinking is a "progressive disease." Once you start viewing your first drafts as just a way station en route to the paper shredder, this soon becomes a self-fulfilling prophecy. Before long, you'll have to write double-digit drafts to produce acceptable copy.

Instead, Meredith advises, "Write each page of your first draft as tightly and carefully as if it had to be sent to the editor the moment it was pulled out of the typewriter." In fact, it's a good exercise to pretend that your first draft will be your *only* draft. What if you were a newspaper reporter, writing on deadline, with an editor panting to snatch your copy away by ten o'clock? How well could you write? Probably better than you think.

After all, think of all the groundwork you've already done. You've focused your research and interviewing, selecting the best material even as you gathered it. You've solved all your organizational and transition problems. You've found a lead that springs naturally out of your material and, in turn, leads you into the heart of your story. The hard work is done!

And your first impulses, when writing, are often not only the freshest but the best. That adjective you had to look up in a thesaurus might just be too labored, too contrived. Writing as people speak—telling your story as naturally as you can, as it comes out in your first draft—is often the best "style" with which to capture readers.

"Style" can be a terrible distraction, anyway. You're better off not worrying, at least not consciously, about your style; rather, write your first draft as plainly and clearly as you can. Keep in mind the old anecdote about the cub reporter who, when his city editor was caught short-staffed, was sent off to cover the Johnstown flood. Flush with "style," the raw reporter cabled back 5,000 stylish words almost utterly devoid of facts. Most of the story read like this lead: "God sits tonight in judgment at Johnstown. . . ." Frustrated and fuming, the city editor wired back: "Forget the flood. Interview God."

Forget style; tell your story.

If you keep that in mind, you'll also be less likely to burden your first draft with what Richard Lanham, in *Revising Prose*, calls "the lard factor": fat, unnourishing words and phrases that you'll eventually have to cut out anyway. It seems obvious, but I'll say it nonetheless: Why write them if you're going to wind up cutting them?

Even at the sentence-construction level, certain telltale words are almost always "lard." Avoid such extra words as "very," "so to speak," "as it were" and "as a matter of fact" unless they clearly contribute to your meaning and message. Shun in particular the lazy "There is/are" construction at the start of a sentence. And guard against the cardinal sin of passive voice. Remember that the Bible opens, "In the beginning, God created the heavens and the earth"—*not* "In the beginning, the heavens and the earth were created by God." Make nouns and verbs do the work of your sentences, instead of spending precious minutes typing extra adjectives and adverbs. Excess verbiage wastes time in the writing and in the ultimate excising; backwards and wimpy sentences take time to write and then to rewrite. Get the basics of your writing right, and free of extraneous words, the first time!

Whenever you sense your draft beginning to veer into "lard," quickly consult your notes and your outline and concentrate instead on communicating the facts and points you've set out. Use that outline like a lodestone, to keep your story always on course.

About this point in my preaching, a significant number of you, scarred by misguided writing teachers or equally misbegotten notions of the writer's life, are probably wondering: But aren't you supposed to overwrite, the better to boil down later on? Isn't writing sort of like making a fancy sauce—you whip up too much, then cook and condense it until it's just right? The late Jerzy Kosinski, for example, once spent twenty-seven straight hours writing a nineteen-page chunk of his novel, *The Painted Bird*. Then he revised and revised, until those twenty-seven hours and nineteen pages were boiled down to a single sterling page. Isn't that how it's supposed to work?

Only Kosinski's garbage can will ever know for sure whether he condensed the right page out of those nineteen, or whether perhaps the novel would have been better with the original draft intact. This much is certain, however: That way of working is a good way to starve. How many writers these days are so successful that they can afford that kind of indulgence? Not me, and I'll bet not you either.

But don't fret: Writing for the trash can doesn't necessarily produce the best prose, anyway. I prefer the approach of John McPhee—every bit Kosinsky's master as a prose stylist, at least in my humble opinion: McPhee likens writing to the sport of curling, in which the greatest effort is expended sweeping the ice clean to advance each shot. Sweep the ice clean in the path of your words, and your first draft will glide effortlessly toward its goal.

PERFECTIONISM VS. PRODUCTIVITY

The other extreme from "first draft-itis" is a fussy perfectionism that keeps you from writing smoothly through your first draft, because you're forever stopping to polish each word, each phrase, like a fine jewel. Perfectionists hate to actually write anything in the first place, since the real words on the page can never be as perfect as they'd imagined. Once they do buckle down to write, it's agony: They spend more time rewriting than writing, more effort with the thesaurus than culling the best from their notebook. The end result is usually precious, overwritten prose.

So, while you want to write as clean and final a first draft as you can, it's important not to swing over to the opposite sin and worry your words to death. Take each chunk of your story as it comes. Write it straight through, then move on. If you didn't use a piece of information or a quote where your outline said you would, don't stop and try to work it in; maybe it didn't belong there in the first place. Circle it on your outline if you think you still might need it later but don't know where, or pencil it in further down in the outline where it might now fit. As you zoom through your outline, turning it into reality, don't leave any sentences that you're really unhappy with and don't write "lard"—but don't break your momentum by fussily revising over and over, either. (This is particularly dangerous with a word processor, which makes tinkering with what you just wrote so painless and seductive.) If Mrs. Griswold back in elementary school were grading it, your goal would be a first draft that's about an A–/B +.

If you still find yourself tending toward perfectionism—if you find yourself frequently backtracking and it's slowing you down—you can try some self-discipline tricks. Once a sentence is written, don't even let yourself read over it. Just write the next sentence and tackle the next item in your outline. This approach will make perfectionists mighty nervous, so here's how you reassure yourself: At the beginning of each writing session, allow yourself to re-read the pages you wrote the day before. Let yourself do some minor tinkering, just to get it out of your system. (But no wholesale rewriting and no more than two trips to the thesaurus!) Take out a comma here and there, change a "glad" to a "happy," and by all means cut out any lard words that slipped through your defenses. Then you're ready to write the next section, your self-confidence bolstered.

This approach has two advantages. First, it forces you to put off your polishing to a point in your workflow when it won't interrupt your momentum. Second, reading what you wrote the day before is a good way to get your head back into the story, to recapture yesterday's "flow."

THE BIG "MO"

Part I: Appreciating the Humble Paragraph

I keep talking about "momentum" because it's every bit as important to speedy writing as it is to a winning sports team or a political campaign. Both within a given work session and from one day to the next, you need to build and maintain a sense of forward progress that carries you through the rough spots. All the hard work you've already done—researching, interviewing, outlining—has served to build up this head of steam. Now you've got to ride it to the final paragraph.

How not to get derailed en route? Let's first talk about an individual writing session. Efficient writing is all about building blocks, and putting them one after another to make a story. In a day's writing session, your building blocks are as basic as words, phrases, sentences and paragraphs. I've already talked about how to strike the right balance between sloppiness and fussiness in your word choices, phrase construction and sentence structure. The key to putting these building blocks together in a way that creates momentum is that much-misunderstood element of English composition, the paragraph.

For the speedy writer, the paragraph is the ideal unit with which to build a story. Words, phrases and sentences are all best thought of as means to the end of creating a solid paragraph. At the same time, the paragraph is not so large a unit that you can't write it in one gulp, one burst. Moreover, the paragraph meshes nicely with the outline you used to plan your story; it's easy to see how one or two items in your outline will translate into a paragraph. And a paragraph is not too much to think about: You can juggle the main point and the three or four supporting points in your head, keeping them straight long enough to actually set them down in words.

Admittedly, what you learned in English class about the paragraph and what you'll see in published prose don't always match. Newspaper writers tend to write paragraphs that are no more than a sentence or two. Some literary authors — William Faulkner comes to mind — have written paragraphs that ramble on for pages. Perhaps surprisingly, many advisers on how to write better prose (William Zinsser and Herbert Read, for example) downplay the importance of the paragraph, advocating what might be called a laissez-faire approach (though Strunk and White, in *The Elements of Style* weigh in definitively with, "Make the paragraph the unit of composition."). Here is a case where what you learned in junior high is probably the best advice: Begin with a topic sentence and fill your paragraph with sentences that support that topic sentence, then move on to a new paragraph.

I don't say this for English-class reasons, and in practice your "topic sentence" can be mighty loosely defined. If you do stick to this basic, old-fashioned notion of the paragraph, however, you will find that your first drafts flow much faster and more smoothly. (Just look at this paragraph: That's a terrible topic sentence, but the paragraph does pretty well round up one argument and one argument only, namely that the reason for following this rule is practical rather than theoretical.)

I discovered the marvelous utility of the humble paragraph several years ago, when I was writing a travel piece on Catalina Island for *TWA Ambassador* magazine. I had a lot of information to impart in not much space — less than eight manuscript pages — and my efforts to cram it all in kept me backtracking and starting and stopping. Finally, for reasons I forget, I realized that I could build my story with paragraphs. Each paragraph was like a coat tree, on which I could hang a bunch of similar information. As long as the last bit I hung gave me some link, some transition to the next bunch of information,

I could assemble a whole story out of these paragraph-sized units. Simple as it sounds, this was a tremendous psychological breakthrough for me. Suddenly I was zooming along, one paragraph at a time.

Here's a sample paragraph, from the first third or so of the story, about the town of Avalon on the island:

> Avalon proper seems suspended in time since William Wrigley, the chewing-gum magnate, first turned it into a haven for Hollywood types and for his Chicago Cubs, in the twenties. "The houses are sort of 'early Calvin Coolidge' style," is how Carlos puts it. They climb the staircases of narrow streets into greenscrub foothills, giving the town a look somewhere between San Francisco and a small town in Illinois in the 1890s. Already steep freight charges from the mainland are doubled for automobiles, and everything in Avalon is within ten minutes' walk of everything else, anyway. So golf carts, a bit reminiscent of "The Prisoner" television series, suffice for trips to the Safeway or Chet's Hardware or the Buoys and Gulls clothing store. Signs imply other options: "Danger — Walk bikes down hill." "No dogs, vehicles or skateboards beyond this point." Streets are marked with chocolate-brown signs in the distinctive diving-fish shape of the island.

Everything that supports the notion of Avalon being "suspended in time" — particularly relating to its geography and old-fashioned transportation style — went into that paragraph. Note that I wasn't compulsive about my topic sentence; I didn't have to write, "Everything about Avalon's geography and transportation seems to be suspended in time."

How do you decide what makes an efficient paragraph? Newspaper editors will command you to make them shorter, but for most other stories an average paragraph of about four to nine sentences, covering one to three points or subpoints, is a good unit to work with. Pick a major point on your outline and concentrate on expressing it, along with its supporting evidence and "local color," if you will. That should make a pretty good paragraph. Move on to the next, and the next after that; before you know it, you'll have written a section, or a chapter, or your whole story.

Moving on to the next paragraph will be considerably easier if you end your paragraphs with some thought to making that transition. Your major transitions should be taken care of in your outline, but it doesn't hurt to pass the baton to the next paragraph with a little extra oomph. For example, by the time I was actually typing that line about the "distinctive diving-fish shape of the island," the opening of my next paragraph was beginning to form in my head:

> Avalon was built roughly where the fish's eye would be, on a perfect half-moon harbor. . . .

This sort of split-second transition, a sort of verbal pirouette that lets you dance on into the next subject, becomes more important the shorter your story runs. In a longer article, I might have devoted whole paragraphs each to Wrigley's motives for building the town, descriptions of the houses, and Catalina's unusual transportation system. Here, however, those facts all became supporting evidence of the town's "suspended in time" qualities. The next paragraph had to quickly pick up on "perfect half-moon harbor" and talk about the boatloads of tourists who arrive there. In a longer story, I might have more lazily segued from a discourse on transportation . . . to a paragraph on the harbor . . . to a paragraph devoted entirely to the tourist boats . . . to perhaps another paragraph on their passengers. On a shorter course, you need to make tighter turns.

Transitions, leading you (not to mention the reader) smoothly into the next paragraph, are crucial to maintaining your writing momentum. Ideally, you should never have to stop to ponder where the story is going next, or how you'll get there. Just let the momentum of your writing carry you along. That's how you establish "flow." That's how you write a first draft faster than you ever thought possible.

Part II: Day by Day

How often have you had a really good day of writing, only to sit at the keyboard the very next day and not be able to summon up a single usable word? Where did that momentum go? Of course, it went into all the other aspects of your life. Your writing "flow" was dissipated among your daily chores, your day job, your family, paying bills, even reading the paper and falling asleep.

Short of writing yourself to death (not to mention divorce!), how can you keep your writing momentum from day to day? How can you pick up where you left off with the same creativity and enthusiasm? The secret, you might say, is to trick yourself.

"Wait till I get to a good stopping point." Sound familiar? You're right not to stop writing except at a good stopping point, but your definition of that point is probably backwards. Don't work until you've completed a paragraph, a thought, a section, a chapter and then stop.

Instead, force yourself to break away in mid-thought, even in mid-sentence.

Talk about creative pressure! Interrupting yourself in mid-creation keeps that creative head of steam from dissipating. Instead of walking away from the keyboard with a smug sense of satisfaction at all you've accomplished, you end the work session with an itch. If your work was going well, the itch to pick it up again where you left off will put your writing momentum in high gear the minute you sit down to work again.

Stopping in mid-work, even mid-sentence, fuels your momentum in an even more basic way. If you broke for the day in the middle of a sentence, well, the odds are pretty good that you know how you were going to finish that sentence. So when you start work again the next day, you know you can at least finish the sentence you started. And that leads into finishing the paragraph, the section, the chapter. Before you know it, you really have picked up where you left off.

As your words and sentences begin to pile up, seek a steady pace rather than exhausting bursts. Once you realize that you can indeed quit for the day and then start up again, just like an assembly-line worker who knocks off at the 4:00 whistle and then tackles a new set of widgets tomorrow, you can pace yourself. Getting a first draft done, after all, comes down to a matter of mathematics: At 1,000 words a day (of a first draft that's very nearly your final draft, remember), you can write a 4,000-word magazine feature from Sunday through Wednesday. You can polish off a 75,000-word novel in two and a half months. Even a blockbuster won't take you much more than two seasons to write.

For first drafts, that 1,000-words-a-day figure is a pretty good rule. You should be able to crank that out in your spare time. (I can write about 1,000 words an hour, for example, which means I can write a chapter in a week, an hour or so a night after my daughter's tucked in.) For serious, full-time writing, 2,000 to 3,000 words a day is a respectable — and achievable — pace. Unless you have a deadline breathing down your neck, there's little reason to push yourself much harder than that. The key to writing "fast," really, is writing steadily and efficiently. You'll be further ahead with your 1,000 "keeper" words a day than the disorganized writer who churns out several thousand words in a creative frenzy, only to trash most of them in subsequent drafts.

What you've been aiming toward, with all your focusing and outlining, is putting the "Pareto Principle" to work for you. That's the principle, also known as the 80-20 rule, that states that 20 percent of your efforts usually produce 80 percent of the value of your work. All of what goes before is designed to turn your first-drafting into that concentrated 20 percent of highly productive work.

You'll find another, less-scientific principle also holds true in your first drafts. It's a Spanish saying: "Life is short, but wide." You'll be amazed at how much productive writing you can fit into what's really only a short slice of time—how wide your writing life can be, once you get it organized.

WRITING TO FIT: HOW TO MAKE EDITORS LOVE YOU

One of my staff writers and I were talking about her problem the other day— *her* problem which inevitably becomes *my* problem once her story is done. She writes well, sure. But she writes too much. Even after she's exhausted her creative energy and willpower trying to hack her first draft down to size, it's still too long. So I have to spend almost as much time pruning her copy as she spent writing it.

Editors hate this. Editors hate writers who tell them, "I wrote it 2,000 words too long, but I figured you could just use the parts you like." That's what *writing* is all about: selecting the telling details among many and making a coherent whole out of them. When an editor asks for 2,500 words, that's generally all he or she has room for. So when you blithely turn in 4,500 words, it's unlikely that the editor will be so overwhelmed with your brilliant writing that he'll add pages to the project or drop somebody else's work to make room.

Naturally, you want to make editors love you. But that's not the only reason to learn to make your first drafts fit: You'll also save an enormous amount of wasted work.

Think about my poor staff writer. For a 4,000-word story, she may write a 7,000-word first draft. Right there, she's wasted the time it takes to write an extra 3,000 words. But that's not all: Now she's got to burn another few agonizing days trying (in vain) to chop her opus down to size. If only she could have written about 4,000 words, no more, to begin with, she'd have finished in less than half the time. (Imagine if Lee Iacocca had to churn out 7,000 Chryslers for every 4,000 that make it to the showroom; he'd go broke faster than you can say "Toyota.")

When I told her that I hardly ever overwrite—no more than 5 or 10 percent over the allotted length—her eyes popped. The secret to writing to fit, I emphasized, is to never put those extra words down on paper in the first place. Once you let them out of the bottle, they're mighty hard to get back in: They become your words, your offspring, and cutting them starts to feel uncomfortably like infanticide.

Keeping your story to the right length begins way back, several chapters ago, with focusing your idea. Figure out what this story is really about and what it will take to get it done. A 1,500-word column does not require the same amount of legwork and facts as a three-part *New Yorker* saga. A short story does not require as much scene-setting or character development as a 500-page novel suitable for lugging to the beach.

Then you have to keep that focus in mind all the way through your research and interviewing. Resolutely forbid yourself to go off on tangents that will later tempt you to weave them into your writing. Edit as you go, marking material you're sure to use and disregarding as early as possible anything that's outside your focus.

Your outline, then, becomes your chief weapon against writing too much. Here's where you must be the most ruthless, leaving out anything that takes your story astray or that, deep down, you know there's no room for. Eliminate it now, when it's just squiggles in a notebook and a line in your outline! Don't wait until it's hatched into wonderful prose in your story, when it will be much harder to excise.

Finally, when you're writing your first draft, use your outline as a kind of ration book. If you're one-third through the outline, you must not be much over one-third your total word allotment. If you *are* over, the earlier you recognize it and start reining yourself in, the better. One of the advantages of composing on a computer is that most word processing programs will count the words for you, at any point. (Some count only characters; divide by six to approximate the word count.) Check this "gauge" frequently. Think of it as a sort of reverse gas gauge: If it's almost full and you still have a long way to go, start conserving fast!

On the bright side, checking the mounting tally of your words also gives you a terrific feeling of accomplishment. Yes, by golly, your first draft really is happening. It's adding up. You're almost there.

CHAPTER TEN

WRITING FASTER FICTION, SCRIPTS AND HUMOR

• • •

A USEFUL WAY TO KILL TIME?

Ah, I can see that by this point all the nonfiction writers in the house have scurried off to their keyboards and are deep into their faster-than-ever first drafts. It's the novelists and screenplay writers, short story authors and humorists who are still out there with their hands on their hips saying, "Yeah, that might work for articles, even nonfiction books, but I want to create Art. You can't rush Art. It must spring from the creative pools deep within." Or words to that effect.

Well, I might say something about your use of hackneyed metaphors ("creative pools"? Give me a break!), but since this is a book on writing fast I'll concentrate on, er, dispelling your misconceptions like dropping a stone into the still waters of a pond. Sorry. Bear with me, OK?

Of course you can write spontaneously, waiting for your creative springs to leak or whatever. Joan Didion, for instance, told a *Paris Review* interviewer that she dives into her fiction with no theme or plot in mind, only a vague character and "a technical sense of what I want to do." Her story line, such as it is, doesn't emerge until *after* her first draft is done; she'll mark uncertain spots "chapter to come" and simply skip over them. Or there's Joseph Heller, who missed the deadline for his novel *Catch-22* by half a decade. "When I started *Catch-22*," he once revealed, "I thought writing novels might be a useful way to kill time."

If you have time to kill, you should probably skip right over this chapter and go do your nails or something. Most writers, particularly beginning and struggling ones, don't have the luxury of approaching their writing without any planning, or missing their deadlines by several years.

Take William Shakespeare, for example—a hard-working and hard-pressed author if ever there was one. His publishers, Heminges & Condell, marveled, "His mind and hand went together, and what he thought, he uttered with that easiness that we have scarce received a blot from him in his papers." A "write fast, write clean first drafts" model author, no doubt about it.

Or, on a less lofty plane of penning, consider Shakespeare's fellow Briton, Edgar Wallace, a British mystery writer (1875-1932) and sometime playwright. Wallace wrote his play *On the Spot* in just two and a half days, and not one word had to be altered in production.

Yes, fiction writers of all stripes can learn to write faster, too. In fact, if you've been paying attention all along, you already know the basics.

FOCUSING ON SETTING

Just like a nonfiction writer weighing whether his work will be an article or an opus, and what the angle will be, the fiction writer must focus his efforts long before the first word hits the page. It's not just a matter of length, but of the implications of length and ambition for the total project. Obviously, a novel means greater scope than a short story; a movie script brings larger challenges than a half-hour TV comedy; a book-length satire has a wider focus than a humorous essay for the local newspaper's op-ed page. But more length doesn't necessarily mean more of everything. It might mean a longer time span in which your story unfolds—but not necessarily: James Joyce's mammoth, *Ulysses*, after all, takes place in a single day. It probably does mean more variations on your theme, which means you'd better be darn sure of what your theme is.

Focusing, in any writing, demands an awareness of what you're writing and why: how the pieces work together to create a greater whole. How many times have you heard, in advice about fiction writing, to put in only what advances the story? That's focusing.

Since in fiction you're *inventing* what happens rather than picking and choosing strictly from the real world, focusing can be especially difficult. With infinite possibilities at your keyboard, you may find yourself trying to explore them all—and wind up not doing a good job at any.

Take the question of setting, for example. You can set your story anywhere (and anywhen) you want: in your hometown, in Paris, in second-century Rome, on Mars, in an alternate universe in which Genghis Khan conquered Europe. Or all of the above.

But if you want to write fast, you'd be wise to restrict your possibilities to those closest to home, to your own experiences or what you can readily research and extrapolate. That's not merely a recipe for speedier writing; "write what you know" is also sound advice for authentic, believable fiction. Not only is it easier to set a scene in the neighborhood McDonald's than it is to conjure up the frigid steppes of Siberia—you'll also write better about Big Macs than about, um, frozen food.

Remember: Find the story that only you can tell, and write it.

This doesn't mean that you ought to spend your whole fiction career penning epics set in your backyard and at the local Minute Lube. It does mean that you should paddle awhile in your own pond before trying to swim the Atlantic. And when you do dive into a more exotic setting, remember my rapid-research tips and don't bite off more than you can chew. If you're writing a short story set in Australia, for example, focus on the theme, the characters and the plot; keep the setting a secondary or tertiary focus. Don't go overboard on description of things you've only seen in *National Geographic*! Sketch in a few details, drop in a fact or two from the ol' *Geographic*, and let your action and dialogue do the heavy lifting for you.

GETTING TO KNOW YOU: QUICK TAKES ON CHARACTERS

At least with settings you have something real to start with (even in science fiction you know that Mars is red); with characters you've got *terra incognita*. Sure, you can base them on bits of people you know, or on aspects of your own character—but there's no encyclopedia you can turn to for quick facts about your characters. ("Let's see, I'll look under 'E' for 'Emotions'. . . .")

And yet how many times have you heard that "you can never know too much about your characters"? It's true, and that's where preparation pays off, just as it does in nonfiction. When you reach the climax, you'll *know* whether your hero will run or make a stand—because you'll know all you need to know about him. With properly prepared characters, a story begins to write itself once you turn them loose.

That's why the Gordons, the mystery-writing team, used to write biographies of their principal characters before starting a new puzzler. If they didn't develop a "feel" for the key characters, they'd abandon the whole novel. Or why Barbara Taylor Bradford, author of

A Woman of Substance, details each character on index cards. She'll note their fictional backgrounds, ages, motivations, even sketch family trees.

Not only do you need to know the intimate details of your characters; you should also think about how you plan to reveal what makes them tick. Of course, you're not going to write simply, "Janet was a nervous woman, probably because she'd had an unhappy childhood." No, you'll *show* her biting her nails and have a picture of her mother turned to face the wall. (C'mon, you can come up with better stuff than I'm whipping out here!) Whatever specifics you plan to use to bring your characters to life, the magic word is *plan*.

How do you keep this preparation from eating up all your creative time — so you wind up with a villageful of imaginary people but no story? Again, you've got to focus. Develop the characters that will drive your story, whose decisions will make your tale twist and turn. Don't waste equal time on minor characters — those that are mostly functionaries in your saga. Yes, know everything you can about your photographer-turned-secret-agent hero. But settle for quick strokes about the woman behind the camera counter who passes him the crucial film (and never appears again in your story), the taxidriver who speeds him to the airport, and the airline agent who takes his ticket. Besides, telling too much about minor characters gives your readers the wrong impression: that these are *major* characters who will turn up again later (surely you wouldn't flesh out that ticket agent so thoroughly if she's not going to return as the spy's love interest?).

Even characters who play a major, yet purely functional role can be treated as stereotypes, or variations on a type. It's probably not necessary, for example, to create a family tree for the ex-Marine who gives your spy hero his orders. He's an ex-Marine, OK, and you know what he looks like and talks like, and maybe just to make him more interesting he's a ballet fan to boot. Chances are that's preparation enough to make him come alive (enough) on the page.

Your focus instead must be on your major characters, because they must change from your first page to "The End" — and that change becomes the motivating force for your story. Remember *Casablanca*? Rick (Humphrey Bogart) starts the story as an aloof bystander, content to cope with whatever hand the war deals him. As the closing credits roll, however, he's ready to join the French Resistance. Or think of Don Quixote and Sancho Panza. As Kenneth Atchity has observed, in the course of the story Don Quixote's faith is shaken — doubt replaces his tilting at windmills — while his loyal companion makes the opposite transformation, from realist to idealist.

Screenwriting theorists, Atchity further points out, hold that a successful screenplay must contain two major turning points—each related to the hero's motivation. So, for example, our tale of the photographer-spy might have an early turning point, in which the hero's decision to abandon espionage for the simpler pleasures of his Nikon is reversed when the fate of the Western World suddenly hinges on his secret-agent skills. (His underlying motivation, of course, is to help humanity—and he just can't stop himself.) That leads him into a series of adventures and obstacles and, ultimately, to turning point number two. That's the pivotal point where our hero's decision determines how the story will come out.

All these turning points, decisions and determinations—essentially, your plot—spring from your own decisions about your major characters. So before you send anybody off to save the world, you'd better know all you can about him or her.

THICKENING YOUR PLOT

How many times have you heard, "I have a great idea for a story"? Ideas are a dime a dozen. But an idea does not equal a plot, and a plot is what you need to make a story. Plotting demands putting your vague, general idea into focus: What ought to happen to bring this idea to life and (just as important) what should you leave out? As Richard Martin Stern, author of *Tsunami*, once observed, fiction writing is largely a process of selection—of choosing what is necessary and of having the willpower to omit what is not.

If that's beginning to sound a lot like the process of focusing your *non*fiction writing, you're right. And, just as with nonfiction, you can work through that process of selection in advance—or you can write a lot of pages that wind up in the trash can. The fastest approach to plotting, of course, is to maximize your self-confidence and minimize wasted writing by deciding where your story is going and how you'll get there.

Barbara Taylor Bradford, for example, not only plans her characters but also creates a ten- to twenty-page outline of her plot before ever sitting down to craft a first draft. For his circus novel *Spangle*, Gary Jennings diagrammed his story on a twenty-foot sheet of brown wrapping paper, using different-colored inks to track his multitude of characters through the twists and turns of sixteen years. He further divided the sheet by date and location, and scribbled his research notes on what was going on in the real, historical world vertically along his timeline. Even Sidney Sheldon, who dives into his own books with only a character and no plot in mind, dictating to a secretary as the story strikes him, has said that any beginning writer ought to use an outline.

Sure, these are blockbuster sagas, multihundred-page beach-reading books where you can't tell the players without a scorecard. What about a frothy little humor book, maybe 200 pages—surely you don't need a plot outline for a frolic like that? Well, P.G. Wodehouse, the master of the brief humor novel, would disagree. Humor, Wodehouse once told a *Paris Review* interviewer, requires perhaps the most careful planning of all forms of writing: "For a humorous novel you've got to have a scenario, and you've got to test it so that you know where the comedy comes in." Before he'd start one of his oh-so-English romps, Wodehouse would pen 400 pages of notes, then build an outline that would make your old teacher Mrs. Griswold beam with pride ("A. Bring in Florence's husband . . ."). All this planning paid off, Wodehouse insisted: "You can more or less see how it's going to work out. After that it's just a question of detail."

You can choose or adapt any of an endless series of schemes for the actual planning of your plot, depending on your needs and the nature of your story. For example, mystery writer William J. Reynolds—author of the "Nebraska" series, including *Things Invisible* and *The Naked Eye*—relies on what he calls "a kind of free-form stream-of-consciousness document, a 'road map' of how I see the story going." Parts of this free-form road map are quite detailed, he says, right down to bits of dialogue that may actually end up in the finished book. Other parts he leaves as vague as can be ("Somehow he finds out that . . ."), meaning Reynolds must work out the details later.

Even if you opt for letting the muse guide you through the specific twists and turns of your tale, at minimum you should write down your beginning and ending and what changes in-between. You wouldn't, after all, set out on a safari without at least knowing where to start and where you're hoping to go. Reynolds, for example, admits that he seldom consults his outline once he's made it, and sometimes doesn't even create his outline until he's a few chapters into the book. ("But I need to have that outline before I feel comfortable really getting into the book," he says.) Nonetheless, his stories always *begin* and *end* at the points indicated on his "map."

So make sure you know at least how your story will start and where it will wind up. Your whole outline might be no more than this: "Chapter 1: Norbert sets out to find his true parents. . . . Chapter 22: Norbert finds his true parents, but decides his adoptive parents are his 'real' parents after all." That's not much, but it's better than plunging into a first draft without knowing whether "Norbert" will succeed in his fictional quest.

For a surer "safari," you'll want to know a little bit more about the journey before you step into the jungle. For example, screenwriters say that Paramount studios sometimes uses the plot of *Bad News Bears*, of all things, as its model of a successful screenplay. It couldn't be much simpler, but it does show how a well-planned plot hooks the reader and keeps him there until the credits roll. It's a couple of steps more complicated than simply beginning-and-end, going on to sketch out the fundamental reversals along the way. You can "analyze" the plot of *Bad News Bears* — or a zillion other successful stories — this way:

The hook: A lousy Little League team suddenly starts winning.
The complication: The team starts losing again.
The response: The team begins the difficult journey back to victory.
The conclusion: The team triumphs.

Your own story — whether screenplay, short story or novel — might be drafted along similar lines, to give yourself a guide to the key plot points:

The hook: Norbert discovers that he's adopted.
The complication: But his true parents vanished in Alaska thirty years ago.
The response: Norbert begins a long and difficult journey to learn the truth about his heritage.
The conclusion: Norbert learns that "there's no place like home" — that is, that the parents who raised him are his "real" parents.

Perhaps his birth parents turn out to be rotten criminals, while something his adoptive parents taught him saves his life in Alaska. (Incidentally, unless you recently took a lengthy vacation in Alaska, this frivolous example is even more unlikely than it seems — because it would shatter the rule about "writing what you know" that we just learned a few paragraphs ago.)

To take your planning one step further still, you might detail how your story develops over a series of chapters — breaking the action down into, say, twenty pieces instead of just these four. Not that the plot should be distributed evenly, five chapters per story element. Your hook and conclusion might each be no more than a chapter or two; your complication not much more. The bulk of your chapters will be devoted to the response to the main complication, and to the miniresponses to the minicomplications (Norbert is attacked by a polar bear . . .) along the way.

For this level of detail, you might use a simple notebook, one page per chapter. Then on each page you could write a sentence or two telling what each chapter is supposed to accomplish. (If it doesn't accomplish anything, for gosh sakes don't write it!) You could note which characters will be introduced in which chapter. (Generally, it's a good idea to get all your major characters introduced within the first quarter of your story—but not to bring them in all at once, confusing the reader.) You might also note each character's reaction or response to the events in the chapter. Then rough in your time span: When does each chapter take place?

Finally, consider what screenwriters call the "backstory"—what has gone on before your story opens. What elements of the backstory will you inject, when and where? How does the backstory affect your characters, their motivations, and the complications of your plot? Part of the backstory in our little Norbert saga is the truth about what happened to his parents before our story opens. Another part might be some key lesson that Norbert learned in his prechapter-one childhood, which comes into play just in the nick of time to save him from that polar bear.

You could accomplish the same as this chapters-and-note book scheme with a combination of index cards and manila folders. If you take your research notes on index cards, you could then distribute them into folders so they're ready when you need them: Your notes on the structure of an Eskimo village should go in the folder for chapter seventeen, when Norbert wakes up in one after being dragged off the ice floe by his loyal sled dogs. Ditto for your cards on characters, placing them in the chapters where they'll be introduced, and your cards on conflicts, plot twists, setting and so forth. The key is to arrange your pages or cards or whatever to make sure that you are constantly giving the reader something new, something to hold his attention and advance the action toward your ultimate goal in the final chapter.

MAKING A SCENE . . . AND ANOTHER ONE . . . AND ANOTHER

However many chapters you have—and it really doesn't matter—your story will ultimately be composed of a series of scenes. These scenes, in turn, add up to your chapters or acts. By thinking in terms of scenes, you can break your writing task into more fundamental building blocks. As we've already seen with other types of writing, that compartmentalizing—cutting your story into bite-sized chunks—is crucial to achieving both the organization and self-confidence necessary to write faster. If you think in terms of scenes, you can concentrate on writing the scene at hand, on making it the best you can. Then move on to the next scene, and the next. Before you know it, you're typing "The End."

For a hundred-minute feature film, for example, you'll probably need about twenty-five different scenes. For a novel, you might have several scenes per chapter, or you might label each scene a chapter. A short story might be no more than a handful of scenes.

Each scene brings a sampling of your characters together for some sort of interaction that advances the plot. You can think of your scenes as miniature stories: Each must "work" as a dramatic unit—with a beginning, middle and end. Within each scene, just as with your overall story, you might start with some goal that your protagonist wants to achieve. (Norbert wants to charter a plane to fly into the Alaskan wilderness.) Then you'll introduce your minicomplication, which might not seem so "mini" to your hero. (The only available plane must first deliver a vaccine to an even more remote outpost.) And then you can mix in some twist—logical but unexpected—that throws your main character for a loop, that seems to send him even further from his primary goal. (The plane runs into a blinding blizzard en route.)

But of course your story can't be just a jumble of disconnected scenes. Each scene has to lead into the next—which is the point of the twist, or hook, or outright disaster at the end of each scene. Between scenes you need a sort of mortar, stuff that holds the bricks of your story together. These transitions must do the basic business of sequencing and pacing your story (jumping ahead five minutes or five years). They summarize and condense the narrative that's not worth developing into a full-fledged scene. (Norbert's uneventful flight from Seattle to Fairbanks, where he tries to charter the plane that turns into an event.) Most important, they have to link the turnabout at the end of one scene to a new goal at the start of the next. (Norbert wants to survive the blizzard.)

The principle that links your scenes, one to the next, is causality. Not only should each scene advance the plot; it should also have consequences for subsequent scenes. In the movie *High Noon*, for example, based on John W. Cunningham's short story, "The Tin Star," ex-marshal Will Kane learns that a killer he sent to prison has been pardoned and is coming on the noon train to get revenge. (Here's the backstory informing the main narrative: Before our story opened, Kane was a marshal who sent killer Frank Miller to the slammer.) As a result (another scene), Kane's pacifist Quaker bride tries to convince him to leave town with her rather than fight. When he decides to stay and face Miller, the consequence is that his bride decides to leave him. And so on. Cause, effect, another cause, another effect—so your scenes run one into the next like falling dominos.

What scene should start this chain reaction? How should your story begin? With a bang, of course—a bang that, as we've already explored in the chapter about leads, doesn't stand alone but rather flows naturally from and into the rest of your tale. Don't waste time—yours or the readers'—penning many scenes of what should properly be relegated to your "backstory." Instead, start with a scene that introduces some change into your hero's life, a change that triggers all the toppling dominos that are ahead. As confession-magazine editors used to advise, "Start on the day that's different." Open with a discovery, an arrival, a conflict. If you're writing a suspense thriller, launch your story with a battle or a bomb: Tom Clancy, for example, opened his blockbuster *Red Storm Rising* with a fiery scene of sabotage at a Soviet oil refinery; all the suspense that follows is triggered by this scene. If you're writing a murder mystery, get that corpse onto page one. If you're telling of a tangle of interpersonal relationships, start with a phone call, the return of an old flame, or the day he walks out on her.

In our imaginary story about Norbert, for example, let's not fritter away a half-dozen scenes on Norbert's ordinary life: Norbert goes to the grocery store, Norbert watches TV, Norbert mows the lawn. No, let's open with Norbert making the stunning discovery that everything he thought he knew about himself is wrong. If our story is a ski slope, let's skip the long, boring ride up the lift. We'll start instead with our hero poised for a long, thrilling ride—and then we'll give him a push.

SECRETS OF SMOOTHER STORYTELLING

So your story is mapped out and you're ready to write your first draft. If you were paying attention in the previous chapter, you really already know how to write faster, smoother, more polished first drafts in your fiction—for the psychological principles are the same whether you're pounding out an article or a novel.

Start with creative pressure. It's important not to write your novel or short story or screenplay or humorous essay until you can't stand *not* to write it. William Faulkner once said that his novels began with an image that "haunted" him until, finally, he had to write the novel to answer the questions that materialized around this haunting image. Your first draft must be a sort of exorcism, transforming those creative ghosts inside you into scenes on the page.

All your preparation—researching your setting, getting to know your characters, outlining your plot—can almost be thought of as a productive way of delaying your actual writing. To write an effortless first draft, you have to build the creative pressure through these "delaying tactics." Start too soon and you'll run out of steam before "The End."

Once you are finally ready to start, don't fall into the trap of thinking that because this is fiction, make-believe, your writing can be any less precise. "I'll fix it later" is even more tempting for the fiction writer, who must spin all the solutions out of his own head. Indeed, because fiction often requires a greater emotional involvement on your part, "later" is even less likely to provide answers. Later, you will be less "hot" on your story, more bored with your characters; your emotional involvement will be at a lower ebb. So write it right—right now, not later, because you'll never be better suited to do it than at your first, most intense draft.

"I don't do drafts," says mystery author Reynolds. "I think they're a waste of time. I try to be satisfied with any given section—page, chapter, paragraph, whatever—before I move on to the next bit. The idea of producing 400 or 500 pages of 'rough draft,' then going back to page one and revising into a second draft, then going back again, etc., etc., sounds so tedious that I doubt I'd ever get past the first draft." (He does, of course, go back over previous work as he progresses, and polishes the whole manuscript—"dotting the i's and crossing the t's, not wholesale revision"—before dropping it in the mail.)

Because you are making it up, fiction first drafts are also particularly prone to "lard" words. If the rain is only in your imagination, it's too easy to make it a "driving" rain—like a zillion other fictional rainstorms. Those stars that only your characters see are probably going to be "twinkling," the fog "thick as pea soup," and the stairs "steep." But don't just replace these tired words with odd new words you've plucked out of the thesaurus: If they don't serve your story (and, after all, don't *all* stars twinkle?), don't waste time writing them in the first place. Save that thesaurus time to spend on nouns and verbs, instead of pondering whether to write "old" or "aged" to describe a ninety-year-old character.

Ah, the temptations of the thesaurus. Fiction writers may be even more prone to perfectionism than their nonfiction kin. Because this is, by definition, Art, the desire to make your fiction perfect can be so strong as to keep you from writing anything at all. Such pressure, to follow in the footsteps of Shakespeare and Tolstoy, Austen and Proust! Keep in mind, when perfectionism starts putting the brakes on your productivity, that much of what today we revere as great literature was written under deadline pressures for commercial purposes. The giants of literature had to eat, too. Whether you write a novel that endures for the ages has far more to do with how large your soul and talent may be, and little to do with one more trip to the thesaurus.

Finally, for the fiction writer no less than for a newspaper reporter on deadline, getting it written demands discipline: putting your seat on the chair and your fingers on the keyboard. Even as daunting a project as a novel can be reduced to willpower and mathematics: If you can write just two to four pages a day of really good prose, you'll finish a novel in a hundred days. If you can manage ten pages a day, five days a week, as the prolific novelist Dean R. Koontz says he does, you'll produce ten novels a year and be considered a phenomenon of productivity. Heinie Faust, who wrote literally hundreds of westerns under the pen name of "Max Brand," used to write only two hours a day. His secret? He wrote two hours *every* day, and he wrote fourteen pages in each two-hour session.

Writing regularly, Reynolds notes, not only makes the words add up faster but also makes it easier to slip into the harness at each writing session. When he made himself keep to a schedule on his first novel, *The Nebraska Quotient*, he soon discovered "it took less and less time to get back into the groove when I began each evening's session. Pretty soon I could just sit down and pick up where I left off the previous evening, with little or no warmup."

Suddenly, Reynolds adds, a project that had kicked around in his ambitions for years was on its way to reality. You get into a groove and the pages start to pile up. You keep at it, and pretty soon there's a book sitting there.

But you must approach your fiction writing as *work*, the same as anything else worth doing in life. Having a story that you're burning to tell isn't enough, or there'd be successful novelists and screenplay writers on every block. Like any other work, fiction writing requires preparation, planning, discipline and drive. That's the bad news. The good news, as you've seen, is that it does not require anguish, hair pulling, alcoholism or long nights staring at an empty page.

Go on, start filling those pages. Get to *work*.

CHAPTER ELEVEN

HOW TO PUT YOUR COMPLETION DRIVE IN HIGH GEAR

• • •

GAUGING YOUR COMPLETION DRIVE

"Finish what you start" is one of those admonitions we all heard from our mothers. But it's easier said than done, as any writer knows. You've crafted a solid lead, you're steaming through your first (almost final) draft, and then. . . . Well, somewhere between that initial burst of creativity and enthusiasm and typing "The End" you run out of momentum. You can't quite wrap it up. The art of writing becomes the drudgery of writing, and you begin to wonder if maybe you should have followed some of mom's *other* advice and become a doctor instead.

You're not alone in struggling to finish what you've started. Virgil, it's said, took a whole decade to complete his *Aeneid* — and still thought it needed another three years' work when he gave it up. Sinclair Lewis spent seventeen years laboring to bring his best-known novel, *Main Street*, to fruition. And Katherine Anne Porter needed more than two decades to finish *Ship of Fools*.

But it's not just writers who have such a hard time finishing what they start; nearly everybody does, to a greater or lesser degree. Psychologists say that we all have a built-in drive to complete what we've begun — it's not just mom making us feel guilty — but some of us seem to be better at harnessing that innate force. For the would-be speedy writer, learning to make the most of your inborn "completion drive" is critical to getting things done. You can write as fast as your keyboard will handle, after all, but if all you have to show for it is a pile of half-written first drafts you're not really *writing* anything; it's just typing practice.

"Know thyself" is probably the first step in getting your completion drive into high gear. Imagine that you're typing along and your typewriter ribbon suddenly gives up the ghost. (Yes, some folks still do use old-fashioned typewriters; if you're in the computer age, just bear with us and use your imagination.) What do you do? Do you calmly change the ribbon and get right back to work? Or do you decide that, gee, now's a good time to go shopping for a new brand of ribbon, or maybe a whole new typewriter? Or perhaps, in the search for a fresh ribbon, you get distracted and end up sorting through stuff in the closet all the rest of the afternoon. The rest of that chapter can wait, sure, while you clip and file those really important back issues of *Procrastinator's Digest Magazine.*

If that latter putting-it-off persona sounds like you, then you might indeed have a completion drive in need of revving up. To see if you really suffer from "finishphobia," try answering this quick completion quiz:

1. Look around your house. Is it packed with half-completed projects you can't throw out? I'm not talking only about writing chores here, but also about that afghan-in-progress, the VCR you bought but never finished hooking up or learning to program, and the Christmas cards from two years ago that you never finished addressing.

2. Try listing the major projects—again, not just writing work—you've started and finished in the past six months. Now make a list of those you've begun that are still "pending." Is the latter list a good deal longer than the first?

3. Would you describe yourself as "impulsive" rather than "driven," impatient" more so than "stubborn"?

4. In a typical week, do you often find yourself coming back to tasks or chores that you've already picked up and abandoned once or more?

If most of your answers were "yes" or "yeah, I guess so" (or if you couldn't even finish this little quiz!), then you probably need a completion-drive tune-up to be the most efficient writer you can be. If none of these quiz questions sounded like you, your completion drive is likely working pretty well for you. It's possible, in fact, that you're one of those rare individuals whose completion drive works overtime—who suffers from a compulsive "finishmania," if you will, and needs to learn to slam on the brakes. Moderation in all things, after all. You can skip the rest of this chapter, in that case, and get an entirely different kind of help. (Of course, the really compulsive completer won't be *able* to skip the rest of this chapter; once begun, the finish-aholic has to read through to the last page.)

For the vast majority of writers who daily struggle with finishing what they start, don't despair. Force yourself to read on. No, no, don't wander away now and work on that half-completed needlepoint you started three years ago. Stay with me here; there's help for you yet.

WAITING FOR THE OTHER SHOE TO DROP: UNDERSTANDING "CLOSURE"

To a Gestalt psychologist, your drive to finish what you start is more than just good advice from mom. It's a real psychological drive they call "closure." And it's as simple and basic as "waiting for the other shoe to drop." The more you really don't care whether that other shoe drops or not, the more your completion drive needs revving up.

Here's a little exercise that can show you how closure works—and that demonstrates how, even if you're a "finishphobic," your mind still has a natural need to finish things, a need that you can put to work to finish your writing projects. Try sketching a circle, but leave the last little bit of the loop unconnected. Now take another look at your almost-circle. See? Your brain fills in the blank, completing the circle so it almost seems as though that final arc is there after all. Kurt Koffka, a pioneer of Gestalt psychology, explained this trick of perception as the tensions of "imperfectly formed neural patterns . . . leading inevitably to their own completion."

What do "imperfectly formed neural patterns" have to do with getting that story done? Well, put yourself in the place of the composer who (as the story goes) loved to sleep late. To get him out of bed and down to breakfast, the great composer's clever wife would play the first three chords of a series on the piano downstairs. One . . . two . . . three . . . but where was the fourth and final chord? The composer would toss and turn upstairs until finally he could stand it no longer. Downstairs he'd come to finish the chord series and, by the way, to eat breakfast.

Just as closure worked like an alarm clock for this sleepyhead composer, you can program yourself to "wake up" and finish your writing. Learning to use closure can pay dividends beyond finally learning whodunit in a murder mystery or getting your Christmas shopping done before New Year's Day. After all, it doesn't do much good to write fast for three-quarters of a story if the final fraction comes agonizingly slowly, far after deadline, or not at all.

So how do you exercise your "closure" muscles and build the mental biceps it takes to finish fast? We're getting to that. First, though, there's another little psychology lesson.

THE ZEIGARNIK EFFECT AND YOU

The "Zeigarnik Effect" sounds like some high-tech phenomenon, perhaps a gimmick in a science fiction story that enables the noble astronaut to outwit the planet-devouring alien. But it's much more mundane—and useful—than it sounds.

The Zeigarnik Effect is named after a Russian psychological researcher, Bluma Zeigarnik, who discovered it in an experiment conducted in 1927. Zeigarnik's subjects were a group of 138 children, whom she gave a series of simple tasks to perform. With half of the tasks, she let the children work straight through to completion. With the other half, however, Zeigarnik interrupted the children partway through and made them move on to something else. Then she quizzed the children an hour later to see what they recalled of the work they had done. She found that 110 of the 138 children remembered more of the *interrupted* tasks than the completed ones.

Zeigarnik concluded that we tend to forget completed tasks, because the motivation to finish them has been satisfied. Unfinished tasks, however, stay fresher in the memory because the original motivation behind them remains unsatisfied.

So when you're writing a story, it's not just the piles of notes and the image of an angry editor that nags you to finish: The Zeigarnik Effect keeps the memory of your work-in-progress fresh in your mind. Once you've tucked that story into a manila envelope and licked the flap, however, the Zeigarnik Effect lets the memory of that writing task fade into a dim glow of accomplishment.

Or at least that's how it's supposed to work. A writer with a healthy sense of closure and a fully functioning Zeigarnik Effect nagging him ought to zip right through to the final page without a hitch. Indeed, you should hardly be able to stop yourself from finishing!

Alas, countervailing psychological forces sometimes keep your natural completion drive from doing its job. You may think of these counterforces as "writer's block" or just plain laziness or inefficiency. But understanding the *real* causes of your failure to finish is crucial to conquering them and getting your story in the mail.

WHY YOU DON'T FINISH WHAT YOU START

Every writing project has its share of frustrations. The secret to keeping up your pace until the finish line is how you handle these rough spots. "Low frustration tolerance" is what psychologists label the problem of quitting too quickly, of not sticking with a task. Sports stars have a simpler phrase: "No pain, no gain."

Remember all that talk early on about the d-word, *discipline*? You may not like it any better now, but it remains a key to overcoming your low frustration tolerance and seeing your writing projects through to completion. You've got to have the discipline necessary to keep writing even when you hit a roadblock. Instead of getting detoured and distracted — "discomfort dodging," as some psychologists dub this trick of steering clear at the first sign of frustration or difficulty — you've got to stick with it.

Low frustration tolerance, however, isn't the only explanation for failing to finish what you set out to write. Unrealistic expectations, a related foible, can also short-circuit your best intentions. I don't mean simply that you set your sights too high; it's fine to have ambitious goals. But unrealistic expectations can trip you up when you forget about all the steps between the present reality and your dreams. If you don't have the discipline to "pay your dues" en route to the top, you'll have a harder time staying the course.

You can't expect to write the Great American Novel, in other words, the first time you sit down at the keyboard. You can't give up just because your first nonfiction effort doesn't wind up serialized in *The New Yorker*. And that principle holds not only for your writing career but for each writing task you tackle. Having a bunch of ideas isn't enough; you've got to follow through on them. Thinking that ideas, even talent, are enough to make your story succeed — in the absence of plain old hard work — is a classic sign of a noncompleter. Didn't I already say, a few chapters back, that there's no magic wand in this business?

Fear of failure can also lead you to put off finishing what you start. That may sound almost contradictory — failing because you're afraid of failing — but it's a common cause of procrastination. After all, if you never finish anything, your work can hardly be criticized, can it? And there's always the will-o'-the-wisp that if only you fiddle with your story a little while longer, if only you put off finishing it, you can still somehow make it perfect. If a story is done, you have to send it out into the hard light of day that will reveal its flaws. A work forever in progress, however, is a work forever straining for perfection.

You may even fail to complete your writing projects because you're afraid of *success*. Deep down, you may feel that you really don't deserve to succeed as a writer. So you subtly sabotage yourself, shortcircuiting stories before the final chapter. Maybe succeeding as a writer would mean you would quit your day job as an accountant or a public relations executive — a job that, gosh darn it, you actually enjoy.

A fear of completion may even be linked to fear of that ultimate finish, death. Do you know the old superstition that if you complete your life's work, you'll die? Well, finishing a writing project that means a lot to you can seem like a little death.

With all these powerful reasons not to finish what you've started writing, it's perhaps a wonder that anything ever gets written at all. But some lucky souls simply have an equally powerful innate completion drive, pushing them along to the final word. What about the rest of the world, the not-so-lucky and not-so-driven ones? You've just got to build up your mental muscles. Once you begin to grasp why it's often so difficult for you to complete a story (at least in time to meet that deadline!), you can "pump iron" to overcome those obstacles.

FLEXING YOUR FINISHING ABILITIES

Time-management experts are full of suggestions for planning and organizing your working life to increase your odds of finishing what you start. In fact, we've already seen a lot of these ideas as they apply to writing. But conquering your "finishphobia" goes beyond time-management. (For one thing, you're likely to keep procrastinating on all those good time-management ideas, just as with everything else.) The best tactics for turning yourself into a writer who completes his or her work promptly combine traditional time-management with smart psychology.

The basic principle is to train yourself to finish things by helping yourself to finish small tasks, or pieces of tasks. Once you get in the completion habit and see how good it feels, you'll be motivated to finish ever-larger projects. So, if you're a finishphobic, do not, for example, start by tackling a blockbuster novel or a lengthy nonfiction exposé. Write some things—a short story, an op-ed essay, a simple profile—that you have a better chance of seeing to the end.

In other words, develop willpower in small doses. By forcing yourself to complete something, even a small story or "fluff" article, you'll gradually strengthen your inborn completion drive—just as a weight-lifter builds his muscles by repeated use. Each time, try something a little bit longer or tougher, a longer sprint; eventually you'll be writing marathons.

Your initial completion exercises can even be smaller than a whole story. Break your projects down into their component parts, and reward yourself for finishing each section. Did you finish a page? Terrific. Did you make it to the end of the scene? Wonderful. Do it again tomorrow. Pretty soon you'll *really* be done.

Think in terms of a writing *schedule*. How long will each part of the project take you? Don't fool yourself here—it's important, if you're not to fall victim to unrealistic expectations, to develop a realistic sense of how long writing chores really take. If you can break the job down into finite, completable parts, and figure out about how long each part will take you, you can apportion the time between now and the deadline.

Let's say you're writing a 4,000-word article for a magazine, and the editor has given you a month in which to work. You estimate (honestly, now!) that researching and interviewing will take you two weeks. Organizing your notes and getting ready to write, you think, will eat up another week. That leaves you just over a week to write your first draft, polish it and get the manuscript in the mail. To leave a margin for error and for revision, you'll probably have to write about 1,000 words a day once you start at the keyboard. That's not nearly as hard as it sounds: Remember, you've done all the hard work of planning and organizing before you ever write word one.

The same principle applies to longer works. As we saw in the previous chapter, mystery writer William J. Reynolds labored in fits and starts for a couple of years on his first novel, *The Nebraska Quotient*. He'd write a bit one Saturday but not the next and, ultimately, didn't seem to be making much progress toward getting the book done. Then he says he "got serious" about finishing and made himself write every single day for one hour. "An hour was a manageable time," he says, "not so long as to be daunting after a full day at my regular job, so brief that I didn't dare waste any of it sharpening pencils or unhooking paper clips, and yet significant enough that I made real progress if I shoulder-to-wheeled it." An hour at a time, the book marched along to completion—and publication, which launched a whole career as a mystery novelist.

Whatever daily quota you set for yourself, and whether it's weighed in words or minutes, once you've finished (yes, *finished*) what you set out to do for the day, resist the urge to keep on going and gain a little extra ground. Rest on your laurels for today, so that tomorrow you'll have the self-confidence and creative energy to do it again. Successful speedy writers are like the tortoise in the race with the hare: Slow and steady finishes fastest.

Only hares, by the way, think of themselves as "thriving on deadline pressure." Do your editors and yourself a favor and plan to finish your story a little *before* it's due. Scheduling your time otherwise is a plan for failure, and that's exactly what we want to avoid here. You're seeking to build a sense of success—so give yourself a little leeway in which to succeed.

Another way in which you should give yourself a little leeway is your own attention span: Work *with* it rather than against it. When I was a newspaper columnist and really had to crank out copy, the newspaper would keep a big pot of coffee—free!—down the hall in the cafeteria. Whenever I felt my attention begin to wander as I wrote, or reached a point where I knew the story would benefit from a few moments' extra cogitating on my part, I'd get up from my computer and wander down the hall. I'd get a cup of coffee. I'd slowly walk back to my desk. And by the time I sat down again I'd be ready to work some more.

You don't have to single-handedly support Juan Valdez and his family, of course. When your attention wanes, you could hop up and walk around the house, do a couple of push-ups, jump up and down, try some isometrics or go and get a glass of water. It was the stroll, really, rather than the free coffee that made my trips to the cafeteria a handy break.

The key, however, is to limit your interruptions—allow them, since you're only human, but keep them in check. Some people, when their attention begins to wander during a writing stint, let themselves get so distracted that they never come back to the keyboard. If your "coffee break" turns into a couple of hours of puttering around the house or watching the Game of the Week, you'll never finish your writing chores. Conversely, if you force yourself to sit at the keyboard for hours without a brief respite, you'll soon turn your writing into drudgery. Don't fight that limited human attention span; fool it.

Think of this working pattern in terms of simple mathematics: If your attention span is about fifteen minutes and you take a one-minute minibreak whenever you start to flag, in an hour you'll squeeze in fifty-six minutes of work and "waste" just four minutes. Those four minutes represent a worthwhile investment in keeping fresh.

Finally, to finish what you start to write it's important to keep your goal in mind. Keep reminding yourself what you're trying to accomplish: a lively article, a moving short story, an amusing screenplay, a mystery novel that will keep the world on the edge of its collective chair. This is a principle that applies to almost any human endeavor, from writing to sports. When Billy Jean King was turning the tennis world topsy-turvy, for instance, she would spend twenty minutes several times each week just staring at a tennis ball. That odd-sounding exercise, she said, helped her build her concentration for the game situations when she had to keep her eye on the ball.

It sometimes helps, between writing sessions, to read prime examples of what you're seeking to write. Keep the rhythms of good writing going through your brain. If you're writing humor, keep P.G. Wodehouse or Robert Benchley by your bed at night. If you're trying to finish a nonfiction piece, read some John McPhee or Tom Wolfe or Barry Lopez. The point isn't to subtly plagiarize successful writers, or even to inspire a pastiche, but rather to remind yourself of where you're headed and to keep on that track.

Learn to keep your eye on the ball. You'll find it helps along the way to game . . . set . . . and match.

RECOGNIZING THE FINISH LINE

It sounds ridiculous to suggest that sometimes writers *don't know* when they're done with a story. But, in fact, one of the greatest hurdles to completing what you start to write is simply recognizing the finish line. In writing, unlike more linear and straightforward endeavors, there's no signal that says, "That's it. You're done. Finito. Hang it up." Golfers play eighteen holes and — aha! — there's the clubhouse, beckoning with a tall cold one. Lawyers work until the case goes to the jury. Plumbers labor till the sink is fixed. But writers must write until the story is finished, which is exactly — when? How do you know the last page is the last page?

This is yet another reason your earlier stages of focusing, planning, organizing and outlining are so important. Without a road map, how will you know when you get there?

Focusing your story clarifies your goals. What is this story really about? (If you don't know, how do you know whether you've completed telling it?) You can't start off with some amorphous, unfocused goal — "I'd like to write a story about Hollywood" — and expect to recognize when or whether you've achieved it. Are you setting out to write a 3,000-word movie-star bio for a women's magazine? A book-length exposé of Hollywood deal-making? Or a latter-day *The Last Tycoon*? Not only will your writing route be different depending on your answer; so will your destination.

Planning and *organizing* your story will flow from your choice of focus. Once you decide where you're going, your plan will tell you how to get there — and will provide the basics of a signal that you've arrived.

Outlining your story, as we've already seen, gives you that road map from your lead to your boffo conclusion. Your outline should be pretty specific about your conclusion, even if (as is often the case with fiction) it's sometimes foggy about the exact steps along the way. Your actual closing words may even be pencilled in right on your outline, which makes the finish line pretty hard to miss. For my story on computerized business simulation games for *Databar*, the lead of which we talked about back in chapter eight, I concluded my outline with:

i.e. see aggressive customer . . . just ltd by imag, he sez (16)
hard to remember — it's only a game

In the actual copy, drawing upon a quote I'd carefully flagged on page 16 of my notes, that became:

"The real power of videodiscs is in simulation and scenarios," says Cavagnol. "Say you're teaching somebody proper sales technique. You confront him with an aggressive customer on the videodisc. Okay, here's the situation: How does he handle it? He can immediately see the feedback of making a particular choice. In management training, this could be very powerful. It's one of the most powerful delivery mediums we have. It's just limited by your imagination."

As you imagine simulated sales calls, market-share wars on videodisc and computer mock-ups that do everything but give winners a raise, try to remember: It's only a game.

That's not notably brilliant or witty, but it did let me close the story. And, of course, I knew when I reached it in my outline that I was indeed done. No more blathering on for several thousand words, wondering if I'd covered all the bases. I had. It was done. Polish it up and pop it in the mail.

Your outlining may, as we've already discussed in the chapter on leads, bring you full-circle at the finish line, so your conclusion springs from your opening. That's a good way to give not only you, the writer, but also the reader a satisfying sense of *closure*. It's no accident that the brain naturally jumps to complete an almost-closed circle: We like circles, and stories, to finish that way.

In any case, your conclusion has to somehow come out of the fundamental focus of your story — to grow out of what's gone before, rather than being artificially grafted on it. The Greeks got away with *deux ex machina* — literally, "god out of a machine" endings, in which Zeus or Hera or somebody equally divine would magically appear and resolve everything that had seemed unresolvable. But today's toga-less audiences won't sit still for such trickery. A kindly uncle, never before alluded to, cannot suddenly show up on your hero's doorstep and pay off all those crushing debts. A secret message from the Kremlin, utterly unprepared for in previous chapters, cannot instantly call off what seemed to be the brink of World War III. And your heroine cannot wake up to discover, on the last page, that "It was all just a dream."

What this means is that your ending will be only as good as the rest of your story. "What's wrong with my third act?" an aspiring playwright once asked George S. Kaufmann. To which Kaufmann archly replied, "Your first." The ending must deliver on the promises made to the reader in the body of your story. As you outline, you must find the ending that your focus demands, mark it down and then write until you get there.

Two other, perhaps obvious, points should be made about knowing the finish line when you come to it. The first is the importance of learning to meet deadlines. Editors will put up with a lot from writers, but not even the most sainted editor will long tolerate a writer who consistently turns his copy in late. For the writer of whatever stripe, the deadline must represent the ultimate finish line: Your challenge is not only to bring all of a story's component parts and complications into a coherent whole, but to do so within a given time frame.

Most deadlines are missed because the writer either underestimates the time a task will take (a variant of our old friend, unrealistic expectations) or, almost conversely, overinflates the time spent on a story (a close relative of that familiar bugaboo, perfectionism). To ward off the first, you've got to learn to gauge your own working habits and speed in relation to common writing assignments. It sounds compulsive, but it's actually not a bad idea to time yourself a few times when writing a chunk of something you regularly tackle (that is, if you're normally a screenplay writer, time yourself in a screenplay-writing session—not an odd excursion into humorous essays). How long does it take you to write 1,000 words . . . or five pages of screenplay . . . or some other convenient unit of writing? You'll also need to be able to estimate your prewriting time—researching, interviewing, outlining—to add it all up and get a realistic guess at how long a typical project takes you. If you discover that, from preliminary research to final draft, a 3,500-word magazine profile takes you three weeks of solid work (woven around the rest of your life), don't wait until a week before the deadline to start!

Overinflating the time spent on a story typically comes from, if you will, writing *Moby Dick* when the task is a 2,500-word essay on whales. While you should always do your best on every story—the mark of a true professional—you should never waste time on overkill. If an editor expects you to talk to every single astronomer in America for a story on black holes, he'll probably make that clear; otherwise, a half-dozen astronomers are likely enough. If an editor wants a light, breezy piece on meter maids, don't turn it into a book-length investigative treatise, the last word on our women in uniform.

I've known too many writers who, faced with an assignment they could easily complete on time and to the editor's full satisfaction, make the job bigger than it has to be. Losing their focus, they let the story control them instead of the other way around. "Gee, this is an interesting sidelight," they'll say—signaling a month-long detour into what is, however interesting, still a *sidelight*. I once asked a writer to survey the city's health-care scene as part of a special "city guide" issue. Cover the basics, I said: hospitals, finding a doctor and dentist, maybe how to find a pharmacy open on holidays. Seizing on this last suggestion, the writer proceeded to call every pharmacy in the metropolitan area and burden me with a 50-page chart of drugstores. Not only was the story delivered after the deadline; it was more work than either the writer or I had bargained on.

This tendency to inflate stories beyond their focus leads me to the second point (a bonus to all of you who still remember that I owed you a second point!) about recognizing the finish line: writing to fit. We've already talked a little about the challenge of making your story fit its "box," but it's a subject that also relates to finish lines. Many writers pooh-pooh the importance of writing to fit; typically, these are writers who've never been editors. If your story must fit on four magazine pages, or in a sixty-minute (minus commercials) TV segment, no amount of artistry on your part will make more copy magically fit on those pages or more minutes squeeze into an hour. "I wrote it long, figuring you could cut what you didn't like," a writer will often say when submitting an overlong manuscript. To editors, however, that translates into, "I was too lazy/disorganized to be selective myself, so you have to do the hard work for me."

Writing to length is an integral part of recognizing the finish line. As you see your length limit approach, you must be ever more vigilant about what you allow into your story. Count words and pages every step of the way, just as you'd watch the gas gauge on a long trip. Apportion your allotted words throughout your story, so you don't spend most of them on the first half of your material and then have to both short shrift the second half and cut copy from the first.

And if you've reached the end of your outline and used up your word count, apply one of the great secrets of speedy writing: Stop!

CHAPTER TWELVE

BEING YOUR OWN EDITOR

• • •

THE POINT OF DIMINISHING RETURNS

By now you've learned enough about efficient writing to appreciate the trouble and the truth inherent in the old saying, "No work of art is ever finished; it is only abandoned." Letting go of a story, pulling the plug on the potentially endless process of writing and rewriting, can be the hardest part of the creative process for many people. As science and science fiction writer Arthur C. Clarke once put it, "Sometimes it is as hard to *stop* work on a piece as it was to start in the first place. . . . You must learn to recognize the point of diminishing returns, and send your 99.99 percent completed masterpiece out into the cruel hard world."

Literature is full of authors who had a hard time recognizing that point of diminishing returns, and there's no telling how many masterpieces we've been deprived of as a result. How many more great novels might Thomas Wolfe have written if he could have mastered the work of revision? As he wrote to his editor, Maxwell Perkins, "Revision is simply hell for me. My efforts to cut 50,000 words may sometimes result in my adding 75,000." In the phrase of his contemporary, F. Scott Fitzgerald, Wolfe was "a putter-inner." He kept putting more into his books, taking more out, then putting more back in again. Wolfe no doubt put in and took out enough to make several good-sized novels.

Even Ernest Hemingway, known for his ability to "go for the kill" as a hunter, had a hard time finishing some of his novels. He rewrote the last page of *A Farewell to Arms*, it's said, nearly forty times.

The modern record for compulsive revision, though, has to be held by Harold Brodkey. His novel originally titled *A Party of Animals* was contracted in 1960 but didn't materialize until 1991, several zillion revisions and a new title later. Brodkey, according to his publisher (which at one point, eighteen years into the process, gave up on him, only to pick the novel up again a few years later), would change his thinking, axe a chapter, add several more—until "the novel became sort of a life in progress."

OK, OK, so you get the point already. At some juncture, the time-conscious writer needs to recognize that enough's enough and it's time to move on to the next project. But you also know all too well that there's nothing more time-wasting than sending a story to an editor too soon, only to have it bounced back to you for a lengthy revision session. "Do it right the first time" was good advice when your mom first shared it with you; it still is. So the writer's inevitable dilemma is how to minimize the time spent revising, while still "touching all the bases" and producing a manuscript that meets the most exacting standards.

Tackling that dilemma is what this chapter is all about.

FIRST AND LAST DRAFTS

If you've ever sat around listening to writers talk about their work, and stayed awake long enough to remember any of the conversation, you probably heard some sort of exchange along the lines of, "How many drafts do you do?" Some writers take pride in the vast number of versions of the same story that they churn out on the road to supposed perfection. It's tempting to crack that there's a name for such folks—"unpublished writers." But of course there are all too many published writers who fall into that time-wasting trap as well. Jerzy Kosinski, for example, would do more than a dozen drafts of his novels. (Even that wasn't enough tinkering for him, though: To the dismay of his publishers, Kosinski would rewrite the typeset galleys a couple of times—and then rewrite again when he got the page proofs.)

So how many drafts *should* you do? Assuming you've been paying attention to the previous chapters, you know by now that, if you're properly prepared, your first draft can be pretty close to your last draft. You should always go through it at least once more, for a light polish. On really big or complicated stories, it couldn't hurt to revise a little harder on the second run-through, then add a third, light polishing draft. (If this is starting to sound too much like a car wash and wax, console yourself by remembering how rapidly cars move through one of those gadgets!) How many drafts should you do? Let's say no more than three.

But though that's as good an answer as any, it's not really the right question. Revising the right way isn't about counting drafts. Better to ask *when* in the process you should revise, and *how much*.

Although you might want to change a word here or there, fix a typo or adjust a comma if you read through what you've written the day before, to recapture your writing momentum, that doesn't really count as another draft or as genuine revision. For your first serious look at what you've written, I'm of the school that advises waiting until you get all the way to the end. For one thing, you may stumble over some problem in chapter ten that requires that you fix something way back in chapter three. (If you've seen the movie *Bill and Ted's Excellent Adventure*, you might recall how those time-traveling teens must keep reminding themselves to go back — later — to a point earlier in time and "plant" a way out of their present jam.) Best in that case to go all the way through to the end and know everything that needs doing in chapter three before you spend time revising it; otherwise you might have to fix it more than once. For another, interrupting the forward progress of your story to tinker with what you've already written is asking for completion-drive trouble. Once you start looking backward instead of forward, the temptation to endlessly revise instead of finishing what you've started can be irresistible.

How much should you revise? While every writer and every story will be different, as a general rule it's better to err on the side of restraint. Don't forget that you wrote your first draft (after careful preparation!) at the peak of your writing momentum and emotional involvement with the subject. Here is probably when you were speaking most "truly" as a writer. When you revise, that creative drive is history. You're thinking more dully and routinely; if you're overzealous, you might revise your story's emotional vigor, freshness and originality right into oblivion.

Over-revising can put overworked prose in place of the freshness of your first draft. Rewriting — as opposed to careful self-editing — can lead to precious writing that smacks of a thesaurus overdose. If you find yourself thinking, "What more colorful or unusual adjective could I use here instead? — you're revising too much. If you start replacing every instance of "he said" or "she said" with "he ejaculated" or "she tittered," try a walk around the block. Then get that story in the mail before it's too late!

A further peril of relying too much on revising and rewriting is becoming *too* familiar with your own material. Soon you know your story so well that you lose perspective. You can no longer tell what the reader needs to know. You cease being able to judge what will interest a reader who, unlike you, comes to the material fresh. At some point, even the most skillful writer loses touch with what ought to stay and what ought to be cut; it's all the same to him.

Some writers grapple with this challenge of perspective by what's been called the "refrigerator" system: They put a completed first draft in the refrigerator — or, more likely, a bottom drawer — to "cool" for several weeks or even months. This sounds promising, but you can never really attain the complete objectivity of someone — like an editor — seeing your story for the first time. And putting a story in the "fridge" too long can cause you to lose all your original creative drive, and even your interest. How many stories have languished indefinitely in the metaphorical refrigerator, wilting like old lettuce?

HOW TO THINK LIKE AN EDITOR

Part I: The Big Picture

To avoid having your manuscript bounced back to you for time-consuming reworking — as well as to minimize the time and maximize the return of your own, presubmission revising — learn to think like an editor. If you've never been an editor, don't worry: You can train yourself to look at your own story through an editor's eyes.

To start thinking like an editor, you might begin by having some sympathy for this misunderstood and underappreciated breed. Whether the editor is laboring at a small community newspaper or following in Maxwell Perkins's pencil marks at a big Manhattan publishing house, chances are he or she faces a similar set of problems: too much work, too much copy, too little time. To survive, to keep from being buried by the relentless march of deadlines, successful editors develop certain habits and thought patterns that enable them to get the most out of the time they spend on each manuscript.

Your own goal in efficient revision is pretty much the same. If you imagine that you're a harried editor in a cramped, manuscript-strewn office, besieged on the one hand by writers and on the other by designers eager to get stories into production, you'll be in the right frame of mind to tackle your own copy. Under those circumstances, you're unlikely to suddenly decide to rewrite the whole thing, weaving in a theme you'd never thought of before. But you're also unlikely to overlook any really important glitches — because you don't want to be back at square one a month from now, going through this all over again.

Most editors look at copy from two different perspectives, each with its own informal, usually unwritten checklist. First they consider the big picture: Does the story hang together? Does it make sense? As you read over your first draft with an editor's eye, here are some of the big-picture questions to ask yourself:

• Does the lead grab readers' attention and flow smoothly into the body of the story? Editors are obsessed with leads, and good editors rarely let a bad lead slip past. All too aware of how busy and fickle readers are these days, editors also know the lead is the key opportunity—maybe the only opportunity—to "sell" the story to a potential reader. Don't forget that your lead may in turn be your only chance to "sell" an editor: Many editors, confronted with a mountain of "slush pile" manuscripts, understandably read only the leads—unless something grabs them and makes them keep reading.

• Does your story immediately follow-up the lead with some kind of "hook" that makes clear what this story is all about and why anybody should keep reading? Particularly in nonfiction, if your story lacks this essential "nut graf" or "cosmic graf," you and it are in trouble. Beat the editor to the punch and fix it now.

• Is your story organized? Does it flow logically from point to point or scene to scene, with all the appropriate material grouped together in each point or scene? Try thinking in subheads, and make sure that what follows each possible subhead belongs there. Remember the editor with the scissors and tape, or the modern-day word processor. Editors are more likely than anybody—writers and readers included—to be finicky about organization, because their ultimate goal is clarity of communication. Of course, that should be *your* goal, too.

• Are your transitions smooth and seemingly effortless? Check each jump in your story line to make sure the narrative flows over it without a lurch. Sometimes, though, you get stuck on a transition that simply can't be done without seeming awkward or forced. (Remember those ludicrous segues on the old "Wild Kingdom" TV show? "A python with a stranglehold like the one that snake has on Jim can squeeze the life out of a human in five seconds. If you feel financial worries getting a stranglehold on you, Mutual of Omaha. . . .") In that case, rather than rewriting the entire story to fix the underlying problem, consider the editor's favorite last resort: Simply leave an extra line of space. Voilá! Instant transition.

• Are there chunks of your story that seem to belong in another story? Root out these prose detours. If you're writing an article, consider chopping out these chunks and transplanting them as sidebars.

• Are there unanswered questions? This is particularly important in revising fiction. Suspense novelist Phyllis Whitney, for instance, once said that whenever she rereads one of her pages, she notes questions that must be answered in subsequent chapters. If those questions aren't resolved, the whole plot chain breaks and the reader is left miffed and frustrated. But answering the questions that your story raises is important for nonfiction, too. As you read over your first draft, look for gaps and holes; then plug them.

Part II: God Is in the Details

Editors in general and copyeditors in particular empathize with an often-quoted axiom of architect Mies Van de Rohe: "God is in the details." You may think that paragraphing, sentence structure, careless word choices, misspellings and grammatical lapses are just "picky details," but your editors won't. That's the second "lens," if you will, through which they examine a manuscript.

Again, though, it's possible to get bogged down endlessly in honing the fine points of your manuscript. You can spend hours debating whether you should use "compose" or "comprise" (or maybe "constitute"?) in a sentence. You could go over your manuscript a dozen times, on each pass trying to eradicate a different compositional or grammatical sin.

Obviously, editors don't have the time to tackle a manuscript this way, any more than you do. They've got three more manuscripts teetering atop their "IN" box, a dozen phone calls to return, six meetings to go to and a nasty stack of galleys to proof. Yet, at the same time, they must get each chunk of copy as close to perfection as they can. How do they do it?

They've got a system, written or (more likely) unwritten. From experience, most editors develop a mental checklist of points they watch for in all manuscripts — "pet peeves" might be a less-charitable way to describe it. Each sentence, each paragraph, gets scanned with this checklist in mind. Sure, a few things that are so uncommon they're not on the list might slip through — though their sheer oddity is likely to call attention to them. Once an editor has run a manuscript through his checklist, he can pass it on secure in the knowledge that he's made it 95 percent perfect.

If you, as a writer, can learn to revise your manuscripts to the point where, from an editor's point of view, they arrive 95 percent perfect, you'll get more work than you can handle even with your new, speeded-up writing habits. (You should see some of the dreck that crosses editors' desks in the guise of a manuscript!) And of course it is not only possible but relatively easy, given a little discipline, to achieve that state of manuscript near-nirvana. All you need to do is start thinking like an editor. All you need is your own mental checklist, and the willpower to apply it.

Every editor has his own checklist — or "pet peeves," if you must — but all are pretty similar when it comes to the basics. (You'll notice that some of my checklist points, below, are already familiar from cautionary notes in previous chapters. See? There's not so much to learn; the key is consistency in application.) Below are some basics to get you started on speedy revision. We'll start with a few broader things to watch out for—how paragraphs are put together, how sentences follow one another—and then move into a closer inspection of individual phrases and words. Whether consciously or not, that's how most editors approach their task: *Does the paragraph hold together? How's the sentence rhythm? Any unnecessary words I should cut? OK, next paragraph.*

• **Paragraph breaks.** Check each time you begin a new paragraph to make certain the break is logical and (the heck with logic!) that it helps to keep the reader reading. While you needn't be a slave to grammar school notions of topic sentences, each paragraph should have some clear reason for being and for being a distinct unit. See if the two strongest sentences in each paragraph are the first and the last—where they carry the most weight with readers; if not, maybe your paragraphing needs reshuffling. Paragraphs must also march the story along: If you have a lot of long paragraphs in succession, maybe you need a shorter one for a change of pace.

• **Sentence rhythm.** Watch out for short sentences. Watch out for long sentences. Consider your use of clauses. Is there a sameness like this? As you revise, you should try to "hear" your sentences in your head, almost like music. Powerful prose contains a powerful rhythm within it, a variation of short and long, simple sentences and complex ones, just as great music waxes and wanes, races and slows. Listen to the music of your writing without regard to the actual words: Does it go *dum-dum-dum* or *di-dum/di-dum/di-dum*? Or does it achieve a more elegant and interesting rhythm, a *di-dum/dum/di-dum-di-dum/dum*? Read great writers until the sound of their writing fills your head, then create your own symphony of sentences.

• **Passive voice.** A symptom of our bureaucratic, responsibility-avoiding society, passive voice runs rampant in feeble writing: "Thousand-dollar toilets were purchased by the department . . ." instead of "The department bought thousand-dollar toilets." "Cost overruns were incurred by this office . . ." instead of "This office spent too much." "Civilian casualties were created by pilot error . . ." instead of "Pilots mistakenly killed civilians."

As you scan your own sentences, watch for that telltale "object . . . were + past tense verb . . . by . . . subject" construction. Question every sentence that has something being done *by* somebody. Shouldn't the somebody come first, as in: "subject . . . action verb . . . object"? Instead of "The ball was hit by the girl," write "The girl hit the ball."

Not every instance of passive voice must be hunted down and destroyed. (The nitpickers among you, I know, are already combing through this book from chapter one on to find passive-voice examples of not practicing what I preach. Cut it out!) But if a manuscript is turned in by you that seems to be all effects, no causes, soon the editor's patience will be exhausted by you. (Now go back and revise that last, flat sentence to: "But if you turn in a manuscript that seems to be all effects, no causes, soon you'll exhaust the editor's patience.")

• **Backwards sentences.** A close kin of passive voice, backwards sentences likewise shun the powerful "subject-verb-object" sentence structure that makes your prose run like a locomotive. Critiquing the stilted "Time-ese" of Henry Luce's *Time*, *Life* and *Fortune* magazines of the 1950s, Wolcott Gibbs wrote, "Backward ran sentences until reeled the mind." (And he wrapped up his critique with the equally arch, "Where it will all end, knows God!") Scout your stories for similarly convoluted prose. Ask yourself, "Does this sound natural? If I were telling this story to a friend, is this how I would say it?" If the answers are *no*, forwards turn your sentences so convoluted they will not be.

• **Present participles.** Yet another way of avoiding direct writing, present participle-itis, isn't as grammatically fancy as it sounds. It's simply the padding out of otherwise straightforward verbs: "The car was driving over the bridge" instead of "The car drove over the bridge." "He was running the bases" instead of "He ran the bases." Unless you've got a good reason for using the present participle — "He was running the bases when the ball hit him" — avoid it.

• **Wimpy verbs.** If you've noticed that verbs dominate this checklist so far, good — you're catching on. Verbs are the fuel of the English language. You could toss all your adjectives in the trash and still be able to say something, but without verbs you have no writing, only collections of words. Verbs make things happen. That's why it's crucial to use the strongest, most concrete verbs you can summon up. When you revise, watch out (as I've already preached) for sentences that begin with "There is . . ." — a sure sign of wimpy verb use. But also seek out and revise sentences that use mushy, nonspecific verbs: "She showed unhappiness" instead of "She sobbed," "The plane abruptly descended" instead of "The plane crashed." Check whether your verbs are hidden in a thicket of excess words: "have a need for" instead of "need"; "make a requirement for" in place of "require."

Warning bells should go off when you come upon words like "take," "have," and "make" clogging up your verbs.

(Speaking of verbs, make sure your tenses match throughout. Few things drive editors crazier faster than stories that begin in the present tense and then slide into the past, or vice versa. A tip-off for trouble can be found in your labeling of quotations: See if you start off with "he says" and then somewhere switch to "he said.")

• **Other vague writing.** Weak writing doesn't infect only verbs, of course; it's a plague on all aspects of prose. As Strunk and White advise so succinctly in *The Elements of Style*, "Prefer the specific to the general, the definite to the vague, the concrete to the abstract." As you check over your first draft, look for instances where you say nothing instead of something, where you write around a subject instead of through it. If you catch yourself sounding like a bureaucrat or one of those overwrought academics sometimes dubbed "educationists," pare your prose back to the essentials.

To illustrate how much more powerful are the specific and definite than the general and vague, Strunk and White cite an experiment by George Orwell, who rewrote this passage from Ecclesiastes in the King James Bible: "I returned, and saw under the sun, that the race is not to the swift, nor the battle to the strong, neither yet bread to the wise, nor yet riches to men of understanding, nor yet favor to men of skill; but time and chance happeneth to them all." Here's Orwell's bloodless translation of that passage: "Objective consideration of contemporary phenomena compels the conclusion that success or failure in competitive activities exhibits no tendency to be commensurate with innate capacity, but that a considerable element of the unpredictable must inevitably be taken into account." Get the point?

• **Avoid clichés like the plague.** Some of what might be called "clichés" will inevitably sneak into your prose, since after all what makes a phrase a cliché is its common use — even in the prose of careful writers. In revising, you need not chop or change every single phrase that sounds familiar; too much of that approach will make your writing sound like it's written by a Martian or a machine, alien to American idiom. You can even brighten up your writing with deliberate clever turns on familiar phrases. But do watch out for the easy, lazy use of clichés where a fresher phrase could do more. Don't let clichés substitute for specifics or familiar phrases squeeze out original thinking. "The scene at the gallery was as colorful as a rainbow" tells the reader nothing more than that it was, well, colorful. But if you replace the cliché with a simile suited to the occasion, you can paint both a more vivid picture and increase the thematic unity of your writing: "The scene at the gallery was as colorful as a Jackson Pollock painting" (suggesting both color and a busy, buzzing scene).

• **Mixed metaphors.** And scrambled similes and metaphors that just plain go on too long, for that matter. Study those "Block That Metaphor!" items that sometimes appear in tiny type at the end of stories in *The New Yorker* for a sense of what *not* to do in your own writing. If, in revising your stories, you run across phrases like "As captain of the corporate ship, the CEO has to get his team across the goal line and into the end zone while dodging the tomatoes and brickbats so often hurled by the 'audience' of investors," a screaming red danger signal ought to go off. One metaphor or simile per sentence, please, and don't stretch any metaphorical structure so long that it collapses into silliness.

• **Excess verbiage.** Oops! Make that just plain "verbiage." If you paid attention when I harped on "lard words," you should already be on the alert for the extraneous words that weigh down your writing. Again quoting Strunk and White: "A sentence should contain no unnecessary words, a paragraph no unnecessary sentences, for the same reason that a drawing should have no unnecessary lines and a machine no unnecessary parts." In addition to the wasteful words warned about above, you should be on the lookout for:

1. *Overloaded adjectives* — Be wary of nonspecific, content-free adjectives. If you can eliminate an adjective without any loss of information, do so: "The beautiful sunset filled the sky with reds, pinks and purples" works just as well without the self-evident and nonspecific "beautiful." Keep in mind the "nice" test: Adjectives like "nice" (or "interesting" or "meaningful") add nothing to your writing; if you can't say something more specific than "nice," don't say anything at all. Also keep an eye out for adjectives trying to do the work of verbs. If an adjective can be replaced with a verb, by switching the sentence around, try it: "The intense sunlight was painful" can become "The sunlight hurt my eyes," losing two adjectives and no information.

2. *Adverbs* — Reading most writing these days, you'd be tempted to conclude that English would be better off without adverbs. See? I could have written, "better off without adverbs entirely," but what would I have gained? Look out for adverbs that are empty intensifiers: "very," "extremely," "especially," "particularly," "totally," "absolutely," "unusually" and their meaningless ilk. Ditto for wishy-washy qualifying adverbs: "ordinarily," "generally," "fairly," "rather," "somewhat."

When revising dialogue, check for spots where you gave in to the temptation to tack an adverb onto every "said": "he said eagerly," "she said lustily," "he added forlornly."

3. *Redundancies and tautologies* — Don't repeat yourself unnecessarily by saying the same thing twice without cause. (Now try taking the redundancies out of *that* sentence!) Warning flags to watch for when revising include adjectives that duplicate the meaning of the nouns they're attached to ("old antiques," "new innovations," "noisy cacophony," "excess verbiage") and words followed by synonyms ("each and every," "separate and distinct," "wild and unruly").

4. *Circumlocutions* — Don't use a wagonload of words when one will do. When revising, watch out for mouthfuls like "at this point in time" ("now"), "in advance of" ("before"), "in the event of" ("if"), and "as to whether" ("whether").

If you've made it this far, successfully juggling the big picture and the details as you revise your first draft, you're almost home. You've almost succeeded in "thinking like an editor" and giving your manuscript the quick polish it needs. Now there's just that little matter I mentioned before, those additional "details" of grammar, punctuation and spelling. But that's a section unto itself. . . .

FEAR OF GRAMMAR, PUNCTUATION AND SPELLING

Ridiculous as it sounds, many writers can't spell. Others don't know — or care about — the essentials of grammar and punctuation. Often they even build up a phobia about these "details," to the point where they can't cope with this fundamental aspect of revision. You don't need to panic, however, when confronted with grammar quandaries or spelling mysteries; all it takes is a willingness to look things up and an efficient approach to doing so.

Admitting your ignorance, as Socrates once observed, is the first step toward knowledge. So don't try to bluff your way through grammar, punctuation and spelling. Keep a handful of essential reference works at your side when you're revising and consult them whenever you're in doubt. You can also speed up this process by recognizing some common trouble spots and committing their solutions to memory.

Ready for the world's quickest course in English grammar, punctuation and spelling? Here goes:

• **Grammar and usage.** The single best reference for sticky points of grammar and usage is Roy Copperud's *American Usage and Style: The Consensus*, cited back in the chapter on research and reference books. Add to that the slim but invaluable *The Elements of Style*, often referred to as "Strunk and White," and a standard stylebook (I recommend either the *New York Times* or the AP style manuals), and you can look up almost anything that stumps you. Any question you can't settle by checking one of these books is probably too obscure to worry about; leave it for the editor.

While English usage has a zillion twists and tricks, if you can keep a few quick-and-dirty rules in mind, you'll save a lot of time looking up answers to the most common quandaries. Here's one editor's top ten grammar and usage traps to watch for in revising your writing:

1. *Among vs. between* — Use "among" for more than two, "between" for two.
2. *Compose vs. comprise* — The whole "comprises" the parts; the parts "compose" (or "constitute") the whole.
3. *Farther vs. further* — "Farther" refers to actual, measurable distance — yards and miles; otherwise, use "further."
4. *However* — Avoid using at the beginning of a sentence.
5. *Importantly* — Instead of "most importantly" or "more importantly," write "most important" or "more important." Ditto for "first" instead of "firstly," and so on.
6. *It's vs. Its* — "It's" means "it is." The possessive is "its."
7. *Less vs. fewer* — "Less" refers to quantity, "fewer" to number. If you can count them, use "fewer."
8. *Literally* — Don't use "literally" in combination with a metaphor, since it means that something is actually the case. "He ate so much that he was literally bursting" means that the poor fellow was coming apart at the seams and spilling his entrails into the dining room.
9. *Unique* — Never modify "unique" with an adverb, as in "very unique" or "somewhat unique." "Unique" means "one-of-a-kind," and is not a synonym for "unusual."
10. *Which vs. that* — If the sentence would make sense without the clause, use a comma and introduce it with "which." Otherwise, omit the comma and opt for "that."

• **Punctuation.** The above-mentioned references will also address your punctuation woes; most good dictionaries also include a quick reference to punctuation. Some issues of punctuation (commas before "and" in a series or the niceties of plural possessives, for example) are more matters of editorial style than right or wrong, so don't sweat them too much. Just try to be consistent (a style manual, such as the *Times* or AP books, will help here).

The punctuation problems that give editors fits are actually relatively few and simple:

1. *Commas vs. semicolons* — If you could substitute a period and have two sentences, use a semicolon; otherwise, opt for the comma.
2. *Exclamation points* — Use with discretion! Don't make everything an exclamation!
3. *Hyphens* — Topic number one for editorial catfights. In general, hyphenate compound adjectives if the hyphen aids clarity. Omit the hyphen after "ly" adverbs ("solidly built").
4. *Quotation marks* — Commas and periods go inside quotation marks; semicolons and colons go outside. Question marks go outside unless the quotation is a question (*What do you mean by "rewrite this"?* vs. *How long should the story be?" he asked.*)

• **Spelling.** This is the easiest one, of course, yet somehow the aspect of writing that gives more folks the heebie-jeebies. Get a dictionary and look it up, for gosh sakes, the way I just looked up "heebie-jeebies." Keep a hand-sized, abridged dictionary close enough to consult without getting up from your chair. You'll also want an unabridged dictionary somewhere in your office or work area, to check more obscure or technical terms. Specialized dictionaries are a must as well if you often write about some technical field, such as medicine, law or science.

If you write on a computer, you should also get a spell-checking program. (Many word processing programs now have spell-checkers built in.) These are most useful for catching simple typos and mental slips. But don't forget that if your misspelling accidentally spells some other word, the computer won't catch it. That's why it's safest to use the spell-checker as a last resort, running it right before you print out a story to catch any errors you've missed as well as any new ones you may have created in revising. Don't rely on it as your only spelling tool.

THE GRAMMAR TRAP

Having laid it on pretty thick about put-upon editors and the divinity of details, I'd like to add a quick cautionary note. Don't let concern over the details of grammar and usage and the like become an obsession. Here's yet another trap for the time-pressed writer: You might end up becoming a darn good copyeditor, but never get anything written. Get it right. Be careful. But rely on the sort of systematic approach I've laid out in this chapter to get your revising done without letting the quest for correctness erode your efficiency.

Proper writing, as important as it is, can also be a breeding ground for pedantry. A glance through *American Usage and Style: The Consensus* will reassure you that many of the "errors" your grade school teachers browbeat you about aren't worth worrying about. Don't lose sleep, for example, over split infinitives or sentences that end in prepositions. Allow yourself to begin occasional sentences with "But" or (more sparingly) "And." Sentence fragments can be a powerful device. When used in moderation. Not overdone. Like this.

Make the language work for you. It's a wonderful, versatile thing, this language of ours. Learn to get the most out of it.

WHEN THE EDITOR CALLS

OK, you've written a solid first draft and polished it to (what seems to you) 95 percent perfect. What do you do when the editor calls and says, gee, he or she doesn't think your story is so perfect. Just when you thought it was safe to move on to your next writing project, the (blankety-blank) editor wants you to do some more revising.

Go ahead (after you say, "Sure, no problem," through gritted teeth and carefully set the phone down instead of hurling it across the room), rant and rave about tyrannical, stupid, insensitive editors who wouldn't know great writing if it bit them on the nose. Take a deep breath. Then go back to your desk and *do exactly what the editor wants — but no more.*

Leaving aside whether the editor is right or a demented idiot who should switch to a more suitable line of work, like operating a jackhammer, the editor is the one you've got to satisfy to get your work into print. Unless you have the clout of a Norman Mailer and can storm off in a huff to a new publisher, it's best to play ball.

In fact, it's best to pay close attention to what the editor asks you to do. Take notes on your phone conversation. If the editor sends your manuscript back, with notes or a separate letter, resist the urge to tear it into teensy pieces. Follow the editor's instructions as precisely and literally as possible: If the editor wants more of X but less of Y, give him more X and less Y.

Ah, but resist the temptation to also take this second chance to fiddle around with Z! Don't waste time and court trouble by spinning out a whole new draft if you don't have to, or by changing things the editor didn't mention. Heck, you might inadvertently alter something the editor *liked*. No, leave well enough alone.

Editors will appreciate writers who take their suggestions seriously—and who get the revised manuscript back to them promptly. Few editors have lengthy author-revision times built into their schedules. They know what they want, and they want it now. Or yesterday, if possible.

So give it to them. Get that manuscript back in the mail—and hope it's the last you see of it until it's printed with your byline attached.

CHAPTER THIRTEEN

TIPS AND TRICKS OF THE FAST WRITER

• • •

NUTS AND BOLTS

The first and most important tip in this wrap-up chapter is that if you're writing a "how-to" book you should always have a final chapter in which you can stuff all the things you couldn't figure out where to put in the other chapters. No, seriously folks, this is the chapter that will give you a head start on the rest of your writing life — your faster, better writing life. Here I'll try to answer some of the questions you may still have about how to speed up your writing, and tackle some of the nuts and bolts of the writing business. Efficiency, after all, isn't a hat you put on and take off; it's an attitude that informs and improves every aspect of your life as a writer.

All right. Any questions? Yes, you in the back, with the ink-stained fingers. . . .

Should I write on a computer?

Yes, yes, a thousand times yes. I sold my first car — a college graduation gift, no less — to buy my first computer, a humble Radio Shack TRS-80 that now looks like an unusually stupid toaster next to today's souped-up models. But even that primitive, 32K beginning was a giant leap forward for me in efficiency and productivity. No more laborious retyping of subsequent drafts! (It didn't help that I was a lousy typist to begin with.) No more messing with bottles of correction fluid.

Buying that first computer also made me a *better* writer, because I no longer had to let things go unfixed simply for lack of time or willpower to retype yet again. The computer can be enormously liberating for a writer, both as a time-saver and as a creativity-enhancer. Aside from word processing, it also opens up a world of possibilities in on-line research, database management of your notes and your queries, and speedier financial record-keeping. (Tax time can be a nightmare for self-employed writers; a computer and a little record-keeping discipline year-round can make April 15 just another day.)

Computer-owning writers, like the rest of the computing world, are essentially divided into two camps: IBM (along with all the various IBM clones) and Macintosh. Yes, yes, I know that there are plenty of other oddball brands out there, along with those weird hybrids called "word processors" (either smart typewriters or stupid computers, depending on your point of view). But it's simply not efficient to be an oddball or a pioneer, unless technology is your main job rather than just a tool. A computer can help you do many things in your writing life besides write, so it makes sense to go whole hog and buy a real computer rather than some hybrid half-measure. To get the greatest power and variety of software for your computer, you've got to buy one of the Big Two operating systems. Editors, who increasingly want writers to submit manuscripts on disk to save *them* typing time and money, will also appreciate your adherence to one of the two most popular disk formats.

So, if you haven't already leaped one way or the other, which should you buy—IBM or Mac? The main arguments for IBM are: compatibility with a large installed corporate base (usually not a factor for a writer); slightly more competitive pricing, because of the pressure from all the IBM knockoffs; and a huge variety of available software. Since presumably you're going to buy just one kind of program for each purpose—word processing, data management, etc.—this last would be telling only if the Mac option suffered from a paucity of programs. One heft of a Macintosh magazine, obese with ads, should reassure you that, while the Mac doesn't have quite the software explosion that the IBM world enjoys, you won't have any problem finding something that does what you need.

The advantages of the Macintosh are ease of setup and learning, a more intuitive interface (which the IBM world has tried to copy with Windows software—but the original is still better), and readier integration with the Mac-dominated publishing world. If that sounds like I'm stacking the deck in terms of which is best for the speedy writer, I am. People will disagree about IBM vs. Mac almost as violently as about politics or religion or how to make the perfect martini, so there's no sense hiding my biases. For the writer who wants to work faster and more creatively and who doesn't care about speed of "number crunching," the Macintosh is the clear choice in my book. If you're already comfortable with the IBM world, don't switch; the alien Mac environment will just slow you down. But if you haven't yet made the jump to computers, the Mac offers both the least painful way to get started and the fastest, most natural way to work once you plug yourself in.

What software and other hardware do I need?
Somebody could write a whole 'nother book on what software and peripherals you should choose—and lots of people have. From the speedy writer's standpoint, though, I want to offer just a few shopping guidelines:
• Buy the most powerful word processing software for your chosen operating system that you can afford. Don't worry about learning all the features right away—just enough to get you started. But it's better to have outlining, a spell-checker, a thesaurus and all the other bells and whistles when you need them. (Don't, however, confuse writing-related features with those that lap over into desktop publishing, unless you're planning to create newsletters on the side.) All other things being equal, it's wise to buy one of the most widely used programs, to make file sharing with your editors easier. At this writing, that probably means WordPerfect for IBM and Microsoft Word for the Mac.
• Make sure that your word processing program will count words for you, both as a measure of your progress and as a hedge against overwriting. An approximate word count should appear on every manuscript you submit.
• Do get a spelling checker and an electronic thesaurus, either built into your program or separately. The former is more important than the latter—you already know my concerns about spending all your time consulting the thesaurus.
• Don't waste money and time on any of the so-called "grammar checkers" or other would-be guides to better writing. Someday one of these programs may be smart and powerful enough to improve your writing rather than wrecking it, but that day has not yet dawned.
• Do buy a simple financial-management program. It will save you time in managing your writing business—time better spent writing.
• Do buy a simple database or file-management program, the sort of thing that lets you organize and keep track of your contacts, queries and ideas. A "flat-file" database will do fine for this chore; don't waste time learning the more complicated "relational" databases.
• Spend a few extra dollars and buy a hard disk drive one notch bigger than you think you'll need. Once you start computing, it's amazing how fast these things fill up; you don't want to wind up spending a lot of time trying to free up and manage space on your hard drive. A 20-megabyte hard drive is probably not big enough. Go for 80 megabytes if you can afford it, so you never have to worry

about having enough room—or at least not until the next dandy but disk-space-demanding program comes out that you simply must have.

• Buy a printer that produces clean, readable text; eschew dot-matrix printers. But there's no need to turn your office into a typesetting shop by buying a multithousand-dollar PostScript laser printer. Assuming your output will be mostly words, not pictures, on paper, settle for an inkjet printer or a low-end laser printer.

• As soon as you can afford it, add a modem to open the world of on-line databases. (You'll also need some basic telecommunications software.) Not only will your modem let you access some incredibly efficient information sources; it will also let you mail your manuscripts electronically to editors who are suitably state-of-the-art. Talk about saving time! Instead of waiting for your story to print out, addressing an envelope, and trekking to the post office to see how much postage it requires, you can just dial up and transmit. When shopping for a modem, by the way, consider getting one that also lets your computer operate like a fax machine—yet another efficient way of both receiving information and sending manuscripts.

Do I have to back up my work?
Glad you asked. My last word on computers doesn't have anything to do with ever-higher technology. Rather, it's a reminder that computers have not yet succeeded in repealing Murphy's Law: Whatever can go wrong, will go wrong. The surest way to lose a lot of time when writing on a computer is to lose all your work to some unpredictable "glitch." Maybe your software will act up. Maybe the power will suddenly go out. Maybe your hard drive will "crash." Maybe your floppy disks will mysteriously become unreadable. So let me give you some invaluable advice:

Back up your work! Then back it up again!

Only the sternest self-discipline can minimize the potential time-gobbling disaster of a computer failure. You must rigorously save and re-save your work at every step along the way. Here's a suggested plan for protection:

1. Save constantly as you work. Whenever you pause to think, shuffle your notes or sip some coffee, save your work in progress. If you can't remember to do this, get a "utility" that saves your work every few minutes automatically. You should save every few paragraphs or every ten minutes, at a minimum.

2. Whenever you take an extended break, save a backup copy of your work in progress on a floppy disk, to guard against hard drive failure.

3. At the end of a writing session, save two backup copies of your work on separate floppy disks, to guard against a floppy-disk glitch. At this point you should have a justifiably paranoid three copies: one on your hard drive and two on floppies.

4. If you are working on an extended writing project, such as a book, periodically make a fourth complete copy of your work on a floppy disk. Take this copy somewhere else — your daytime office, the house of a friend or relative, a safe-deposit box. Think about it: What if you had a flood or a fire? You could replace the computer, but not six months of work.

How do I make my office more efficient?
Most writers fall into one of two extremes when it comes to setting up a place to work: Either they waste a lot of time picking out office furniture and Oriental rugs, time that could better be spent at the keyboard, or (more commonly) they spend no time or concern at all on their work area, trying to create in the midst of a disorganized mess.

The happy medium is that, yes, as we saw back in chapter two, you do need a defined and organized place to write, but, no, you don't need a palace. You need a desk, some shelves close by for reference books, a filing cabinet and a comfortable desk chair. Efficiency-wise, the most important thing to remember is to put things away. File things as they come to hand; don't wait until you have a pile of papers threatening avalanche. A simple alphabetical filing system will work just as well for most writers as anything elaborate or more "scientific." File things under obvious keywords, so you can find them again: Think of a "slug" (as newspapers would call it) for your stories — "Special Effects" for a story on Hollywood's movie magicians, for example — and stick to it. It also helps to think of file folders as being made that size for a reason: A single folder will only hold so much, which is probably also the limit of how much you can stuff in a single folder and hope to efficiently retrieve it.

But let's get back to that business of the desk again, before we move on. Your desk doesn't have to be fancy, but it does have to be neat. I've seen writers' desks that were a foot high in papers, magazines, and heaven knows what else. A few neatly organized piles are OK, but you must not think of your desktop as some sort of horizontal filing cabinet. Discipline yourself to keep on your desk only what you need for what you are working on right now — notes for the chapter-in-progress, for example, not everything for your whole book — and to put away anything that you're finished with.

How can I get better control of my time?

The same time-management techniques that apply to busy executives can help writers squeeze the most out of their working time. (Except that you probably don't have a secretary or a staff to delegate tasks to!) You'll find bookstores full of how-to tomes that purport to solve all your time-management troubles, and indeed many of them contain some useful ideas. I'd like to distill and adapt for the harried writer four bits of advice that are common to many time-management systems:

1. Handle each piece of paper only once—well, OK, no more than twice. A working writer sometimes seems to get as many pieces of paper as he or she sends out in manuscripts: mail, magazines, rejection letters, clippings, maybe even contracts and checks. It's easy to get bogged down in all that paperwork, and to let the chore of dealing with it start to eat into your writing time. So you need to force yourself to deal with each piece of paper the first time you touch it; resist the temptation to set it aside in the vague hope of doing something about it later.

Every piece of paper that you handle should be dealt with in one of three ways:

- Trash it. As a *Business Week* wag once observed, "Man's best friend, aside from the dog, is the wastebasket." How often have you saved something for weeks, even months, pondered what to do with it several times, and then wound up trashing it after all? Throw it away now and save yourself some time and uncertainty.

- File it. You don't have to hop up and run to the nearest file cabinet right away, but you should put anything file-able into a clearly marked "To File" folder. Do it now, not later. Then force yourself to really file all that "To File" stuff once a week.

- Act on it. OK, you might not be able to act immediately and completely on every "action item" that comes your way, but at least you can clearly identify each as a "To Do" and tag it with some indicator of priority. Then make yourself do all the things in your "To Do" file; again, once a week will probably keep you from being swamped.

2. Make the most out of small chunks of time. Remember D'Aguesseau, who wrote a whole novel in bits and pieces while waiting for his wife to come down to dinner? Even if a chunk of free time is too tiny to actually start writing anything, you can still use it to do your filing, clip magazines, or make a phone call.

3. Work on several things at the same time. How many things that

you do really require your full attention? You can open your mail and chat on the phone at the same time. While your computer is printing or spell-checking, tackle that pile of filing or clean up your desk.

4. Group tasks. Everything you do has a certain warm-up time: cranking up the computer, driving to the library, gathering your notetaking materials. So it pays to group together tasks that require the same kind of preparatory action. Once you've turned on the computer, do all the computer-related tasks at hand—instead of turning on the computer and waiting for it to boot five times for five different chores. (This is also easier on your computer's delicate circuits, by the way.) If you have several stories to research, get them all to the point where you're ready to go to the library before you make the drive downtown.

How can I save time in marketing my writing?

We've already stressed the importance of writing queries instead of trying to find a home for a completed manuscript. But there are other ways to trim the time it takes to sell your skills and ideas as a writer.

First and most important is simply to make sure that every query you send goes to an editor or publisher with a high probability of "biting" on it. If you're going "fishing," which is a good way to think about queries, it's not enough to have good equipment and wriggly bait; you've got to cast your line where the fish match your bait and tackle.

Consider magazine markets, for example. You'd be amazed at the number of fiction, poetry and personal-essay submissions I used to get at my city magazine—even though, as the merest glance at the magazine would have revealed, we ran no fiction, poetry or personal essays. Talk about writers wasting time! Similarly, we got dozens of queries on topics that had nothing to do with our city or region— when, clearly, that was the focus of our magazine. I even had writers argue with me over the phone (and of course I hate phone queries to begin with), insisting that I should be interested in a story utterly outside the scope of our magazine.

Don't waste time querying a magazine until you've at least seen a copy of it. Study the contents page. Try to imagine your story listed there; if it requires a stretch of the imagination, maybe you're fishing in the wrong waters. As we saw in chapter three, contents pages make a perfect ready-reference to not only what a magazine is buying but also how it is seeking to position itself. That's why I keep a file of contents pages torn or photocopied out of magazines stapled to the magazine's masthead so I have the editor's name and address.

You can also collect book catalogs if you have your eye on longer writing projects. Again, try to envision your book idea among a publisher's offerings before you fire off that proposal. Don't fall into the trap of thinking that your idea is so wonderful that any smart publisher, regardless of its list, will snap it up. If a publisher doesn't do mysteries, sending it your proposal for *Murder Most Wicked* is just an arrogant waste of your time and the publisher's. A children's book house will not suddenly transform itself into a romance-novel publisher just for you. A regional press won't want your book about some other region of the country. Trust me on this and save yourself a lot of time and confidence-shaking.

You should also evaluate your ideas in terms of their marketability. If you find only one magazine or just two book publishers where your idea could conceivably find a home, maybe pitching that particular idea isn't the most efficient use of your time. The odds are pretty high, after all, that you'll collect a rejection or two in the process—which might then leave you with an orphaned idea. (An exception here would be if you're trying to build a relationship with a particular market, even one that might be *sui generis*, such as your local city magazine or a trade publisher in a field where you already have lots of salable expertise.) Yes, every query should be tightly targeted to a specific market. But the best ideas are those that you can twist and retarget for multiple markets if at first you don't succeed.

Once you have identified appropriate targets for your ideas, you need to turn into a querying machine. Take your list of potential markets for each idea and prioritize it from most likely to least likely. Start at the top and start sending queries. Here again you'll find your computer to be a godsend: Write a terrific, specific query letter—then save it. If your idea doesn't fly with the first market you try, call up your query letter on your computer again and fiddle with it until it's right for market number two. No need to start from scratch! Much of what you have to say in your letter—the details of the story, your qualifications to write it—will be the same from one query to the next, anyway.

You can take this "automation" of your idea-marketing a step further and use your word processing program to create a query "template." Write the skeleton of a query letter—your address, a paragraph about your writing experience, a pleasant closing paragraph and so forth—and then start each new query with this document (save the new query as a different file, to preserve your original template). This won't save you more than a few minutes—but, as I hope you've learned by now, a few minutes saved here and there can add up to major steps toward writing faster.

Where do I go from here?

Back to work, of course! By now you've seen how a focused, organized, disciplined approach to the writing life can lead you to write not only faster but better. You know that by clearing away all the clutter—both physical and mental—that keeps you from writing efficiently, you can free yourself to become the best writer you are capable of being.

But writing faster and better is a habit that must be practiced every day of your writing career. Don't let yourself think, "Oh, yeah, I know how to do this more efficiently, but just this once . . ." You've got to make the habits of focus, organization and self-discipline as much a constant in your life as brushing your teeth.

One of the appeals of being a writer, I think, that draws so many people to it as either a dream or a career is that writing is ultimately up to the individual. It is not a team sport. Writing is just you, alone in a room with your inspiration and imagination, doing something only you can do exactly that way. Only Dostoyevsky, with his unique combination of talent and life experience, could have written *Crime & Punishment*. Only Edgar Rice Burroughs could have created Tarzan. No one but Mark Twain could have made us laugh at that jumping-frog contest. And only you can create the works of reporting and make-believe, of comedy and tragedy, that will be your gift to the readers of the world.

All things considered, doesn't it make sense to write as much as you can, as well as you can? You owe that to your readers—and to yourself.

INDEX

• • •

OTHER BOOKS OF INTEREST

Annual Market Books

Artist's Market, edited by Lauri Miller $21.95

Children's Writer's & Illustrator's Market, edited by Lisa Carpenter (paper) $17.95

Guide to Literary Agents & Art/Photo Reps, edited by Robin Gee $15.95

Humor & Cartoon Markets, edited by Bob Staake (paper) $16.95

Novel & Short Story Writer's Market, edited by Robin Gee (paper) $19.95

Photographer's Market, edited by Sam Marshall $21.95

Poet's Market, by Judson Jerome $19.95

Songwriter's Market, edited by Brian Rushing $19.95

Writer's Market, edited by Mark Kissling $25.95

General Writing Books

Beginning Writer's Answer Book, edited by Kirk Polking (paper) $13.95

Discovering the Writer Within, by Bruce Ballenger & Barry Lane $17.95

Freeing Your Creativity, by Marshall Cook $17.95

How to Write a Book Proposal, by Michael Larsen $10.95

Make Your Words Work, by Gary Provost $17.95

Pinckert's Practical Grammar, by Robert C. Pinckert (paper) $11.95

The 28 Biggest Writing Blunders, by William Noble $12.95

The 29 Most Common Writing Mistakes & How To Avoid Them, by Judy Delton (paper) $9.95

The Wordwatcher's Guide to Good Writing & Grammar, by Morton S. Freeman (paper) $15.95

The Writer's Book of Checklists, by Scott Edelstein $16.95

The Writer's Digest Guide to Manuscript Formats, by Buchman & Groves $18.95

The Writer's Essential Desk Reference, edited by Glenda Neff $19.95

Nonfiction Writing

The Complete Guide to Writing Biographies, by Ted Schwarz $6.99

Creative Conversations: The Writer's Guide to Conducting Interviews, by Michael Schumacher $16.95

How to Do Leaflets, Newsletters & Newspapers, by Nancy Brigham (paper) $14.95

How to Sell Every Magazine Article You Write, by Lisa Collier Cool (paper) $11.95

The Magazine Article: How To Think It, Plan It, Write It, by Peter Jacobi $17.95

The Writer's Digest Handbook of Magazine Article Writing, edited by Jean M. Fredette (paper) $11.95

Fiction Writing

Characters & Viewpoint, by Orson Scott Card $13.95

The Complete Guide to Writing Fiction, by Barnaby Conrad $17.95

Cosmic Critiques: How & Why 10 Science Fiction Stories Work, edited by Asimov & Greenberg (paper) $12.95

Creating Characters: How To Build Story People, by Dwight V. Swain $16.95

Dialogue, by Lewis Turco $13.95

The Fiction Writer's Silent Partner, by Martin Roth $19.95

Handbook of Short Story Writing: Vol 1, by Dickson and Smythe (paper) $10.95

Handbook of Short Story Writing: Vol. II, edited by Jean Fredette (paper) $12.95

Manuscript Submission, by Scott Edelstein $13.95

Mastering Fiction Writing, by Kit Reed $18.95

Plot, by Ansen Dibell $13.95

Theme & Strategy, by Ronald B. Tobias $13.95

The 38 Most Common Fiction Writing Mistakes, by Jack M. Bickham $12.95

Writer's Digest Handbook of Novel Writing, $18.95

Writing the Novel: From Plot to Print, by Lawrence Block (paper) $11.95

Special Interest Writing Books

Armed & Dangerous: A Writer's Guide to Weapons, by Michael Newton (paper) $14.95

Comedy Writing Secrets, by Mel Helitzer (paper) $15.95

The Complete Book of Feature Writing, by Leonard Witt $18.95

Creating Poetry, by John Drury $18.95

Deadly Doses: A Writer's Guide to Poisons, by Serita Deborah Stevens with Anne Klarner (paper) $16.95

A Guide to Travel Writing & Photography, by Ann & Carl Purcell (paper) $22.95

Hillary Waugh's Guide to Mysteries & Mystery Writing, by Hillary Waugh $19.95

How to Pitch & Sell Your TV Script, by David Silver $17.95

How to Write & Sell Greeting Cards, Bumper Stickers, T-Shirts and Other Fun Stuff, by Molly Wigand (paper) 15.95

How to Write & Sell True Crime, by Gary Provost $17.95

How to Write Mysteries, by Shannon OCork $13.95

How to Write Romances, by Phyllis Taylor Pianka $15.95

How to Write Science Fiction & Fantasy, Orson Scott Card $13.95

How to Write Tales of Horror, Fantasy & Science Fiction, edited by J.N. Williamson (paper) $12.95

Powerful Business Writing, by Tom McKeown $12.95

Successful Scriptwriting, by Jurgen Wolff & Kerry Cox (paper) $14.95

The Writer's Complete Crime Reference Book, by Martin Roth $19.95

The Writer's Guide to Conquering the Magazine Market, by Connie Emerson $17.95

Writing the Modern Mystery, by Barbara Norville (paper) $12.95

The Writing Business

The Complete Guide to Self-Publishing, by Tom & Marilyn Ross (paper) $16.95

Business & Legal Forms for Authors & Self-Publishers, by Tad Crawford (paper) $4.99

A Writer's Guide to Contract Negotiations, by Richard Balkin (paper) $4.25

The Writer's Guide to Self-Promotion & Publicity, by Elane Feldman $16.95

Writing A to Z, edited by Kirk Polking $22.95

To order directly from the publisher, include $3.00 postage and handling for 1 book and $1.00 for each additional book. Allow 30 days for delivery.

Writer's Digest Books, 1507 Dana Avenue, Cincinnati, Ohio 45207
Credit card orders call TOLL-FREE
1-800-289-0963
Prices subject to change without notice.

Write to this same address for information on *Writer's Digest* magazine, *Story* magazine, Writer's Digest Book Club, Writer's Digest School, and Writer's Digest Criticism Service.